Portals

people, processes and technology

Edited by
Andrew Cox

facet publishing

© This compilation: Andrew Cox 2006
   The chapters: the contributors 2006

Published by
Facet Publishing
7 Ridgmount Street
London WC1E 7AE

Facet Publishing is wholly owned by CILIP: the Chartered Institute of Library and Information Professionals.

First published 2006

British Library Cataloguing in Publication Data
A catalogue record for this book is available from the British Library.

ISBN-13: 978-1-85604-546-9
ISBN-10: 1-85604-546-3

Typeset from editor's disks by Facet Publishing in 10/13 pt Revival and Zurich.
Printed and made in Great Britain by MPG Books Ltd, Bodmin, Cornwall.

Contents

Introductory preface

Purpose

The meaning of the word 'portal' is elusive, fuzzy, but people persist in using it. It captures something people want to say. It is a valuable property that can sell software, websites and projects. At some level it expresses what users and organizations are looking for.

The purpose of this book is to draw together authors from multiple perspectives to explore themes and sectoral experiences as a way of increasing our general understanding of how the concept of the portal is being realized in different contexts. Many previous books have focused on the latest technology. Others have tended to concentrate on web, corporate or academic portals – ignoring the potential and reality for cross-sector learning. This book tries to bring many different views together, both to capture directly lessons and wisdom about portals and to stimulate the reader to think about what cross-linkages can be made. The primary focus is the efforts of organizations to create portals for their own members, rather than general web portals, but their relevance as models is recognized in most chapters. The chapters are probably more suggestive and stimulating than conclusive. I hope the reader will feel they have learnt a lot from reading the book, but they will probably not have found simple or easy answers.

In the first section of the book authors tackle broad themes such as technologies, personalization, usability and management issues. Even if one questions the value of the term 'portal', it is clear that these are now key issues in information service management. The second section focuses more specifically on the role of information professionals and libraries in portals. In the third and fourth sections, authors explore the experience of portals in different sectors, sometimes capturing a particular institution's experience, sometimes reflecting on whole industries. The three chapters in the final section deal specifically with an issue that is present throughout the book: the future of portals.

Each author speaks in their own voice, with the section introductions setting some context, adding some points that have not been covered by the chapter authors and suggesting a few of the many connections and contrasts that can be made between chapters.

Audience

The main audience for the book is the growing number of information practitioners interested in developing or contributing to a portal or supporting users in their use of portals. Most of the authors are themselves from the information management world. The book will interest other information professionals simply for current awareness. Each chapter stands alone as useful reading with implications beyond the topic of portals as such.

Students of information management will also find much of interest relevant to their study of increasingly technological information services. The portal as a historical experience may be a good case study of the patterns of change – partly technically driven – that are passing through the information world, often starting on the net, then propagating themselves locally as people transfer what they learn on the web to internal practices.

Acknowledgements

The editor would like to acknowledge Stephen Emmott and Stephen Musgrave's influence in choosing the wording of the sub-title for the book.

Every effort has been made to contact the holders of copyright material reproduced in this text, and thanks are due to them for permission to reproduce the material indicated. If there are any queries please contact the publisher.

Section 1

Core themes

The first section of this volume addresses two fundamental clusters of questions about portals. First, what is a portal? What distinguishes one from any other service? What functions, features or affordances can or should we expect to find in a portal? What types of portal is it useful to identify? A second set of questions revolve more around how a portal is designed, especially how to incorporate users in the design process – and how to manage the portal on an ongoing basis. These will be questions that all the chapters of the volume address, but in this section authors tackle them at a more general level.

My own chapter encourages the reader to re-examine their own experience of different services that call themselves, or are called by others, portals, and to ask: what is the common ground? What common themes emerge? The discussion suggests that it may be possible only to identify themes – not a hard and fast definition – but this helps us understand the emergent character of the concept and to identify the existence of less recognized counter-trends. The chapter also begins to ask what forces operate to control the development of the portal as a project; what organizational influences are likely to govern the shape of its evolution? Andrew Madden's chapter reflects further on the evolution of the web portal concept, in the context of internet searching behaviour.

Franklin and Hepworth, Probets, Qutaishat and Walton address the first cluster of questions. Franklin reviews underlying technologies, again trying to explore the need organizations have for a portal and what is achievable. The examples are from the university sector, but the principles are probably generic. There is recognition again that the portal is an evolving concept. The stress on middleware and on access management is notable. Simplifying sign-on is a key objective (as Schelleman demonstrates in Chapter 14) and it is the bedrock on which things like personalization will be achieved. Hepworth et al. concentrate precisely on personalization, drawing on a very wide range of models to consider what could be useful to users, what is realistic. Looking at most existing portals what has actually been done in the way of personalization is quite limited, so this chapter is inevitably relatively conceptual. Yet there seems little doubt that personalization/customization/adaptivity will be a continuing major theme in portal development. However, it is also going to be far more difficult to work out what will be really valued by users than was once thought. Of course, this begins to address our second set of questions: where do users fit into the design?

The chapters by Zaphiris, Dellaporta and Mohamedally, and Emmott focus more exclusively on the second cluster of questions, about the design and management of portals. Zaphiris et al. address what is increasingly understood to be a key responsibility in information work: systematic user needs analysis and usability testing. It is probably the complex and novel requirements of portals that have pushed us to realize how inadequate previous web design practice was in this area. The chapter outlines the major methods of user needs analysis and offers a short case study of a portal evaluation. Emmott looks at core management issues, supplying both a general conceptual framework and comments on seven central issues in managing portals, based on his practical experience.

1

Definitions and debates

Andrew Cox

Many writers who have written about portals have been worried by the difficulty of defining exactly what the term itself means. The authors in this book again tussle with the issue. The evidence of the book seems to be that however diverse the meanings attached to the word, it does seem to encapsulate important issues for those working to support the use of information. Thus information professionals are likely to find themselves not only explaining to users what different forms of portal are and how they work, but also developing online services which work within wider organizational portal frameworks, and perhaps actually helping to develop or manage their own portals.

This chapter starts the reader thinking about some of the key questions, explored in greater depth in subsequent chapters, and also provides a guide to some of the relevant literature.

Definitions

The reader might take a moment to consider which (if any) of the following they would consider to be a portal:

- Direct.gov (www.direct.gov.uk/)
- University of Durham's duo (Murray, 2003)
- My Caledonian, Glasgow Caledonian's portal (McKay, 2003)
- Metalib/SFX at Loughborough library – 'eResource portal' (http://metalib.lboro. ac.uk/)
- CSA MultiSearch (www.csa.com/e_products/multisearch_login.php)
- Ingenta connect (www.ingentaconnect.com/)
- National electronic Library for Health (NeLH) (www.nelh.nhs.uk/)
- The NHS core content collection
- The National Library for Health (www.library.nhs.uk/)

- The North East Regional Portal (www.northeastofengland.com/)
- SOSIG (www.sosig.ac.uk/)
- Yahoo! (http://uk.yahoo.com/)
- Google (. . . Amazon, eBay, Wikipedia, the BBC).

When this chapter was being written the top hit on the UK web in Google for the single search term 'portal' was Direct.gov. Interestingly, in its own description of itself the word portal is never used. Rather, it would seem that other people have decided it is a portal, by describing it as such in the descriptive text associated with their links to it. On this basis Google has labelled it a portal. Both duo and My Caledonian are 'institutional portals' – the university equivalent of enterprise information portals – but though screenshots suggest a strong similarity in what is being offered it seems that the underlying technological base is very different: one is built from an e-learning system (a virtual learning environment) and the other from the student record system. This suggests that they might be run by different people, have different paths of development, etc. The implementation of metalib and SFX at Loughborough University at the time of writing is described on the library website as an 'eResource portal'. For an information professional this is something radically different from a single publisher's or aggregator's service offering cross-search of multiple databases (such as provided by CSA or ingenta). In fact, often publishers are using exactly the same search technology that the library portal uses, and in a sense they are competitive offerings – the user might not really be very interested in the distinction. The comparison of NeLH and the NHS core content collection forces us to think about the differences between a gateway to evidence, 'virtual communities of practice' and unique publications and a more traditional-feeling library-orientated collection of bibliographic databases and full-text e-journals. Is the familiar self-styled web gateway to social science information SOSIG a portal? It resists the definition. Is Yahoo! a portal? Was it one in 1996, is it one in 2006? For that matter what about Google itself, now that it has a directory and is aggregating so many tools, or any of the other classic internet sites that seem to be so influential in defining how we understand the net, such as Amazon and eBay? If they are all portals, what is the value of the word that is so elastic? If they are not, where is the line to be drawn?

To approach the same problem from another angle, what is the difference (if any) between a corporate portal (Collins, 2000) and an intranet portal (the latter being the term preferred by the usability guru Jakob Nielsen)? Are these different from an EIP (enterprise information portal)? Or an EP (enterprise portal)? Looking at the usage of the terms there seems to be little real difference. Further, how different is an EKP (enterprise knowledge portal) or an enterprise system (as used in the special issue of the *Journal of Strategic Information Systems* cited below)? Certainly within organizational portals it is quite common to differentiate B2E, B2C, B2D, B2B, B2G and B2x (business to employee, customer, distributor, business, government, anything). The proliferation of terms is evidently one response to the vagueness of the term.

Not surprisingly, many commentators have complained about the haziness of the meaning of the term portal (e.g. Miller, 2001; Firestone, 2003). Dempsey (2003) describes it as one of the least helpful terms of the last few years. Some practitioners have abandoned use of the term altogether. This is probably also why one of the practical pieces of advice that comes out of portal projects is that whoever is managing the project should define what is meant locally by the term – to manage expectations. What a portal means for a particular organization may be unique to that organization. The continuing problem is that it is not possible to control what is understood by the word – it is in some sense in itself a valuable property which many people are trying to appropriate and use, for their own purposes (often commercial or 'political'). The evolution of the concept on the internet makes it difficult for people inside organizations to influence what it means locally. The JISC has been rather successful in the academic sector in discouraging loose use of the term and trying to make some clear distinctions (Miller, 2001; JISC, 2003). But the concept is evolving: no neat definition can be produced for all times, for all sectors.

Another way of approaching the question of definition, then, is to embrace the flexibility of the word, so that it could be seen as:

> an evolving and elastic concept expressing our desire to background information we do not want and bring the information we want (and the tools to use it) to our fingertips.

This definition neither identifies a particular technology (but most definitions do not) nor even a particular set of functions; rather it focuses on an underlying aspiration. Above all it captures the need we have for a portal as a response to a sense of information chaos on the net and the annoyance of not being able to find what we want when we want it.

One part of this definition focuses our attention on the way the concept continues to evolve. The definition also makes it easier to focus on equally powerful counter-trends, such as:

> our tendency to wilfully change what we are interested in, our aspiration to explore information at will, serendipitously and to organise it for ourselves.

The fact that we frequently change what we are interested in is a problem for personalization of systems such as portals. The way that we like to browse partly to explore what is 'out there' but also as a way of working out what we are thinking defies a neat matching of content and user. The user actively organizing information is again part of the process of learning about a subject of interest. User-driven solutions to information organization such as personal bookmarks have an advantage over centrally driven organization like portals, in their ability to allow the users to gather appropriate information sources around themselves in exploring a topic.

Some definitions of a portal seem to suggest that everything can be neatly integrated and presented to us so that we see just what we need and no more. Thus Ovum's early definition:

> A workspace portal is a single, coherent, integrated portal that presents its users with all the information they need to carry out their jobs.   (cited Winkler, 2001)

Franklin (2004) reports the aspiration for the portal to replace the desktop. Cloete and Snyman (2003, 241) talk about a sign of a portal's success being people 'living in the portal'. Taken to extremes such centralization has its dangers. It goes beyond helping us by filtering out irrelevant information to locking us into a closed environment where access is on a need-to-know basis. From the librarian's perspective it is quite clear that the potential sources of information are just too many and diverse to be easily integrated – except perhaps in the context of the immediate needs of the individual in a very closely defined workflow. Knowledge management ideas have further expanded our understanding of types and sources of information/knowledge that we use to achieve our ends and the diverse paths we use to reach them. The individual's need to organize them flexibly defies a technically driven solution. The problem is that portal frameworks may be too controlling: in an attempt to foreground useful information they may create inadvertent silos. This is at any rate a danger.

In further pursuit of a flexible definition of the portal concept, it does seem that we can identify five aspects of portalization to date:

1 **Organizing** information sources
2 **Aggregating** information services and web-based tools
3 **Personalizing/customizing** of the portal as an environment
4 **Integrating** data
5 **Creating a space**/hosting communities.

These themes are rather neatly summarized by Dolphin, Miller and Sherratt (2002):

> A [thin] layer which aggregates, integrates, personalises and presents information, transactions and applications to the user according to their role and preferences.

Early internet portals such as Yahoo!, which were influential in defining the concept (Techencyclopedia, 2005) – as an internet 'meme' – were a directory of information sources, attempting to help navigate the net as a space, alongside aggregated web-based tools. The benefits of this were recognized and sold to corporations as EIP. Winship in this volume reviews the types of services that may be aggregated (see also Butters, 2003; Pearce, 2003). The issue here is really of all the possible services to collect together what makes a magnetic place to return to – to find the killer application? Self-service applications are often an important feature.

The next theme is personalization and customization. These two terms approach adaptivity from two directions, by matching presentation of information/tools to users on the basis of their broad role(s) and by allowing the end user to make their own choices about look and feel. Personalization was a very strong theme around 2000. Thus the mylibrary concept seemed to solve many information problems (see special issue of *Information Technology and Libraries*, 2000, 19 (4)). In some attempts at definition, personalization is central, thus:

> A Portal is a customized transactional web environment, designed purposefully to enable an individual end user to 'personalize' the content and look of the web site for his/her own individual preference.   (Lakos, 2004)

However, confidence that the benefits of personalization could be easily achieved has retreated, though personalization continues to be a key aspect of the agenda. Smith, Schmoller and Ferguson (2004) stress that it is likely to work best where it is directed to a specific known need. Perhaps personalization is a rather post hoc approach to adapting a system to users that should be addressed earlier in the development process through exploration of user needs and usability testing. Zaphiris, Dellaporta and Mohamedally in this volume reflect an increasingly sophisticated understanding of how to do this. Whereas the early driver was adapting the environment to the individual's interests, now the main driver may be accessibility.

Integrating data is the dominant theme of the moment in the definition of a portal. The JISC definition of a portal focuses on this:

> Technically, a portal is a network service that brings together content from diverse distributed resources using technologies such as cross searching, harvesting, and alerting, and collate this into an amalgamated form for presentation to the user.   (JISC, 2003)

From this perspective 'merely' organizing information sources and aggregating web-based tools and services along side them is not enough to be called a portal (though a portal may have to do that too). The portal has to create a new resource by 'recombination' (Dempsey, 2003).

Working in the background for personalization and integration is access management. Achievement of some simplified sign-on, if only by co-ordinating passwords, is a central part of integrating content and tools.

A final aspect of the portal is that it has always needed to be a place in its own right, not just a gateway to other places. There may also be a case for it being a community or a host of communities – in some sense of that other elastic term. This will be a theme developed in depth in a later section (see introduction to Section 5 below).

Related concepts
Yet another portal (YAP)

Klein argues below that portal development, in the university sector at any rate, has been opportunistic, developed on top of existing core systems such as the student record system or an online learning system to produce a broader gateway. The underlying driving force here is generally self-service. Grand portal visions have also been imagined, but more often development seems to be ad hoc. This explains the yet another portal/portal war phenomenon (Dempsey, 2003; Browning et al., 2002). Without clear organizational decisions being made there is a danger of multiple systems competing to be the portal, the user homepage – 'the interface to everything' (Paschoud, 2002). Klein's chapter explores this in the university context. Many universities seem to have moved towards institutional portals through expanding their student record system or virtual learning environment (VLE). A VLE is in many senses much like a student portal in itself anyway; it is already likely to organize access to most of what the student needs. An institutional content management system (CMS) will doubtless have some relation to these phenomena. The library may also have something called a portal though it is externally focused. The situation is potentially quite confusing, particularly for the user.

Portal as framework: the portlet

The concepts of a portal as a framework into which different portlets or channels can be slotted is a key idea in the development of understanding of what a portal might mean and partly a solution to YAP. The portlet refers to the way that a web-based service can be delivered as a window within a framework. This is a crucial concept in two respects. First, it implies that people close to a particular information source can continue to develop and maintain it – to own it – and have it accessed through its own native interface, yet at the same time the information or tool can also be surfaced inside another system. This addresses the problem of silos of information, through technical means. The need for information to have an owner is observed, but at the same time it can be made available through portals. Thus a library OPAC search screen could sit alongside a course module catalogue search screen.

A second application of the portlet concept is what Dempsey (2003) refers to as unbundling, so that, for example, a small function of the library system could be surfaced within another system, rather than the user having to go through the whole rigmarole of going to the library system, logging on and navigating to the service they require. This means that potentially unbundled services could be repackaged around individual workflows.

People and portals

So far technology has been at the heart of the discussion. Actually a recurrent theme throughout this volume is the challenge of 'integrating' people through technology and process. As integrative projects, portals will inevitably redefine the relationships between planners, developers, data owners, individual users and user communities. Differences of interest and cultural outlook, issues of power and governance are likely to be as critical to success as sheer technical difficulty and complexity. The rest of this chapter explores some of the complexities of these issues to prime the reader to think about these aspects of portals as they read the book. The approach taken is to consider the different drivers that are likely to be in play in a portal project.

> Let's not build portals just because we can – let's build them because they contribute to organisational strategies, because they meet the needs of target user groups, and because the benefits outweigh the costs. (Anderson, 2002)

Anderson's quote articulates eminently reasonable aspirations about what should be the motivation to build portals. It is a stimulating remark because it focuses our attention on defining precisely what we wish to accomplish, but also reveals the limits of its applicability.

In the first place it is evident that technology is often a driver. Klein's conclusions about the priority of technical opportunity over vision have already been cited. An Accenture study also found that portals were IT driven, and by IT departments in the main (Englert, 2003). The chapters by Franklin and Awre below explore the way technical change is opening up new possibilities, and in many ways it is these technical opportunities that are the key to change.

> At Glasgow Caledonian University the development of a portal came about by accident. Hence there was no business case made for it nor did it go through a tendering process. (McKay, 2003)

Clearly many portals are developed opportunistically. This is not unreasonable because what is technically possible does seem to evolve quite rapidly. Gradualist models of development based on technical opportunity rather than abstract visions are less risky.

Anderson's second point is that portals should contribute to organizational strategies. Some of the papers from the recent special issue of the *Journal of Strategic Information Systems* (Howcroft, Newell and Wagner, 2004) illustrate some of ways the proposition is actually quite problematic:

- Tingling and Parent (2004) argue that the process of choosing a system is not a purely rational process; rather it contains elements of ceremony, that is different parties are represented but have little real say in the final choice. The complex, weighted checklists of features designed to help choose a system may not bear that much relation to the reality of how the choice is made.

- Lee and Myers (2004) make the important point that the organizational strategy is not unitary and fixed, rather it is complex, changing and contested. Universities, for example, are often immensely diverse organizations which pursue multiple purposes. One cannot simply latch the portal onto a stable institutional purpose and leave it at that. Developing a portal is likely to be a highly political process.
- Chae and Poole (2005) make the point that a senior management mandate to use a system is always contestable in practice: there can always be reasons found for not participating in institutional portal initiatives even if one is directed to do so.
- Wagner and Newell (2004) make the point that computer systems tend to be based on generalized models of functions, often presented as the best practice of how to achieve some purpose. But it is obviously quite possible that the best practice fits one context (sector, country) not another. Notwithstanding the ability to localize a system, such 'best practices' may actually work very poorly compared with existing practices which have evolved over time to adapt to local needs.
- Volkoff, Elmos and Strong (2004) make the point that the epistemic boundaries between those who are charged with implementing a system and those who are actually going to use it are often very wide. The classic solution of creating local power users is, in some cases, therefore, ineffective.

Musgrave in this volume makes the point very forcibly that there are multiple epistemic divides that need to be bridged to achieve a successful portal project. Actually starting to address such divisions might be a potential benefit of such a project.

These points are probably very obvious to the practitioner on the ground, yet they are rarely reported in full in practitioner writing – probably because they are seen as 'just politics', unavoidable parts of organizational life, about which it is not possible to speak (it draws discredit to the organization) and not analysable within a clear framework (it is just life – not a theorizable category). Schelleman's chapter in this volume is a healthy exception to the rule, reporting very honestly the contingent process through which a portal project happened. Equally, if practitioners often cannot or do not report such factors, for academia these irrational elements are part of the 'forbidden knowledge' that gets left out of most accounts which usually focus on a driving rationalizing logic (Czarniawksa, 2003).

The focus in the Anderson quote on organizational strategies also masks the power of extra-organizational forces, which have already been acknowledged as driving the evolution of understanding of what a portal is. Another example in the specific context of personalization is reflected in the comment by Smith, Schmoller and Ferguson (2004):

> User expectations of services available to the academic community will change as they increasingly experience the advantages (and sometimes disadvantages) of personalisation in commercial services and in many applications of Internet banking and finance.
>
> (2004, 33)

In developing systems what happens in the wider world in terms of the evolution of technology but also our own users' experience of technology is beyond control.

Anderson's next point is to focus on users' needs. The library world is fond of the rhetoric of user needs; often this is realized as passively allowing access. The chapter by Zaphiris, Dellaporta and Mohamedally reflects a developing methodology to understand such needs. Yet the variety and diversity of user groups, the impenetrability of needs (as opposed to stated wants) makes this a difficult area. There is also an argument for providing a service and seeing whether people use it. As we move into the area of introducing portal systems unexpected uses and ironic outcomes of systems must be expected.

Anderson's last point is to stress the need for the benefits to be measurable, with a clear positive return on investment. This is a useful correction to ad hoc efforts in which there is no evaluation. It does not follow that because some users make use of a system that the benefit outweighed the cost. Raw statistics of usage of a library portal do not tell the whole story of its impact on behaviour or value. It will always be difficult to measure the value of a portal in monetary terms. It still seems that evaluation is in its early stages.

So Anderson quite neatly encapsulates what we might ask for, achieving it in reality will be difficult.

References

Anderson, S. (2002) *Portals: what are they good for?*, paper presented at Gateways to Research and Lifelong Learning: portals in perspective, University of London, www.ull.ac.uk/news/portals/sheilaanderson.ppt+ [accessed 21 December 2005].

Browning, P., Fearon, K., Shaw, T., Stanley, T. and Stuckes, J. (2002) *Avoiding Portal Wars*, www.ukoln.ac.uk/web-focus/events/workshops/webmaster-2002/talks/panel/introduction/introduction-portal.ppt [accessed 21 December 2005].

Butters, G. (2003) What Features in a Portal? *Ariadne*, **35** [online], www.ariadne.ac.uk/issue35/butters/intro.html [accessed 16 October 2005].

Chae, B. and Poole, M. S. (2005) Mandates and Technology Acceptance: a tale of two enterprise technologies, *Journal of Strategic Information Systems*, **14** (2), 147–66.

Cloete, M. and Snyman, R. (2003) The Enterprise Portal – is it knowledge management?, *Aslib Proceedings*, **55** (4), 234–42.

Collins, H. (2000) *Corporate Portals: revolutionizing information access to increase productivity and drive the bottom line*, London, McGraw-Hill.

Czarniawksa, B. (2003) Forbidden Knowledge, *Management Learning*, **34** (3), 353–65.

Dempsey, L. (2003) The Recombinant Library, *Journal of Library Administration*, **39** (4), 103–36.

Dolphin, I., Miller, P. and Sherratt, R. (2002) Portals, PORTALs Everywhere, *Ariadne*, **33** [online], www.ariadne.ac.uk/issue33/portals/ [accessed 16 October 2005].

Englert, B. (2003) *Portal Trends in Higher Education*, paper presented at Educause Southwest Regional Conference, www.educause.edu/ir/library/powerpoint/SWR0304.pps [accessed 21 December 2005].

Firestone, J. M. (2003) *Enterprise Information Portals and Knowledge Management*, London, Butterworth-Heinemann.

Franklin, T. (2004) *Portals in Higher Education: concepts and models*, The Observatory, www.obhe.ac.uk/products/reports/pdf/February2004.pdf [accessed 1 November 2005].

Howcroft, D., Newell, S. and Wagner, E. (2004) Understanding the Contextual Influences on Enterprise System Design, Implementation, Use and Evaluation, *The Journal of Strategic Information Systems*, **13** (4), 271–419.

JISC (2003) *Portals: frequently asked questions*, www.jisc.ac.uk/index.cfm?name=ie_portalsfaq [accessed 21 December 2005].

Lakos, A. A. (2004) Portals in Libraries: portal vision, *Bulletin of the American Society for Information Science and Technology* [online], **31** (1), www.asis.org/Bulletin/Oct-04/lakos_intro.html [accessed 21 December 2005].

Lee, J. C. and Myers, M. D. (2004) Dominant Actors, Political Agendas, and Strategic Shifts Over Time: a critical ethnography of an enterprise systems implementation, *Journal of Strategic Information Systems*, **13** (4), 355–74.

McKay, P. (2003) *My.Caledonian: case study of an institutional portal*, www.jisc.ac.uk/uploaded_documents/Glasgow_Caledonian_case_study.doc [accessed 12 December 2005].

Miller, P. (2001) The Concept of the Portal, *Ariadne*, **30** [online], www.ariadne.ac.uk/issue30/portal/intro.html [accessed 1 October 2005].

Murray, M. (2003) *duo – Durham University Online: implementing the Blackboard™ Community Portal*, www.jisc.ac.uk/uploaded_documents/Durham_case_study2.doc [accessed 12 December 2005].

Paschoud, J. (2002) Portals Portals Everywhere . . . why the interface to everything is not an interface for everyone, www.angel.ac.uk/public-files/ppt/OU-Personalisation-Oct02a.ppt [accessed 22 December 2005].

Pearce, L. (2003) *Institutional Portals: a review of outputs*, www.fair-portal.hull.ac.uk/downloads/iportaloutputs.pdf [accessed 22 December 2005].

Smith, N., Schmoller, S. and Ferguson, N. (2004) *Personalisation in Presentation Services*, www.jisc.ac.uk/uploaded_documents/jp-study-15.pdf [accessed 1 November 2005].

Techencyclopedia (2005) *Portal*, www.techweb.com [accessed 21 December 2005].

Tingling, P. and Parent, M. (2004) An Exploration of Enterprise Technology Selection and Evaluation, *Journal of Strategic Information Systems*, **13** (4), 329–54.

Volkoff, O., Elmes, M. B. and Strong, D. M. (2004) Enterprise Systems, Knowledge Transfer and Power Users, *Journal of Strategic Information Systems*, **13** (4), 279–304.

Wagner, E. and Newell, S. (2004) 'Best' for Whom?: the tension between 'best practice' ERP packages and diverse epistemic cultures in a university context, *Journal of Strategic Information Systems*, **13** (4), 305–28.

Winkler, R. (2001) Portals – The All-In-One Web Supersites: features, functions, definitions, taxonomy, www.sapdesignguild.org/editions/edition3/portal_definition.asp [accessed 22 December 2005].

2

Portals or filters? Identifying quality on the internet

Andrew Madden

Introduction

This chapter looks at the changing role of portals, and considers what function they may serve in the future.

It is common for new technologies to be understood by relating them to older, more familiar technologies. Two consequences of this tendency are discussed: problems associated with the new technology's adoption might be ignored, and opportunities that are afforded by it are sometimes overlooked.

In the case of the internet, comparisons with print and broadcast media often ignore the fact that such means of information exchange are subject to a greater degree of quality control than the internet. They are also, however, far more constrained and less accessible than the internet.

Portals, it is argued, can help to compensate for the loss of some of the quality control mechanisms associated with other media, while allowing a level of discussion and exchange that would not previously have been possible.

A change of role

In July 1999, the retail outlet Dixons floated 20% of its Internet Service Provider, Freeserve (DSG International, 2005). The Dot Com bubble was inflating nicely at the time; Freeserve (now Wanadoo) had over a million subscribers, and there was considerable interest in the flotation (Fleming,1999).

In the preceding year, it had become conventional wisdom

> that 'portals' would be the means whereby corporations would capture the hearts and minds of consumers . . . . They were therefore expected by this particular round of soothsayers to command high advertising-rates and click-through fees, plus commissions on resulting sales.
> (Clarke, 1999)

The Freeserve flotation was part of what Tim Berners-Lee (1999) refers to as 'the battle of the portals'. At the time, I remember hearing an interview with a financial pundit who expressed the view that the shares would be a good investment. Freeserve, he explained, provided a way into the internet for over a million users, and with such a large potential audience, advertisers would be as interested in Freeserve as they would in a television channel.

As McLuhan (1964) observed, a common way of coming to terms with a new technology is to relate it to an existing one:

> people feel compelled to look at new situations as if they were old ones (33).

The most common way of encountering information and entertainment through a screen was (and still is) through a TV. What the pundit had not grasped, however, is that web pages have very little in common with television programmes, and so portals are not like television channels. Nevertheless, the prevailing thinking at the time was that portals would be the automatic first port-of-call for large numbers of captive net users (Clarke, 1999).

As more people have become familiar with the web and have grown accustomed to finding their way around it, the need for a fixed entry point has declined. Definitions of portals now stress their value in providing access to useful web-based information, rather than to the web itself. The Microsoft (2006) website, for example, defines a portal as

> a single web interface that provides personalised access to information, applications, business processes and much more. With portal technology . . . you can aggregate and integrate information within a particular working environment, application or service
> . . .

According to RePAH (Research Portals in the Arts and Humanities),

> A portal brings together content from diverse resources, amalgamates it and presents it to the user. The general purpose of a portal is to allow the user to find and cross-reference information from different sources by searching and browsing.
> (Greengrass, 2005)

Portals therefore, are no longer valued as windows onto cyberspace, but as routes to reliable resources.

While few people nowadays would liken the internet to television, it is still common, even amongst expert users, to perceive it as an electronic library (Ratzan, 2000; Madden, Bryson and Palmi, 2006). When viewed in this light, it becomes reasonable to consider the creation of resources that serve some of the same functions as library catalogues: i.e. the introduction of order, and the provision of guidance for the inexpert user.

A key ingredient of any library, however, is quality control. This is present at two levels. No library has an unlimited budget, or unlimited space. The first level of quality control, therefore, is determined by the decisions made for the library users. What should be bought? What should be kept? How these decisions are made depends on the function of the library, the perceived interests of its users, and the views of its managers; but they will shape the library.

A second level of quality control is present because the documents within a library are, in general, books. The production of a book usually involves a collection of interests, comprising not only the authors, but also those of editors and financiers. While this does not guarantee the quality of a book, it is in the interests of several people to ensure that its contents can be defended.

The contents of the internet, by contrast, are not subject to any form of quality control. Documents on the web may be the work of an authoritative body, or they may be the ramblings of a lone juvenile. Unlike a library catalogue, therefore, if a portal is to lead a user to reliable resources, those responsible for the construction of the portal must not merely categorize the contents, they must also review and assess them.

Affordances

The practice of likening a new technology to an existing, established one, is useful in getting the new technology accepted by people who are unfamiliar with it and who could feel threatened by any changes that may follow its introduction. All technologies have their limitations. Arguing that the new is merely an improved version of the old reduces the threat of change, and focuses on recognizable benefits. It can also, however, obscure other activities afforded by the new technology that would not be possible with the older one.

The concept of 'affordances' became popularly associated with technology following the publication of Donald Norman's book *The Psychology of Everyday Things* (1989). The idea arose from the work of James Gibson (1986), who argued that humans perceive their environment and the objects it contains, not in terms of measurable qualities, such as height, weight, colour, etc., but in terms of what actions those qualities facilitate:

> There is much evidence to show that the infant does not begin by first discriminating the qualities of objects and then learning the combinations of qualities that specify them. Phenomenal objects are not built up of qualities; it is the other way around. The affordance of an object is what the infant begins by noticing. The meaning is observed before the substance and surface, the color and form, are seen as such.

Gibson's theories of perception help to explain why children are so adept at learning to use new technologies. Slum children in India, left alone with a PC, learned to use it without instruction (Mitra and Rana, 2001). Similarly, school children searching the internet attempted to improve their searches by performing actions and using facilities that they had discovered for themselves (Madden et al., 2006). Faced with a new phenomenon, adults apply models derived from their experience and learning, while children will construct and test models through exploration during play (Faucher et al, 2002, 348–54).

Old literacies

Discussion on the impact of the internet and other information and communications technologies (ICTs) frequently focuses on new 'literacies' (e.g. Kellner, 2000). These often include references to 'computer literacy' and 'internet literacy'. By implication, therefore, the skills needed to master ICT are being likened to the skills of reading and writing, both of which are considered so fundamental to life in an industrial or post-industrial society that the benefits of acquiring them are rarely questioned.

One of the most familiar criticisms of literacy skills, however, was attributed to Socrates by Plato (Waterfield, 2002). Socrates dismissed text as being a tool for

> jogging the memory, not for remembering . . . [providing readers] with the appearance of intelligence, not real intelligence . . . they will seem to [have] wide knowledge, when they will usually be ignorant. (Sec 275, 69)

Despite the doubts of Socrates and probably many others, literacy spread because it was useful. Not only were written records more reliable than the memories of witnesses, but low levels of literacy helped the ruling elite to retain control of technological and other valuable information, and so remain a ruling elite.

The advent of the printing press increased the availability of texts by orders of magnitude. Where it had taken up to three years to produce a copy of the Bible by hand (Gutenberg digital, 2004), two hundred Bibles were printed by Gutenberg in the three years between 1452 and 1455 (Presser, 1974, 4, 18). Books became cheaper and more widely available. Literacy began to become more commonplace, and information that had been the preserve of a few became widely known.

An abundance of broadcasts

A broadcast was, at one time, understood to be a means of sowing seed. The seed was scattered (or cast) over a surface instead of being sown in drills or rows, as the *Oxford English Dictionary* definition confirms. This was clearly seen as being an appropriate metaphor for media such as television, in which a message from one source is spread across a field of viewers. Arguably, the same metaphor could be applied to books.

Information disseminated in books (whether printed or hand-written) clearly could not reach people as quickly as the newer medium of television. Nevertheless, the relationship between informer and informed is much the same in both cases.

The latter are, for the most part, passive receivers. Socrates' criticism of writing (Waterfield, 2002) remains valid, and applies equally to television:

> if you want an explanation of the things they're saying and you ask them about it, they just go on and on for ever giving the same single piece of information.   (Sec 275, 70)

In both cases there is a 'one-to-many' relationship. One entity (publisher, television company) broadcasts statements, images or sounds to a receiver (reader/viewer), who is incapable of entering into any dialogue (Socratic or otherwise) with what is being broadcast.

Lowering of barriers

The internet may have been compared to television and to book collections, but it is clearly neither. The low cost of publishing online affords 'many-to-many' relationships. Access to the necessary technology and skills, though still uncommon in world terms, is becoming increasingly widely available. In the UK, in the last few years it has become the norm for children of all ages to have access to the internet. In 1998, for example, just 17% of English primary schools were connected to the internet. Six years later, 99% were online. Children, therefore, are learning to use the internet at the same time as they learn to read and write (DfES, 2003).

Madden et al. (2005) have suggested that, because of this rapid increase in access to ICT resources, the educational experiences of students beginning school in the mid-1990s will be very different from those of their predecessors. They argue, however, that the full impact of ICT in the classroom will not be realized until the generation of children that grew up with ICT graduate to become teachers.

One fundamental change that is likely to take place will occur as a result of a many-to-many relationship with information sources rather than today's common-place one-to-many relationships.

Although information broadcast through books or television is not wholly reliable, there are, as has been discussed, mechanisms in place to ensure that certain minimum standards are maintained. Print, in particular, remains a trusted medium, and it is only fairly late in education that students are encouraged to question their sources. Traditionally, the practice has been to persuade children to 'look it up in a book'. Many teachers, attempting to modernize this practice, have translated the instruction to 'look it up on the internet'. Such teachers quickly realize that the internet is not as reliable as a library. A key part of education in the internet age, therefore, is recognition of reliable information resources, and an understanding of the processes by which websites are created.

One strategy that teachers adopt (Madden et al., 2003) is to direct their students to suitable websites, many of which are portals established by recognized bodies (e.g. Spartacus Educational, www.spartacus.schoolnet.co.uk/; BBC Schools, www.bbc.co.uk/schools/).

Searching for quality

Despite the original role of portals as an entry route to the internet, they may nowadays be more valuable because of what they keep out rather than what they let in. They are increasingly gaining value as an adjunct to search engines.

Technological innovations seem to pass through two cycles of invisibility. The first cycle begins with the birth of the technology, when it receives a lot of attention. A caste of professionals acquires the skills needed to operate it. These experts act as intermediaries, allowing those who can afford their services to benefit from the technology with minimal understanding. So, computers were handled by programmers, word processors were operated by trained secretaries, and professional web designers were employed for even the simplest of web pages. Because people tend to deal with the intermediary rather than the technology, they can benefit from the technology's affordances with relatively little understanding of the technology itself; so the technology fades into the background.

As a technology becomes cheaper, the proportion of the cost associated with the human intermediary becomes significantly greater. Organizations and individuals attempt to use the technology without the intermediary. Once more it becomes visible, mostly owing to the frustrations arising from the difficulties that had previously been dealt with by intermediaries. The market for the technology has grown, however, so refinements are rapidly produced, the technology becomes more intuitive, and it begins to fade once more.

At one time, only information professionals would have performed online searches. With the disintermediation of the internet (largely owing to the development of the world wide web), search skills became more widely desirable. internet users who went on courses were trained by information professionals to use a variety of tools (e.g. quotation marks, Boolean operators) in order to refine their searches. Most users, however, received no training; so searches tended to be uncomplicated. Studies of search engine transaction logs (e.g. Spink, Bateman and Jansen (1999), Jansen, Spink and Pedersen (2005)) suggest that 'most Web searches are short and simple'.

In accordance with the pattern described above, search engines adapted themselves to users. Short and simple searches are now adequate for most purposes. Often, however, the most useful part of a search does not take place at the search engine. Ongoing research at the University of Sheffield suggests that searching does not stop when the user leaves the search engine. It is common for people to begin looking for information by using a general search tool (such as a search engine), and to use this to find a specialist search tool (such as a portal) (Madden et al., 2006). Like the teachers referred to above, who direct their students to a website of known quality, searchers will often look for a portal with an associated 'brand' (such as BBC) to identify a reliable source.

Interacting with information

Analogies to recorded sources of information (such as books) ignore the dynamic nature of the internet; but, used as a starting point, such analogies help to clarify what the internet can offer.

Stock (1983) argued that one consequence of the rise of literacy was the development of textual communities: collections of individuals who

> demonstrated a parallel use of texts, both to structure the internal behaviour of the groups' members and to provide solidarity against the outside world (90).

The most obvious examples of such communities are those religions which share sacred texts; but the concept could apply equally well to specialists, who share a common body of texts.

The texts that define such communities are not limited by geography, but the discussion associated with the defining texts is. On the internet, this is not a problem. Portals representing web-using communities can provide a forum for users to evaluate and review websites.

Many websites make use of the interactivity of the internet to gain feedback from users. Some, such as Amazon, do so for commercial reasons, by inviting users to contribute reviews of books. Others, such as the online encyclopaedia (and portal) Wikipedia, do so for ideological reasons. Complete openness, however, can create problems. At best, contributions can be inaccurate; at worst, they can be malicious. In November 2005, for example, in *USA Today*, John Seigenthaler described the problems he had seeking redress after having been maligned by a hoax article in Wikipedia (Seigenthaler, 2005).

Communities both virtual and real

A portal that invites any user to nominate and review websites shares the problems of any forum that is totally open to the public. If there is no formal mediation, then the forum is easy to abuse. Increasingly, though, portals are being developed that invite responses from users, but regulate access. IHR (the Institute of Historical Research), for example, is working to develop mechanisms for peer review of electronic resources (IHR, 2005). Among other objectives, these mechanisms will help to

> establish those types of resource which are of most use and interest to the academic community, contribute to the development of common standards and guidelines for accessibility and usability

In addition to virtual communities, however, physical communities are benefiting from portals. Portals designed to monitor and publicize websites offering services to a particular location are becoming common. In Sheffield, for example, the ITforMe project works through local libraries to provide links to sites of relevance and interest to library users and others living in South Yorkshire.

Summary and conclusion

In the internet's short history, perceptions of portals have changed. Where they were once valued as a first port of call for users entering cyberspace, they are now regarded as a tool for collecting useful websites into an easily accessible package.

In an effort to understand the internet, commentators have tended to compare it to the technologies with which they were familiar when they grew up. Such a practice tends to result in many of the affordances of the internet going unrecognized. Nevertheless, certain things are clear. Like television broadcasts and traditional publishing, the internet frees messages from the confines of geography. Unlike these older technologies, which represent the efforts of groups of people, the internet can genuinely provide a voice to the individual. One potentially valuable role of portals, therefore, is to create an informed sampling of these voices. To non-expert seekers of information, this provides a useful filter. If the portal has a sufficiently trusted brand, such users can find it invaluable for focusing their searches.

Portals, therefore, can impose a limited editorial control over the contents of the internet. Unlike the control of traditional editors, however, what is included in, or excluded from, a portal, can be directly determined by a community, and the portal can change in response to the needs and interests of that community.

Relatively few people have had access to the internet for a longer period than ten years. It is a short history on which to base any speculation. Now, however, a generation of children is growing up that learned to use the internet at the same time as they were learning to read and write. They will relate to the technology very differently from the generation that first introduced portals. How portals will look in future, it is hard to say. At the heart of their construction, however, will be a responsiveness and interactivity that are impossible with today's 'one-to-many' communications media.

References

Berners-Lee, T. (1999) Web of People, Chapter 10 in *Weaving the Web*, London, Texere.

Clarke, R. (1999) The Willingness of Net-consumers to Pay: a lack-of-progress report, *Proceedings of the 12th International Bled EC Conference, Slovenia, June 1999*, www.anu.edu.au/people/Roger.Clarke/EC/WillPay.html [accessed 12 January 2006].

DfES (2003) *Survey of Information and Communications Technology in Schools*, www.dfes.gov.uk/rsgateway/DB/SBU/b000421/bweb05-2003.pdf [accessed 24 January 2006].

DSG International plc. (2005) *Our History*, http://dsgportal01.dixons.co.uk/wps/portal/!ut/p/.cmd/cs/.ce/7_0_A/.s/7_0_GN/_s.7_0_A/7_0_GN [accessed 12 January 2006).

Faucher, L., Mallon, R., Nazer, D., Nichols, S., Ruby, A., Stich, S. and Weinberg, J. (2002) The Baby in the Lab-coat: why child development is not an adequate model for understanding in the development of science. In Carruthers, P., Stich S. and Siegal, M. (eds), *The Cognitive Basis of Science*, Cambridge, Cambridge University Press, 335–62.

Fleming, S. (1999) How Much is that Freeserve in the Window, *The Register*, www.theregister.co.uk/1999/07/12/how_much_is_that_freeserve/ [accessed 12 January 2006).

Gibson, J. J. (1986) The Theory of Affordances, Chapter 8 in *The Ecological Approach to Visual Perception*, Hillsdale NJ, London, Laurence Erlbaum Associates.

Greengrass, M. (2005) *RePAH: Research in Portals in the Arts and Humanities: progress report*, www.ahrcict.rdg.ac.uk/activities/strategy_projects/repah.ppt [accessed 2 February 2006).

Gutenberg digital (2004) University Library, Göttingen, Germany, www.gutenbergdigital.de/gudi/eframes/texte/framere/b42_2.htm [accessed 19 November 2004].

IHR (2005) *Peer Review and Evaluation of Digital Resources for the Arts and Humanities*, www.history.ac.uk/digit/peer/ [accessed 2 February 2006).

Jansen, B. J., Spink, A. and Pedersen, J. (2005) A Temporal Comparison of AltaVista Web searching, *JASIST*, **56** (6), 559–70.

Kellner, D. (2000) New Technologies/New Literacies: reconstructing education for the new millennium, *Teaching Education*, **11** (3), 245–65.

McLuhan, M. (1964) *Understanding Media: the extensions of man*, London, Abacus.

Madden, A. D., Ford, N. J., Miller, D. and Levy, P. (2003) Schoolchildren Searching the Internet: teachers' perceptions. In Martin, A. and Rader, H. (eds), *Information and IT Literacy: enabling learning in the 21st century*, London, Facet Publishing, 234–43.

Madden, A. D., Baptista Nunes, J. M., McPherson, M., Ford, N. J., Miller, D. and Rico, M. (2005) A New Generation Gap? Some thoughts on the consequences of increasingly early ICT first contact, *International Journal of Information and Communication Technology Education*, **1** (2), 19–33.

Madden, A. D., Bryson, J. and Palmi, J. (2006) Information Seeking Behaviour in Pre-literate Societies. In Spinks, A. and Cole, C. (eds), *Information Seeking Behaviour*, New York, Springer.

Madden, A. D., Ford, N. J., Miller, D. and Levy, P. (2006) Children's Use of the Internet for Information-seeking: what strategies do they use, and what factors affect their performance?, *Journal of Documentation* (in press).

Microsoft (2006) *Windows System Server: what is a portal?*, www.microsoft.com/uk/windowsserversystem/portals/what-is/default.mspx [accessed 12 January 2006].

Mitra, S. and Rana, V. (2001) Children and the Internet: experiments with minimally invasive education in India, *British Journal of Educational Technology*, **32** (2), 221–32.

Norman, D. A. (1989) *The Psychology of Everyday Things*, New York, Basic Books.

Presser, H. (1974) *Gutenberg-Museum of the City of Mainz – World Museum of Printing*, Munich, Germany, Verlag.

Ratzan, L. (2000) Making Sense of the Web: a metaphorical approach, *Information Research*, **6** (1), October, http://information.net/ir/6-1/paper85.html.

Seigenthaler, J. (2005) A False Wikipedia 'Biography', *USA Today*, www.usatoday.com/news/opinion/editorials/2005-11-29-wikipedia-edit_x.htm. [accessed 30 January 2006].

Spink, A., Bateman, J. and Jansen, B. J. (1999) Searching the Web: a survey of EXCITE users, *Internet Research: electronic networking applications and policy*, **9** (2), 117–28.

Stock, B. (1983) *The Implications of Literacy*, Princeton, Princeton University Press.

Waterfield, R. (2002) *Phaedrus*, by Plato, translated by Robin Waterfield, Oxford, OUP.

3

Portal architectures

Tom Franklin

Introduction

There has been considerable interest in appropriate architectures for building portals, and a number of solutions have been proposed. In this chapter I do not analyse the architectures in detail, but look briefly at what a portal is and what this means for the architectures and then look at what is needed in an architecture for building portals, using examples from some of the most important architectural models.

What is a portal?

There is no common agreement as to what a portal is. Many point out that the word means doorway (often taken to be a grand doorway such as that found at the main (west) door of a cathedral), with the implication that a portal is simply a way of accessing a number of services, but as Strauss has stated, 'a home page doth not a portal make'.[1] By which he means that it is not enough simply to bring a number of different channels or information sources together on a web page; there is a need to provide some degree of integration and customization. He goes on to describe a portal as a 'Customized Personalized Adaptive Desktop' and it is worth exploring what he means by each of these terms before looking at some of the implications for how one might build a portal, and equally how one can set about shifting the entire organization from where it is now to having a portal.

- **Customized** – The portal adapts to the user, and the more it knows about the user the better it should be able to adapt to their needs, whether the user is a member of teaching staff, administrative staff, a researcher, a student or a prospective student (or someone who occupies several of those roles – for instance a postgraduate student who also teaches). It should also be able to adapt to the type of hardware that the user is currently using (PC on a LAN, PC on a dial-up line, personal digital assistant (PDA) or smart phone). This should be done as the user logs into the portal.

- **Personalized** – Allows the user to change the portal's interface and behaviour to meet the user's needs and preferences. This would include the appearance (colours, fonts, size), channels subscribed to and their location on screen.
- **Adaptive** – Changes its behaviour depending on context. Many people will have multiple roles, and will present information or channels depending on activity. It will also have an understanding of time and be able to support workflows for example around marking exam papers.
- **Desktop** – It replaces the desktop environment, hiding the operating system by providing access to all applications and information that the user needs regardless of whether these are local or networked.

The last of these is the most contentious, and it will be a while before portals can attempt to do this.

Portals started from the idea that it would help users if services from a variety of sources could be gathered together and presented to them in a single place. Initially this included links to services in a single web page. However, people quickly wanted their portals to do more than send users off to other sites. In particular there was an idea that the portal should be designed around the various sources and enable the user to move easily between them all. The concept rapidly moved beyond simple links to the concept of channels. Channels have the advantage that the portal has some control over their behaviour, including the possibility of automatically logging the user into them and of controlling the way the channel looks to keep a uniform look and feel to the whole portal.

Some key concepts
- **Portal** – A portal is a web-based application that provides personalization, single sign-on and content aggregation from different sources, and hosts the presentation layer of information systems.
- **Channel** – Channels are individual applications or information sources which are made available through the portal.
- **Portlet** – Portlets are components of portals to access information sources or applications such as library catalogues, news, e-mail or even learning management systems and compose and display it to the user within the portal. Portlets are a means of implementing channels.

Portal architectures

A wide variety of architectures has been proposed for portals, and the reader can find many of them online; for example:

- Computer measurement group, www.cmg.org/measureit/issues/mit18/m_18_6.html
- University of Bristol, www.bris.ac.uk/is/projects/portal/7_99/mle_arch.gif
- University of California, Davis, http://my.ucdavis.edu/integration/myucdavis_enterprise_architecture_files/image004.gif
- David Viney, www.viney.com/DFV/intranet_portal_guide/before/arch_small.jpg
- IBM, www.128.ibm.com/developerworks/websphere/zones/portal/newto/images/wp-arch-hilevel.gif

JISC's own model can be found reproduced later in this book (see Chapter 15, page 204). The point is to demonstrate the lack of agreement on precisely what a portal is, and therefore on what their architecture should be like. We will not look in detail at any of these, but instead use a very simple diagram (see Figure 3.1), which contains the key features of portal architectures and illuminates the discussion below.

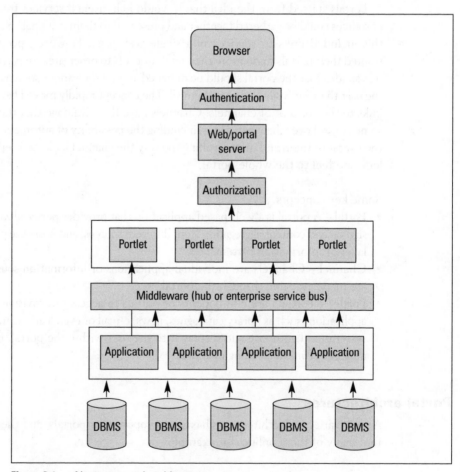

Figure 3.1   Abstract portal architecture

Users access a portal via their web browser, and sign-in to the portal server, which provides them with web pages. Assuming that the user has signed in they will be authenticated to any of the underlying services which they are authorized to use, which could be provided by the institution, or the services could be institutional services, or external to the institution (in which case they may require their own authentication methods which are not shown in this diagram). The services are built as portlets, and these provide the interfaces between the applications and the portals, either directly or via middleware. The applications can be anything from those shown in the JISC Information Environment Architecture – such as cross-searching and aggregating systems – to institutional systems such as student records, virtual learning environments, course catalogues and human resource systems.

From Figure 3.1 it can be seen that two issues are central to portal architectures: these are single (or simplified) sign-on and integration of systems, and we look at each of these in turn.

Single (or simplified) sign-on

Members of most universities currently have a large number of user names and passwords. In some universities this can be more than 20 different user name/password combinations. Each time users start using a different system they will be challenged for their user name and password again. With a portal the user should only have to log into the portal itself, and then the portal takes responsibility for logging the user into other systems as the user starts using them. It is possible to achieve this in a variety of different ways. There are two ways in which single sign-on can be implemented:

- by altering the application so that the user logs on with the sign-on method that the portal uses (this is primarily for on-campus applications which can have their authentication methods altered)
- by intercepting the authentication request when the user switches to a new application and passing the username and password on to the other system without any intervention from the user.

The latter can sometimes be used with external applications as well as internal ones provided there is a way of mapping from the user's institutional user name/password to that of the external system. Thus it appears to the user that they no longer need to log into the systems if they access them via the portal.

Many institutions are moving towards single sign-on, whether or not they are developing a portal, because it provides the user with a valuable benefit of having a single user name and password to remember. There is considerable discussion on whether or not single sign-on improves security. On the one hand, it reduces the likelihood that the user will write down their password; on the other hand, if the user name/password is compromised then all the user's systems are exposed. It is therefore essential that users understand this and treat their user name and password as being as important as the most sensitive system that they have access to. You might lend your keys to a friend to get into your house or borrow your car, but would you give them your bank card and pin number? In part, this explains why many people are now talking about simplified sign-on, whereby a common user name and password can be used for most systems but the most secure systems may require a different method of sign-on. There is also a move towards biometric authentication, whereby you are validated not by what you know (a password) or what you have (a bank card), but what you are (fingerprint, iris). This has the additional advantage that the user cannot forget their fingers or iris, or lend them to their friends.

Integration of systems

The key to creating a portal, rather than a website, is the integration of systems, something that the IT industry has been striving for at least for the last 30 years in a number of different guises (e.g. modular systems and object-oriented systems). In most institutions personal information (name, address, department) is held on multiple different systems (personnel, payroll, library, registry, etc.). Which of these is the authoritative one? Which (if any) of these are correct? There are two issues that have to be resolved here: data ownership and data handling.

In most institutions the 'owners' of systems gain much of their authority and power through that ownership and are reluctant to let go. The personnel department insists that it holds the authoritative name and address of employees, and the registry that it does for students (but someone may be both an employee and a student), and in many institutions the library insists on holding the same information so that it can chase up overdue books. Departments often insist on collecting the information themselves (because they don't trust the central databases to be correct) and so the data multiplies. When someone moves, do they remember (or even know) to tell all these groups that they have moved?

To move beyond this each piece of information should have a single place where the authoritative version is held (we look at how other systems use it below). This means building up a data registry. For each item of information the registry would include what that information is, where it is held, who is responsible for it and optionally how it may be used. Many organizations are now doing this even if they are not creating a portal because it is one of the tools that can be used to understand and manage the information within the organization. For a portal it is essential: without it users will see different information depending on which system they are accessing, and as different systems hold differing (and often wrong) information can destroy users' faith in the entire system.

The transformation towards data being held in a single location and used by many systems will not be easy because system (or data) 'owners' will have to rely on others for information which they may have started collecting precisely because they did not trust that information source, or because the original data owner was unwilling to make the information available in a timely manner that met the other system owners' needs. However, the benefits are enormous both in terms of having better, more reliable data and through the large savings that can be made through collecting and updating data only once and making it available to all systems as they need it. Furthermore, these benefits accrue whether or not a portal is built. If you are considering building a portal then the earlier that this process is started the better. It will take a considerable amount of time to create the data registry, and even longer to negotiate who is the 'owner' of each type of information. It can then be taken to the next logical step, which is determining who has authority to see and to update any piece of information. For instance, in many universities students and staff can update some of their personal information such as address or phone number, while in others they may not. The rules for this need to be determined so that systems can be built that meet these rules.

The implication of this is that systems will be drawing their data from different sources, and in new and more complex ways than hitherto. Historically, in most places data is passed between systems through special purpose routines that have been written specifically to support that transaction. This was manageable as few systems passed data so that the number of such routines that had to be written and supported was very small (see Figure 3.2). However, as the number of systems grows the number of potential links grows exponentially. If the data has been rationalized through the creation of the data registry so that there is a single authoritative version of any data then the number of such links grows very rapidly and soon becomes unmanageable, as shown in Figure 3.3.

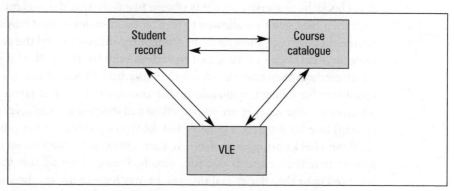

Figure 3.2   Connections between a small number of applications

In fact, Figure 3.3 shows a fairly small selection of applications, but already has over 30 links, each of which has to be developed and maintained, and updated each time any of the applications involved is updated. Most universities have significantly more systems than this, including payroll, estates management, student admissions, research grants management, publications, alumni, etc., and those are just the central systems. Many departments or schools also have their own applications as well so that the number of applications may run into the hundreds in a large university with

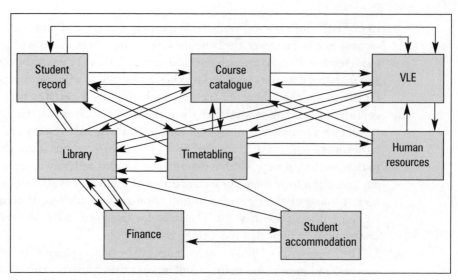

Figure 3.3   Connections in a medium-sized set of applications

the number of potential links running into the tens of thousands. Each time any application is changed an increasing number of routines that interface with other programs must also be changed. Each of these is complex, with the result that the system rapidly becomes unmanageable.

Let us briefly consider an example of the data flows for a relatively simple transaction. A student wishes to register to take a particular module. The system may check the university accounts system to ensure that the student is up to date with their fees, and thus allowed to register on modules, then it may check which degree they are registered on in the student record system and the course rules in the course catalogue to see if that module is valid for them. Next it might check which modules they have already taken (in the student record system) and the pre-conditions for taking the module (in the course catalogue). It could next look at which other courses they are registered on and the course timetables (timetabling system) to ensure that it is possible to take the requested module. Assuming that all these checks are passed it might then check with the course management system that the course is not full. Finally, having done all this the student is accepted onto the course, and the system may have to inform the student record system of the student's registration, then look up in the identity system the student's preferred form of communication (e-mail, SMS, etc.) and send a message confirming the registration. The student would also be registered into the virtual learning environment for the module and module registration system may check the course leader's preferred communication method and inform them of the student's registration. Finally it may post some billing information to financial systems. The information flows are shown in Figure 3.4.

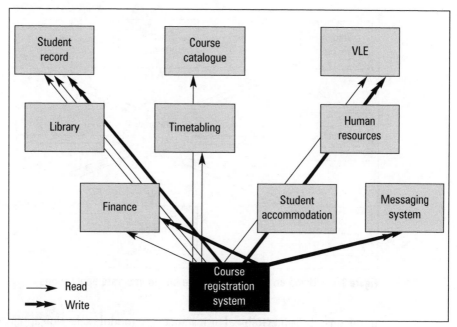

Figure 3.4 Transactions required to register on a module

Integration solutions

There are many ways in which this problem can be addressed. Special routines can be written to interface the module selection system with each of these other systems, but as we have already discussed this rapidly becomes unmanageable. An alternative is to create an enterprise service bus (also known as a hub), which mediates all data requests. Then each application has to write only a single set of routines which interface between it and the enterprise service bus, or a service can be written to handle each type of data request. The enterprise service bus then has an application program interface (API) which can be used by any application that needs to request information from, or pass information to, another application. See Figure 3.5.

An enterprise service bus is the central system, which handles data requests from all applications and retrieves the data from the appropriate system(s), and possibly passes information to other programs as well. It means that when a system is added (or amended) there is a need to build a single set of interfaces between the system and the enterprise service bus. Requests for data are passed to the enterprise service bus, which is responsible for ensuring that the request is valid (i.e. the application requesting it has the authority to access that data and the user of the application has the authority to see the data), and then forwarding it to the appropriate application and receiving the data from that application, possibly reformatting it for the receiving application and returning it. While this is complex enough, the enterprise service bus will inevitably become more complex if updating of information is handled from outside the system that 'owns' the data. And this,

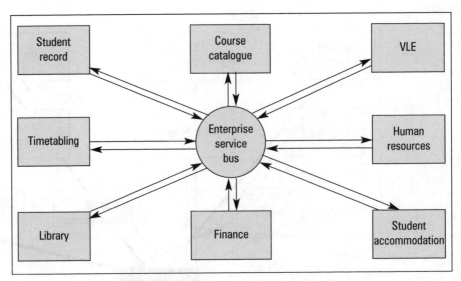

Figure 3.5   Using an enterprise service bus to integrate applications

unfortunately, is inevitable. For instance, the module selection application that we considered earlier may need to update the student record system, the virtual learning environment and the accounting system. These updates all have to be securely handled via the enterprise service bus, which must also have which must also have the ability to roll back if any part of the transaction should fail. The advantage of the enterprise service bus is that the complexity of the systems grows linearly with the number of applications (rather than exponentially with the individually developed links). However, the enterprise service bus will be an extremely complex application, the complexity of which grows as more information is shared between applications. It will also need considerable re-engineering whenever a system is updated or replaced.

Service-based solutions

This has led to interest in using a service-based approach. This goes under a variety of names, including service-oriented architecture (SOA) and web services, where web services is a particular way of implementing a service-oriented architecture. It is worth looking at what service-oriented architectures are, how universities might consider deploying them and some of the issues they raise.

There are many definitions of service-oriented architecture. Here are a couple taken almost at random:

A service-oriented architecture (SOA) defines how two computing entities interact in such a way as to enable one entity to perform a unit of work on behalf of another entity. The unit of work is referred to as a service, and the service interactions are defined using a description language. Each interaction is self-contained and loosely coupled, so that each interaction is independent of any other interaction.[2]

A service-oriented architecture is essentially a collection of services (where a service is a function that is well-defined, self-contained, and does not depend on the context or state of other services). These services communicate with each other. The communication can involve either simple data passing or it could involve two or more services coordinating some activity. Some means of connecting services to each other is needed.[3]

Let us first look at what a service is, then at how we might link the services together. The key point to note in the definitions is that services are well defined and self-contained. Self-contained means that a service can exist and function independently of any other particular service or application. This does not mean that it does not make use of other services. An important part of the concept is that services can call upon other services to provide some of their functionality. However, as the services are independent any service which offers the same functionality and interface could be used since there is no dependence on a particular service. Thus services offer small, reusable pieces of functionality that can be used to support or even assemble other services and applications. The idea is not new, and builds on work of the object-oriented community going back at least as far as the mid-1970s and modular programming which has an even longer history. However, there are two key differences in SOA. First, there is a presumption that the services can be automatically invoked by programs at run time, instead of having to be assembled in advance of need by programmers. Second, with the development of the internet there is the assumption that services can exist (and be run) anywhere in cyberspace rather than having to exist and run on local machines. Arising from this there are further problems to be solved. One has to be able to locate services in order to be able to use them, which means that there need to be directories that list services, their functionality, where they can be found and the terms for using them. These directories are called service registries, and there is a standard for them called Universal Description, Discovery and Integration (UDDI). Second, there need to be standards for describing the services and their interfaces and for methods by which the services can communicate with each other. Typically the interaction between the services is handled by another standard – the Simple Object Access Protocol (SOAP), Web Services for Remote Portals (WSRP) or JSR 168. The format of the data these days is almost always expressed in eXtensible Markup Language (XML). However, XML is a very general language so that a very large number of standards have been developed for more specific purposes which are expressed using XML. Examples of these include the IMS specifications for use in education, the IEEE Learning Object Metadata (LOM) standard, Security Assertion Markup Language (SAML) for authorization, authentication and accounting, and Electronic Business using XML (ebXML) for business transactions.

The advantage that a service-oriented approach offers is that when new functionality is needed only the affected services need to be amended. Because the services have well defined interfaces it becomes possible to replace services which offer new functionality so long as the interface remains the same. Should the interface need to change then the services which it interacts with may also have to change. If the service requires new data then the service that produces the data may also have to be changed. To go back to our example of course registration, if there is suddenly an age limit imposed on some of the courses then that information would have to be passed from the catalogue (which may also have to be changed) and the student's age (or date of birth) retrieved from the student record. Only the services which retrieve data from the course catalogue and the student record need to be changed. Similarly, should a new payment method become available then the accounting system would only need to make use of an additional service which handled the new method of payment (PayPal perhaps), without having to re-engineer anything else.

This provides the infrastructure on which we can build the portal in a unified and extensible way in order to provide the 'Customized Personalized Adaptive Desktop' mentioned in the introduction to this chapter.

Issues

As is apparent from the discussion so far, the situation is extremely complex, with new standards and specifications [4] being developed all the time. In the educational domain there is already a plethora of standards and specifications to choose from, including IMS [5] (which itself has around 20 different specifications including IMS Enterprise, IMS Learner Information and IMS eportfolio), the Schools Interoperability Framework (SIF) [6], Sharable Courseware Object Reference Model (SCORM) [7], IEEE Learning Object Metadata (LOM) [8], Dublin Core (DC), The Open Knowledge Initiative (OKI) [9] and Open Service Interface Definitions (OSID).

Unfortunately, having a standard is not enough. The standards are all extremely complex and many of them contain ambiguities, leaving them open to interpretation, so that even where a service claims that it is compliant with the standard it does not mean that it is capable of interoperating with other services due to differences in interpretation of the standard. There is therefore a need to be able to demonstrate compliance with the standard and thus the need for systems capable of testing for compliance. In the educational context a European Union-funded project called Telcert [10] is creating such as system, and starting with some of the IMS specifications.

Portal developments in UK higher education

A number of universities are in the process of implementing portals (a few have already gone live). The majority of implementations are based on uPortal, [11] either as the free, open source version of uPortal from JA-SIG, or a commercially supported variant such as Luminis[12] from SCT. Much of the early work in this area was supported by the JISC,[13] which has run several programmes in support of the use of portals[14] and service-oriented architectures. Initial work focused on information portals, and was concerned with helping users locate and access information resources through a variety of means including subject portals.[15] It has also part funded some of the early developments of portals within universities, the best known being at the University of Hull,[16] which among other things undertook a detailed requirements study, literature review and introductory information on uPortal.

More recently the JISC has funded an e-learning framework[17] and an e-framework programme[18] (the latter being jointly funded by the Australian Department for Education, Science and Training). These are looking to develop a service-oriented architecture for use in education, and many of the services are likely to be surfaced through portals.

Actions to take now

Whether or not you are planning to develop a portal in the near future there are several steps which will provide benefits, and ease the development of the portal when you decide to implement one. These are:

- **Implement simplified/single sign-on** – This will provide great benefits to users by enabling them to use any of the systems that they are allowed to as soon as they have logged on to the system. It also reduces the number of support calls because users do not forget a single user name/password, or use the wrong one and ask for help.
- **Have a single identifier for each person** – This should be the same for that person regardless of their roles – prospective student, student, alumnus, employee. Note that one individual may occupy several of these roles at the same time, but all systems should be required to use the same identifier, which once issued should be permanent.
- **Create profiles for each role** – Different roles have different rights and responsibilities (lecturers, departmental secretary, payroll staff, deans, etc.). Define the roles and rights of each group so that role-based authorization can be implemented. Without this, it is necessary to define the rights of each individual. This will form the basis for the personalization of the portal.
- **Create a data catalogue or registry** – Define all the data being used in the institution. As far as possible ensure that there is only a single copy of any element (or where there are copies only one is considered authoritative and others are copies of it).
- **Define data owners for each data element** – Define who is responsible for the element, and what their responsibilities are.

- **Implement 'middleware'** – In order to enable the levels of application integration discussed above, implement some form of middleware to dispense with application-to-application communications in order to keep the number and types of interaction manageable and secure.

Bibliography

Gilmore, B., Farvis, K. and Maddock, J. (2004) *Core Middleware and Shared Services Studies: single sign-on report*, JISC, www.jisc.ac.uk/uploaded_documents/CMSS-Gilmore.pdf.

Ingram, C. and Awre, C. (2005) *Contextual Resource Evaluation Environment Literature Review*, www.hull.ac.uk/esig/cree/downloads/CREEliteraturereview.pdf.

The Open Group, *Introduction to Single Sign-on*, www.opengroup.org/security/sso/sso_intro.htm.

Strauss, H. (2002) All About Web Portals: a home page doth not a portal make. In Katz, Richard N. and associates, *Web Portals and Higher Education: technologies to make IT personal*, San Francisco, Jossey-Bass, www.educause.edu/ir/library/html/pub5006.asp.

Notes

1. Strauss, H. (2002) All About Web Portals: a home page doth not a portal make. In Katz, Richard N. and associates, *Web Portals and Higher Education: technologies to make IT personal*, San Francisco, Jossey-Bass.
2. www.whatis.com/.
3. www.service-architecture.com/index.html.
4. A standard has been approved by an official standards body such as ISO (International Standards Organization), the British Standards Institute (BSI) or an organization approved by ISO such as IEEE. Specifications have no such official backing and can be produced by anyone including industry bodies and academia. Specifications may be as important as standards, for instance most of the web is run on specifications produced by W3C.
5. www.imsproject.org/.
6. www.sifinfo.org/.
7. www.adlnet.org/.
8. http://ltsc.ieee.org/wg12/.
9. www.okiproject.org/index.html.
10. www.opengroup.org/telcert/.
11. www.uportal.org/.
12. www.sct.com/Education/products/p_l_index.html.

13   The Joint Information Systems Committee of the further and higher education funding councils of the United Kingdom. This body is responsible for the national ICT infrastructure for universities and colleges in the UK, including the academic internet (Janet) and nationally provided datasets. It also runs a research and development programme to support the use of ICT in teaching, research and the management of colleges and universities. See www.jisc.ac.uk/.

14   www.jisc.ac.uk/programme_portals.html.

15   www.portal.ac.uk/spp/.

16   www.fair-portal.hull.ac.uk/index.html.

17   www.elframework.org/.

18   www.e-framework.org/.

4

Personalization initiatives in the public and academic domains

Mark Hepworth, Steve Probets,
Fadi Qutaishat and Geoff Walton

Introduction

To personalize has been defined as to 'design or produce (something) to meet someone's individual requirements'. That products and services should be focused on a target community and fulfil the demands, wants and needs of that community is accepted as a truism by marketers in virtually all domains. A successful product, whether it is a car seat, a bar of chocolate or a computer game, tends to be inspired by a deep knowledge of the consumer derived either through systematic market research or expert knowledge via practice. Such products tend to satisfy either a long, thin horizontal niche across a wide population or a deep, narrow niche vertically within a population. Information products and services, although paying lip service to user-centred design, have tended not to be geared to the specific needs of the user. However, current developments in personalization are beginning to lead to information products that can be both generic and specific by being able to adapt to the specific needs of the user.

In the past this 'consumerist market philosophy' has only partially penetrated the design and development of information products. Services such as portals as well as libraries, compact discs, online databases, public access catalogues, portals, web-based information services, even the computer desktop itself and most computer applications have tended to be generalized and aimed to meet the common needs of a broad community.

In fact there is still doubt in some quarters about the general value of investing time on personalization. Neilsen (1998), for example, who has gained quite a reputation in the area of human–computer interface design and usability, has stated that it is better to concentrate on general characteristics of good interface design than on personalization. Despite the stress on personalization features in an increasing number of products – portals, online catalogues, virtual learning environments, world wide web search tools, e-messaging services, as well as by e-commerce vendors

– few studies have been conducted into the impact of personalization. One exception is in personalized health information provision where Kreuter and Strecher (1996) showed the benefit of personalized information provision. Whether or not this has similar lessons for information products that serve a less focused need is as yet unproven.

However, the idea of 'tailored' or 'personalized' information products has been present for some time, for example, among library and information professionals who serve people with specific roles. Similarly, electronic information systems and products have had functionality that related to specific roles and subject specific needs. More recently, from the design community, approaches (influenced by an earlier background in ergonomics) such as co-design (Clarkson et al., 2003) and the use of methods such as ethnographic techniques to help understand the world and needs of a particular community of potential users of a product are increasingly common. This has been the outcome of greater emphasis being placed on user requirement analysis in computer engineering, and the notion of user-centred design, leading to changes in the software/system development process.

The advent of e-commerce has also been a driver for personalization. Marketeers who have a knowledge of the consumer goods sector have brought their conception of 'service' and the need to provide a personalized, customer-focused service – one that emulates or even enhances the physical shopping experience and the associated face to face encounter. This has led to attempts to incorporate a personalized experience when the individual is involved in electronic shopping, generally suggesting another similar product or perhaps enabling the user to make choices as to the form of the finished purchase.

At a more fundamental level, thinking has been influenced by a constructivist perception of users: a user is situated in a particular social context that the product needs to embrace to be accepted and integrated. Furthermore socio-political drivers such as democratization, participation and the concept of inclusion and the perceived need for products and services to be able to respond to and be accessible by all people in society have led to changes, some encapsulated and enforced by recent legislation, such as the Disability Discrimination Act in the UK, that require designers to ensure that products and services are accessible to users with different abilities.

However, personalization has been held back by economic constraints, including the labour costs of creating tailored material and of creating computer code that will enable the dynamic authoring of content plus computing and telecommunication capacity. There is also, we would argue, a fundamental lack of knowledge of the interactive and communication needs of the consumers of electronic information products such as portals. Relatively little experience has been developed as to how to respond to these needs, dynamically, in the electronic domain. Nor is there a well defined methodology for gathering these needs at the required depth, despite a growing awareness of the requirement to understand these needs.

Furthermore, there are concerns about the potential intrusive nature of personalization where the user is irritated by inappropriate messages due to faulty assumptions by the system or where privacy is threatened. For example, where access to insecure personal data leads to illegitimate use of the data by third parties or where unwanted e-mail is delivered by automated systems.

Nevertheless, electronic information products are incorporating personalization features and more and more methods of enabling personalization are being explored. The following provides an overview of the form that personalization is currently taking, and what is likely to inform its development specifically within portals.

Levels and forms of personalization

Personalization of information has been described as 'coarse grained tailoring' where prewritten units of material are recommended and chosen, or 'fine grained tailoring' where each page is adapted for the individual. 'Coarse grained tailoring' would be where the user has stated certain criteria such as previously taken taught courses, and the system presents further relevant learning material. 'Fine grained tailoring' could incorporate different material such as smaller chunks of text, images, appropriate language, font, layout, background, etc. and assemble these in a way that is based on a user's profile. User modelling and personalization can also take place while the user interacts with the system via monitoring, logging and processing the user's navigation and selection of material. Personalization tends to take one or more of these broad approaches.

Modelling the user

Capturing enough data about the user to provide a personalized response is difficult. The amount of mediation that the user is willing to undertake and, depending on the degree of personalization intended, the need to gather the data from the user is a source of conflicting demands.

Data can be captured via mediation or non-mediation
Mediation

This implies, at its simplest, the user making a selection, such as choosing items of information to be included on a webpage, the layout and colour of the site, discussion forums. The user could, however, provide various data, such as demographic data, e.g. name, age, gender, education, location; perhaps role, task, areas of interest, knowledge; learning style, e.g. holist/visualizer; physical condition, e.g. sighted; cognitive state, e.g. dyslexia; emotional state, e.g. needing encouragement. The system will then need to process these 'values' and, according to previously defined rules, select, process and present information accordingly.

Non-mediation

This depends on the system being able to make assumptions based on the course of the user's interaction with the system and use of their computer. IF one selects this item/link THEN show this . . . An individual's bookmarks stored in the web browser, in frequently visited sites or even in the content of e-mails, can be a source of data for personalization. This can be used to indicate a person's areas of interest and perhaps expertise, and then to access and filter sources, as well as to enable contact and communication with other people.

Examples of personalization

Personalization tends to be a mixture of mediated and non-mediated user interaction.

Cookies

Cookies are commonly discussed in relation to personalization. However, they are an often non-mediated means of facilitating the storage of information about the user. They are a method of maintaining 'state' information about the user's computer, the user and their selections. Cookies can be created by web servers to identify uniquely a user (or machine), enabling data about the user to be stored. The data can be stored either within the cookie on the user's machine or, more frequently, on a web server. In the latter case the cookie simply maintains a user-identifier which indexes data stored in a database or on the web server. Services such as Amazon and easyJet use this type of approach to create slightly personalized web pages where a 'Hi Mark' type of page may be provided, and specific selections offered. However, data stored in the database can also be used as the basis for personalized e-mails delivering a targeted marketing message. E-mail-based personalization is developing further. GMail, Google's proposed new e-mail service, has recently come under fire due to plans to scan a user's incoming e-mails for the purpose of enabling advertising to be targeted at specific users (BBC News, 2004). IBM has also developed a system whereby e-mails are parsed and analysed to determine people who have similar interests and people with expertise (Marwick, 2001).

It is also possible to identify and log the links in a website that have been selected in a session by a user and on the basis of this suggest other links. A similar approach can be taken in the virtual learning environment, suggesting that certain teaching material be viewed once a person has completed another module or on the basis of an evaluative test.

Collaborative filtering

Collaborative filtering takes a similar approach but uses the information in a different way. If you use Amazon.com, by choosing a book other books will be suggested that may be of interest. These suggestions are based on the captured choices of other people who have made a similar purchase to yours. In other words, collaborative filtering is looking for similarities in the user/system interaction and making 'personalized' recommendations on that basis. Another application of collaborative filtering is to identify other people, based on their user profile and one's own, with similar interests or who may be useful for a specific project due to their skills, knowledge, experience, etc.

Non-mediated personalization can be static but it is likely to be able to adapt dynamically since data can be captured, non-intrusively, throughout the user's interaction and between interactions. However, a mediated system can also be updated and customized.

Mediated personalization is present in a number of information products. In the public domain sites such as MyYahoo! and MyMSN – classic portal sites – enable personal data and personal preferences to be entered and used to provide desktops that can be personalized. These services allow the user to change the appearance of the site in terms of content, e.g. choosing topics such as health and wellness, local, sports, news; colours, e.g. colour of frames, background; layout, e.g. where boxes are on the screen. Font size can also be adjusted. In addition, the user can choose the discussions, lists and blogs that they want to join and get 'feeds' from.

Corporate environment

In the corporate environment, portal vendors such as Plumtree Software or Microsoft's Sharepoint provide a desktop that can be tailored to the user and provide access to a wide range of systems both within and outside the organization. Only the most useful information and services are presented to the user. These include subject-specific, e.g. industry-specific, news stories. E-mails can be filtered; internal resources such as databases, public folders, calendars, training material, knowledge directories and the means to interact and collaborate with colleagues can be made available. External sources such as blogs, newswires, price feeds, etc. can be filtered and delivered to the desktop. In the background the system carries out maintenance, such as checking, changing and deleting links; usage statistics are gathered. Popular and underused sources are identified and acted on.

Academic environment

In the academic environment, the application of personalization to the provision of learning environments is in the early stages of development. Universities teach far more students than before; this has been a key driver for change, along with a greater stress on distance and independent learning, the desire to facilitate access to resources and the evolution of the technology itself. In one area, resources have gone into developing online learning environments, such as:

- portals, e.g. uPortal, COSE, CoFE and Sakai
- virtual learning environments, such as Blackboard
- gateways to online databases, such as Metalib, and learning resources
- computer-aided assessment, which enables students to test themselves as part of a learning package and also radically reduces the time spent on marking for formal assessment.

One area where some degree of personalization has taken place is the library portal that provides integrated access to online sources, such as via Metalib from Ex-Libris or ENCompass from Endeavor as well as the online public access catalogue (OPAC). These services can personalize the process of searching for academic resources. They provide links only to subscribed e-journals or the 'most appropriate copy' for an individual wishing to access an online resource. However, in terms of accessibility, for example providing screen reader access for a person with sight problems, these systems tend to be poor, as do the databases they give access to. The portals will, however, enable the average user to have their own personal space to store searches, references and material. Alerts can be run to highlight new resources that correspond to a user profile. Links are made to the student's reading list. Dynix intends to offer sophisticated adaptive personalization via options as well as logging. The Open University library portal provides easier access to resources as well as personalized alerts. This has led to an increase in the use of resources (Ferguson, Schmoller and Smith, 2004). Researchers at Monash University are exploring the use of intelligent agents that will summarize relevant content and make it available via the student portal.

Creating a personalized work/learning space would naturally enable many of these facets of the e-learning environment to come together. This has enabled students to be presented with material that relates to their profile, including coursework, access to resources, etc. At present this seems to be in a relatively early stage. Figure 4.1 (overleaf) shows the use of Blackboard to provide a personalized working environment in an academic setting.

The opportunity for the learner to personalize their own work space is illustrated in Figure 4.2 (overleaf), which shows the use of COSE to deliver an information literacy learning package where the student can create and save their own notes for each screen.

WHURLE

In the research domain, systems are being developed to provide a personalized learning programme and an environment for the author of learning material. For example, WHURLE (Web-based Hierarchical Universal Reactive Learning Environment) is a prototype learning system developed at Nottingham University that aims to provide adaptive learning content to students in accordance with their perceived needs (Moore, Brailsford and Stewart, 2001). WHURLE encompasses

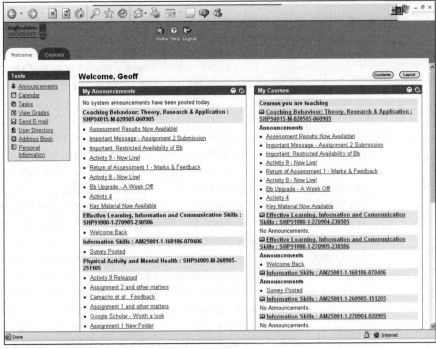

Figure 4.1   Blackboard personalized work space

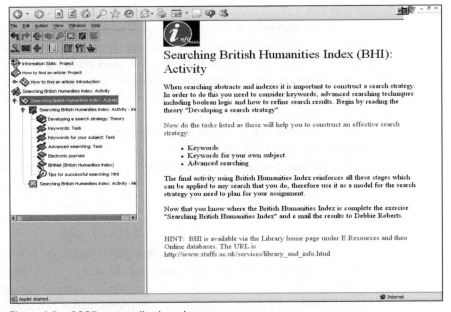

Figure 4.2   COSE personalized work space

the idea of 'transclusion' whereby material can be authored once but presented differently in different contexts. Transclusion is implemented using the Xinclude specifications from the W3C recommendations (more can be found at www.w3.org/TR/2004/REC-xinclude-20041220/). In this technique it is possible, for example, for a document to be built by the inclusion of other resources (text, images, etc.) coming from other documents (DuCharme, 2003). Therefore, content in WHURLE is coded into 'chunks' placed in different XML (eXtensible Markup Language) files. These files are managed and organized using a 'lesson plan' which can be considered as a template that references all the relevant XML files which, when combined, eventually deliver appropriate HTML (Hypertext Markup Language) pages to a student's web browser. The lesson plan includes a references for two types of materials – basic and supplementary. Students are modelled in WHURLE through users' profiles; each student has a profile that stores information such as their skills, level of knowledge, etc. This information is gathered explicitly through mediated approaches (e.g. Q&A) or implicitly through non-mediated means (e.g. time spent reading a page).

In WHURLE, the information contained in a student's profile is taken in association with the lesson plan when creating pages of content. Basic materials are presented first in an appropriate layout, relying on the information stored in that student's profile. If a student profile reflects a low knowledge in the presented subject, links to more relevant supplementary materials become available. On the other hand, if a student profile reflects a high knowledge in the presented subject, links to higher level materials become available. (This is called 'conditional transclusion'.)

AHA

Another interesting research project is AHA (Adaptive Hypermedia Architecture), which has been developed at Eindhoven University in the Netherlands (De Bra and Calvi, 1998). This is an example of an authoring systems for personalized hypermedia documents. AHA enables authors to create systems (in almost any subject) with personalized features (such as adaptive content and link structure) according to a maintained user model. Any system generated by AHA depends on the following key aspects for implementing the adaptation:

- **User modelling based on concept-value pairs** – In this methodology the system builds a user model based on materials offered to the user and the evaluation of these materials. This can occur through reading a page or taking a small test reflecting the gained knowledge. This is accomplished in AHA through using (C, V) pairs where C is the concept that is being read by the user and V is the knowledge value gained for that concept (e.g. the Boolean representation 'False' for unknown or 'True' for known). Other user preferences (e.g. preferred link colours) are modelled using the previous pairs but with different knowledge representation (e.g. red, blue, etc.).

- **Adaptive content** – Here the content is coded in a way that allows filtering processes in the system to include only fragments of information that fulfil some conditions that should be reflected in the user model (see Figure 4.3).

```
<!-if definition and history -->
This part appears if the two "concepts"
definition and history are both known
according to the user model.
<!-else -->
If this is not the case then this
alternative is presented instead.
<!-endif -->
```

Figure 4.3   Conditional inclusion of fragments (De Bra and Calvi, 1998)

- **Adaptive linking** – The links in a system generated using AHA aim to guide users to relevant content based on their knowledge level stored in their user profile. AHA allows authors to choose between three types of adaptive link techniques named link annotation, link hiding and link removal. In the link annotation technique links are coloured differently so that they can be distinguished by users (in AHA, four types of links are distinguished: desired, undesired, neutral and external). The link hiding technique occurs if the links are of type undesired and is accomplished by colouring links so that they cannot be distinguished from the surrounding text. However, the link functionality (i.e. the linking process) remains and can be distinguished when moving the mouse pointer over the link text. (Usually the browser alerts users to the presence of links by changing the mouse pointer into a hand as well as showing the destination of the link in the browser's message line.) By contrast, the link removal technique is implemented through transforming link anchors into a form that allows them to be included in pages conditionally (see Figure 4.4).

In Figure 4.4, if a link is classified under the type desired, the link anchor text and its functionality are included in the provided page, otherwise just the link anchor text is included (i.e. the link will be inactive).

```
<!-- if desired -->
<a href="...">here is the link anchor text
</a>
<!-- else -->
here is the link anchor text
<!-- endif -->
```

Figure 4.4 Using conditional links to implement links hiding (De Bra and Calvi, 1998)

Information literacy

Information literacy initiatives have also led to the development of learning environments that, although not explicitly personalized, do allow the user to learn using examples that relate to their discipline. The debate around information literacy, primarily with regard to schools, higher education and life-long learning, has also led to more focus on learning theory, learning style and thinking skills. Electronic learning environments are starting to be grounded in good pedagogy as well as accessible design. A combination of practice and increasing theoretical awareness has led this community to recognize the cultural aspect of learning information literacy. It is also increasingly appreciated that there is a need to embed information literacy learning in the learner's context, and also to enable a learning culture to evolve through practice, reflection, interaction and discourse. This indicates the scale of the challenge of designing a 'good' virtual learning environment that provides a rich learning experience.

Health sector

In the health domain, since the 1990s, a number of projects have investigated personalization, for example, Healthdoc, Migraine, Patient Advocate (Bental, Cawsey and Jones, 1999). These have included providing information a patient has not already seen, personalized leaflets, automatically completing forms, providing content of a certain tone and complexity. Most projects are ongoing and little evaluation of the popularity and impact of these systems has been done. However, Kreuter and Strecher (1996) found that tailored health information was more likely to be read, it was better remembered and led to better outcomes. Bental, Cawsey and Jones raise the question whether the results are entirely related to personalization and whether personalization may be more effective in certain situations, for example, when people are more open to suggestion. Nevertheless, knowledge is being generated and a better understanding of personalization that should lead to improved personalization strategies.

The personalization effects

Systems that enable personalization:

- capture and store characteristics of the user and on this basis authorize, filter, select, cluster, aggregate and open a gateway to resources and sources
- can alert the user to resources or suggest resources; they can help to ensure the accessibility of (learning) resources
- can enable collaboration by identifying common interests and exchangeable expertise.

Exploiting the potential power of personalization will probably be an increasingly important aspect of portals (and many other information and learning systems).

Some underlying technologies

As mentioned above information retrieval techniques such as collaborative filtering and also relevance feedback and clustering are being applied. In addition various logging software is being deployed.

Log file analysers

Log file analysers read log files (usually generated by the web server that hosts the website) and transform them into a format that provides useful information about the user's behaviour on the website. This can be tremendously helpful when making changes to the website, for instance, changing the content of the page least visited by users to make it more interesting or popular. This software is provided by many online vendors. It is possible to download free trials of their products, such as WebTrends, WebSideStory, Inc., FreeStats, Coremetrics, Inc., eXTReMe Tracking, NetGenesis and DeepMetrix Corporation (*Reading the Log Files*, 2002).

XML and XSL(T)

One technology that is having an impact (and is already the basis for some of the developments described above, e.g. WHURLE) is the eXtensible Markup Language (XML) and the associated eXtensible Stylesheet Language (XSL(T)). XML is a markup language that enables content to be described by tagging it with logical descriptive tags, thereby enabling more flexibility and control over how the content can be used and ultimately presented by a browser. Files of content can be coded (marked up) in such a way that content can be extracted and transformed according to rules specified in associated programs written in XSL(T). An XSL(T) program enables component parts of an XML document to be located and processed, transforming the core data before output to the screen or further processing by a subsequent XSL(T) program. For example, depending on the profile of the user, information can be presented with either more text or more pictorial content and individual sentences or paragraphs can be included or excluded. In addition to determining the logical content to be included, physical considerations such as font size, position of data on the screen, and background can all be determined and personalized in real time.

Standards

To enable and facilitate personalization, as can be seen from the portal solutions, there is often a need to access, on behalf of the user, different systems and retrieve and integrate data. For example, users with a particular health condition may need numerous systems to adapt to their condition. Furthermore, users may want to access the same resources using a variety of devices. To achieve this level of adaptation, the integration of data from different systems standards is essential.

Recognized ontologies, taxonomies and taxonomy environments are required so that, for example, form and content can be identified across systems. Ontologies and taxonomies enable data to be described in a machine-readable way that ensures a common understanding of the terms used within the data. They enable the terminology, and therefore the underlying data, to be shared by co-operating parties. There are many languages for representing ontologies including the Web Ontology Language (OWL), which is 'designed for use by applications that need to process the content of information instead of just presenting information to humans. OWL facilitates greater machine interpretability of Web content . . . by providing additional vocabulary along with a formal semantics' (Web Ontology Language, 2005). If content is to be transcluded or reused between different systems (whether personalized or not) then ontologies will be required to ensure the content can accurately and unambiguously described and accessed.

However, it should be noted that whether information is personalized or not, it is important that accessibility standards and guidelines such as those outlined in the web content accessibility guidelines (www.w3.org/TR/WCAG20/) are adhered to. In addition, standards and protocols are evolving to enable information and data to be found in diverse systems, aggregated and presented to the user in an accessible, and possibly personalized, format. These include standards such as JSR168 for exchanging data, RSLP Collection Description Schema and Open URL.

The future

The future of personalization depends on belief in its value. Current practice, the inertia of the status quo, the potentially higher up-front investment – including the need for highly proficient programmers as well as appropriate technology – may limit progress in personalization. However, general trends favouring realization of increasingly sophisticated personalization are:

- the drive for personalized learning environments that relate to the learning needs of the user and the possibility of improving the learning environment for large numbers of students and people in general
- the hope that personalized electronic sales/product interactions are more attractive to the consumer (as well as providing the opportunity for market growth due to diversification and segmentation) and hence commercially attractive
- the need for government services, such as health, where due to growing numbers of clients, contact via the institution and face-to-face care will become increasingly difficult, leading to information and communication technology being seen as a possible tool to provide or facilitate patient care
- the perceived need by government to promote inclusion and participation in governance via electronic means
- the promotion of information and communication technology literacy throughout society by government and industry.

It therefore seems likely that personalized electronic learning and information management environments will not go away. However, this progress will depend on a more systematic understanding of personalization and the need for and impact of personalization.

References

BBC News (2004) *Google's Gmail Could be Blocked*, http://news.bbc.co.uk/1/hi/business/3621169.stm [accessed 25 April 2005].

Bental, D. S., Cawsey, A. J. and Jones, R. (1999) Patient Information Systems that Tailor to the Individual, *Patient Education Counsel*, **36**, 171–80.

Clarkson, J., Coleman, R., Keates, S. and Lebbon, C. (2003) *Inclusive Design: design for the whole population*, London, Springer Verlag.

De Bra, P. and Calvi, L. (1998) *AHA: a generic adaptive hypermedia system*, Proceedings of the 2nd Workshop on Adaptive Hypermedia HYPERTEXT'98, 20–24 June, Pittsburgh, USA, 5–12, www.is.win.tue.nl:8080/ah98/Proceedings.html [accessed 12 July 2004].

DuCharme, B. (2003) *Transclusion with XSLT 2.0*, www.xml.com/pub/a/2003/07/09/xslt.html [accessed 9 March 2005].

Ferguson, N., Schmoller, S. and Smith, N. (2004) *Personalisation in Presentation Services*, a report commissioned by JISC, www.jisc.ac.uk [accessed March 2005].

Kreuter, M. W. and Strecher, V. J. (1996) Do Tailored Messages Enhance the Effectiveness of Health Risk Appraisal? Results from a randomised trail, *Health Education Research*, **11** (1), 97–105.

Marwick, A. D. (2001) Knowledge Management Technology, *IBM Systems Journal*, **40** (4).

Moore, A., Brailsford, T. and Stewart, C. (2001) *Personally Tailored Teaching in WHURLE Using Conditional Transclusion*, Proceedings of the 12th ACM Conference on Hypertext and Hypermedia, 14–18 August, Århus, Denmark, 163–4, http://portal.acm.org/portal.cfm [accessed 20 October 2004].

Neilsen, J. (1998) *Personalisation is Over-rated*, www.useit.com/alertbox/981004.html [accessed 24 March 2005].

Plumtree Software home page, www.plumtree.com/.

Reading the Log Files (2002), www.searchengineethics.com/logfiles.htm [accessed 25 March 2004].

Sawyer, R. and Bailey, N. (2001) *Personalisation Issues in the Enterprise Learning Portal*, http//:ausWeb.scu.edu.au/aw01/papers/refereed/sawyer/paper.html.

W3C Recommendation (2004), www.w3.org/TR/2004/REC-xinclude-20041220/ [accessed 13 February 2004].

Web Ontology Language (2005), www.w3.org/2004/OWL/ [accessed 25 April 2005].

5

User needs analysis and evaluation of portals

Panayiotis Zaphiris, Aspasia Dellaporta and Dean Mohamedally

Introduction

As specified in the ISO 13407 standard (ISO, 1999), user-centred design begins with a thorough understanding of the needs and requirements of the users. User needs analysis (or knowledge elicitation) and evaluation methods in human–computer interaction (HCI) are a critical function to the success of requirements and design gathering (Maiden, Mistry and Sutcliffe, 1995), usability testing and user evaluation stages of software development (Zaphiris and Kurniawan, 2001).

Examples of knowledge elicitation methods often start with initial questionnaire for feedback, requirements task walkthroughs, interviews techniques and focus group sessions (discussed in further detail in a subsequent section). It can rapidly scale upwards to more complex psychometric, design and evaluation processes: prototype construction of various fidelity levels, direct and indirect observation practices for monitoring user actions, response time comparisons, and various methods for eliciting mental categorization models, e.g. for distinguishing patterns of use between experts and non experts.

The measure of a good experience can vary from person to person; however the appropriate understanding of a usable design comes from gaining the knowledge that it is functional, efficient and desirable to its intended audience (Kuniavksy, 2003). John and Marks (1997) identify three key factors to assess the usability of an interface:

> Usability is measured by the extent to which the intended goals of use of the overall system are achieved (effectiveness); the resources that have to be expended to achieve the intended goals (efficiency); and the extent to which the user finds the overall system acceptable (satisfaction).

The usability of a system is also related to issues surrounding its accessibility. There is a broad range of users to whom web-based services are directed, and the services provided ought to be accessible to them (e.g. the visually, hearing, physically or cognitively impaired or even people with different experience of and attitudes towards technology).

The Disability Discrimination Act (DDA) began to come into effect in the UK in December 1996 and brought in measures to prevent discrimination against people on the basis of disability. Part III of the Act, in force since October 2004, aims to ensure that disabled people have equal access to products and services. Under Part III of the Act, businesses that provide goods, facilities and services to the general public (whether paid for or free) must make reasonable adjustments for disabled people to ensure they do not discriminate by:

- refusing to provide a service
- providing a service of a lower standard or in a worse manner
- providing a service on less favourable terms than they would to users without the disability.

There is a legal obligation on service providers to ensure that disabled people have equal access to web-based products and services. Section 19(1) (c) of the Act makes it unlawful for a service provider to discriminate against a disabled person 'in the standard of service which it provides to the disabled person or the manner in which it provides it'.

An important provision here is that education is not covered by the DDA, but by separate legislation, the Special Educational Needs and Disability Act 2001 (SENDA). This Act introduces to the UK the right for disabled students not to be discriminated against in education, training and any services provided wholly or mainly for students, and for those enrolled on courses provided by 'responsible bodies', including further and higher education institutions and sixth form colleges.

Knowledge elicitation and usability/accessibility evaluation theory

There are many different elicitation and usability/accessibility evaluation techniques (Cooke, 1994) and selecting the 'right' technique in a particular situation is very important. Burge's table of knowledge elicitation methods (Burge, 2001) provides an extensive comparative view of almost all the common KE (knowledge elicitation) techniques found in HCI: see Table 5.1 (overleaf).

In addition, usability and accessibility evaluation techniques are often grouped into two broad areas: user-based (that often include user testing) and expert based (that often include heuristic evaluation and cognitive walkthrough) techniques performed by experts.

Table 5.1 Burge's KE techniques grouped by interaction type

Category	Examples	Type	Results
Interview	Structured Unstructured Semi-structured	Direct	Varies depending on questions asked
Case study	Critical Incident Method Forward Scenario Simulation Critical Decision Method	Direct	Procedures followed, rationale
Protocols	Protocol Analysis	Direct	Procedures followed, rationale
Critiquing	Critiquing	Direct	Evaluation of problem solving strategy compared to alternatives
Role playing	Role Playing	Indirect	Procedures, difficulties encountered due to role
Simulation	Simulation Wizard of Oz	Direct	Procedures followed
Prototyping	Rapid Prototyping Storyboarding	Direct	Evaluation of proposed approach
Observation	Direct Observation Indirect Observation	Direct Indirect	Procedure followed
Goal related	Goal Decomposition Dividing the Domain	Direct	Goals and subgoals, groupings of goals
List related	Decision Analysis	Direct	Estimate of worth of all decisions for a task
Sorting	Card Sorting and Affinity Diagramming	Indirect	Classification of entities (dimension chosen by subject)
Laddering	Laddered Grid	Indirect	Hierarchical map of the task domain
20 Questions	20 Questions	Indirect	Information used to solve problems, organization of problem space
Document analysis	Document Analysis	Indirect (usually)	Varies depending on available documents, interaction with experts

Incremental usability and accessibility evaluation framework

King et al. (2004) presented what they called 'an incremental usability and accessibility evaluation framework for digital libraries'. See Figure 5.1.

Their framework is broken down into seven key activities and addresses all stages of a design of a digital library system:

- **Activity 1**: Conduct query – requirement gathering
  Identify satisfaction levels of current users of the system and establish key positive and negative aspects of the interface and what features they would like to see.
- **Activity 2**: Analysis
  Evaluate current findings and identify issues not yet addressed.
- **Activity 3**: Perform empirical (user) evaluations
  At this stage user testing needs to be conducted to allow the identification of real user problems by observing users interacting with the system. Retrospective

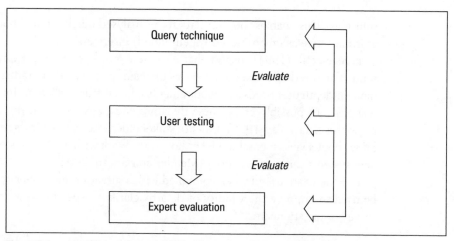

Figure 5.1   Usability and accessibility framework for digital libraries

focus groups or interviews may be conducted after the evaluations which can provide a volume of qualitative data.

- **Activity 4**: Analysis
  Establish key problems and assess if any areas of the service have not been covered by user evaluations.
- **Activity 5**: Expert evaluations
  Conduct expert testing. For this, appropriate modification of expert evaluation techniques may be required so that they supplement previous evaluation findings, and address any areas or issues that have not as yet been covered.
- **Activity 6**: Analysis
  Analyse all data identifying key issues that need to be addressed in the redesign of the service. Establish new usability and accessibility goals for the design.
- **Activity 7**: Iterative process
  Re-conduct all stages in the iterative framework to evaluate redesign.

Methods of HCI knowledge elicitation practices

In this section we describe the key methods that are associated with the above mentioned framework.

Interviewing

This query-based process elicits from users knowledge on a set information topic based on their expertise in the domain in question. It is useful for obtaining behavioural reasoning and background knowledge. Interviews can be categorized as structured or unstructured. Structured interviews elicit limited responses from users, by using a series of closed questions that have to be answered based on given solutions. This enables the user data to be analysed quicker but is not necessarily as informative as unstructured (open-ended) interviews.

Preece et al. (1994) suggest that interview processes are most effective when semi-structured and based on a series of fixed questions that gradually lead into more in-depth user needs and requirements understanding, allowing for open-ended responses to possibly create new dynamic questions based on prior structured responses (Macaulay, 1996). On-site stakeholder interviews allows researchers to bring about a vivid mental model of how users work with existing systems and how new systems can support them (Mander and Smith, 2002).

Interviews are useful when combined with a survey or questionnaire, as they can be used to improve the validity of data by clarifying specific issues raised in the survey or questionnaire.

Surveys

In conducting surveys, three things are necessary: 1) the set of questions, 2) a way to collect responses, and 3) access to the demographics group you wish to test (Kuniavksy, 2003). There are several widely reported templates for acquiring different types of user data, such as the well known Quality of User Interface Satisfaction (QUIS) by Chin, Diehl and Norman (1988), and the Computer System Usability Questionnaire (CSUQ) by IBM with Lewis (1995).

Surveys can be based on open and closed questions, but also allow researchers to acquire scalar results giving indicators of quality in positive and negative statements. Self-filling surveys can be time-efficient to deploy, and results from closed questions can be fast to analyse. Open questions tend to elicit unanticipated information which can be very useful early in design. Existing survey techniques include face-to-face, paper and pencil based, and telephone surveys where the researcher fills in the results (which becomes more of an interview style), but there is modern interest in computer-assisted and web-based surveying techniques.

Focus groups

This activity is useful for eliciting cross-representative domains of knowledge from several stakeholders/users in an open discussion format. Sessions are often moderated and tend to be informal by nature, centring on the creation of new topics from open questions. Evidence shows that the optimal number needed for a mixed-experience focus group is between five and eight participants, with group size being inversely related to the degree of participation (Millward, 1995).

Observation

Observation methods elicit user knowledge from the way users interact with a prototype or a final product. It can be direct, whereby a researcher is present and can steer users to particular points in an interaction. This tends to utilize video camera equipment and note-taking to successfully acquire the timeline of user actions, e.g. 'getting from point A to point D may require steps B or C'. The other model of observation is indirect, whereby all user actions are captured electronically. The researcher has to maintain co-operation between users and should pose questions only if clarification is needed.

Paper prototyping

There are several approaches to paper prototyping, enabling users to create quick and partial designs of their concepts. It is often used in the early stages of the design processes. Though the methodology lacks standardization, Rettig (1994) distinguishes between high-tech and low-tech views, and the more commonly modelled categories are of low-, medium- and high-fidelity prototypes (Greenberg, 1998). Rudd, Stern and Isensee (1996) also distinguishe prototypes according to horizontal and vertical prototypes, with vertical representing deep functionality of a limited view to the final output, and horizontal giving a wide overview of the full functionality of the system but with a weaker depth of understanding. Hall (2001) discusses the benefits of using various fidelities of prototypes.

Cognitive walkthrough

Cognitive walkthrough is an expert-based evaluation technique that steps through a scenario/task by focusing on the user's knowledge and goals. The expert evaluator first starts with descriptions of the prototype interface, the task(s) from the user's perspective, the correct sequence of actions needed to complete the task using the prototype and any assumptions about the characteristics of the user. Then the evaluator walks through the tasks using the system, reviewing the actions that are necessary and attempting to predict how the user will behave.

A series of key questions are used throughout each sub-task evaluation:

- Will the user be trying to achieve the correct effect?
- Will the user know that the correct action is available?
- Will the user know that the correct action will achieve the desired effect?
- If the correct action is taken, will the user see that things are going okay?

Heuristic evaluation

Heuristic evaluation is an expert review technique where experts inspect the interface to judge compliance with established usability principles (the 'heuristics'). It is usually conducted in a series of four steps:

1 **Prepare**: Create a prototype to evaluate; select evaluators; prepare coding sheets to record problems.
2 **Determine approach**: Either set typical user tasks (probably the most useful approach) or allow evaluators to establish their own tasks or conduct an exhaustive inspection of entire interface.
3 **Conduct the evaluation**: Inspect the interface individually to identify all violations of heuristics (the usability problems); record the problem (feature and location), severity (based on frequency, impact, criticality/cost) and heuristic violated.
4 **Aggregate and analyse results**: Group similar problems; reassess severity; determine possible fixes.

Case study

Now we demonstrate how the above framework can be applied to a specific case study from the public sector.

Need2know.co.uk is a portal developed by CIMEX which covers areas such as health, relationships, law, money and travel. Although a cross-government initiative, the portal should not bear government branding. Need2know (www.need2know.co.uk) aimed to be a 'first-stop-shop' for everything in a young person's life with signposts to relevant websites in the public, private and charitable sectors. The goal was to create the de facto online 'life' resource for 13–19 year olds that appreciates and satisfies the differing needs of each age group within the target audience. To inspire movement throughout the site and encourage repeat visits, a regularly updated online magazine called 'n2k' was also developed.

The portal had to be easily accessible by all computers, from 56k modems to broadband users as well as by people with disabilities. Therefore, compliance with accessibility guidelines and standards was an important requirement. Another important requirement was that individual users should feel that the portal is meeting their needs. Figure 5.2 shows a screenshot of the home page of need2know.

To develop need2know a series of user needs analysis techniques and formative evaluation techniques had to be conducted. A variety of methods and techniques had to be used to diagnose usability and accessibility issues early in the development process and as the development built up and evolved. The process outlined in this case study fits within a framework of an iterative development process which evolves through cycles of development and testing.

User analysis/needs analysis

Once the requirements had been gathered following research (interviews, surveys) with over 2000 young people across the UK the requirements had to be analysed and prioritized from a user experience point of view and from a business perspective.

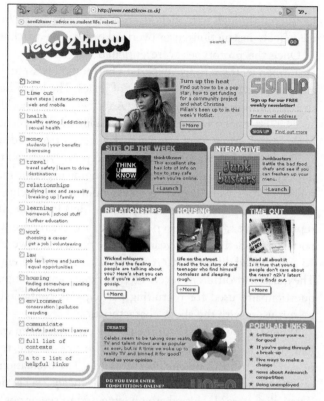

Figure 5.2 Screen shot of need2know home page (May 2006)

A site that really works should fulfil the client's aims and objectives while meeting the needs of the target users and this should be central to the requirements analysis.

What are the tasks the user will be able to do on the site and what needs do they meet? What are the portal's intended functionalities? We had to have answers to these questions well before proceeding to the first evaluation. Also it is of utmost importance that findings from each evaluation activity are built into all the architectures and designs prior to the next test.

Formative evaluations cycle: What to evaluate? How? At what stage?

Once a draft site architecture diagram had been developed and some basic low-fidelity prototypes that demonstrated basic functionalities were designed, the first evaluation was conducted. Cognitive walkthrough was used by one or more evaluators to go through the prototypes in the correct sequence trying to model what the user would do on the system and to assess whether the interaction and dialogue design supported the user tasks. In the case of need2know which has a diverse audience aged 13–19 with diverse interests, a series of prototypes had to be walked through to model different user behaviours. In this way missing steps, inadequate instructions, user overload or poor feedback were identified.

Once the prototypes were enriched and refined, a heuristic evaluation was performed by three to five experts. This method is useful because it is inexpensive and can detect a significant amount of issues. The list of heuristics was customized to cover information architecture. An accessibility checklist was also used by an accessibility expert to ensure that accessibility requirements were met. The results of these evaluations were summarized and prioritized and amendments were made.

The next step was to take the refined prototypes and to do user testing to see if everything was on the right track. The home page, the main menu and important functionalities were tested to assess information architecture, interface layout and navigation design ideas early in the development. It was important that a representative sample of users from the target audience was selected because the portal was aimed at 13–19 year olds. The participants were of various ages between 13 and 19, had different interests and came from different areas and backgrounds. They also had different levels of experience with computers and the web. The questionnaire used for recruiting participants contained questions that helped recruit users with the above characteristics.

When setting the tasks for the testing care was taken with wording. The testing had to be as objective as possible. The one-to-one testing sessions enabled researchers to focus on one user at a time. The evaluation was structured around questions such as: What do you think this means? What do you think will happen if you click here? Is this what you expected to see or not? Why? The participants were encouraged to think aloud so that researchers could understand what was going on in their minds. A short interview followed after the testing to give the participant the opportunity to reflect on their experience with the prototype and capture their overall impressions and recommendations for improvement. The test is best performed in a usability lab where some members of the development team are present to observe the testing behind one-way mirrors. In this way the participant doesn't feel uncomfortable and the development team gains greater understanding of the users.

The next stage was to refine the prototypes and enrich them with additional features. A basic clickable HTML prototype was developed with no images on it or colours so that the users could concentrate on the content and navigation. This prototype had enough content for the users to give feedback about the tone of voice, the layout and the level of engagement with it. Scenarios were also used to ensure that the functionalities inserted remained task-specific and were related to the user needs identified in the requirements stage.

It is very important that the prototype is tested in advance with heuristic evaluations that concentrate on both usability and accessibility. Some scenarios of use can be provided for the experts to make sure they cover the important functionalities the way a real user would. User testing occurred in the same way as illustrated previously. However, this time disabled users from the target audience were recruited as well, to test the accessibility of the prototype. This prototype was clickable and more 'realistic' than the one developed earlier.

The success of this methodology is evident from the fact that the portal was given a 'green light' by the Government's Gateway Review team.

Conclusion

In this chapter we described an incremental user needs analysis and evaluation, usability and accessibility framework and its associated methods and demonstrated how it has been applied to a public sector portal system. Such evaluative processes are increasingly recognized to be critical stages in developing any system, but particularly portals. The days of *ad hoc* development are receding.

References

Burge, J. E. (2001) Knowledge Elicitation Tool Classification, PhD Thesis, Worcester Polytechnic Institute.

Chin, J. P., Diehl, V. A. and Norman, K. L. (1988) *Development of an Instrument Measuring User Satisfaction of the Human–Computer Interface*, ACM CHI'88 Proceedings, 213–18.

Cooke, N. J. (1994) Varieties of Knowledge Elicitation Techniques, *International Journal of Human–Computer Studies*, **41**, 801–49.

Greenberg, S. (1998) *Prototyping for Design and Evaluation*, at http://pages.cpsc.ucalgary.ca/~saul/681/1998/prototyping/survey.html [accessed 30 November 2004].

Hall, R. R. (2001) Prototyping for Usability of New Technology, *International Journal of Human–Computer Studies*, **55** (4), 485–502.

ISO (1999) ISO 13407: Human-centred Design Processes for Interactive Systems, International Standards Organization.

John, B. E. and Marks, S. J. (1997) Tracking the Effectiveness of Usability Evaluation Methods, *Behaviour and Information Technology*, **16** (4/5), 188–202.

King, N., Ma, T. H. Y., Zaphiris, P., Petrie, H. and Fraser, H. (2004) An Incremental Usability and Accessibility Evaluation Framework for Digital Libraries. In Brophy, P., Fisher S. and Craven, J., *Libraries without Walls 5: the distributed delivery of library and information services*, London, Facet Publishing.

Kuniavksy, M. (2003) *Observing the User Experience*, San Francisco/London, Morgan Kaufmann.

Lewis, J. R. (1995) IBM Computer Usability Satisfaction Questionnaires: psychometric evaluation and instructions for use, *International Journal of Human–Computer Interaction*, **7** (1), 57–78.

Macaulay, L. A. (1996) *Requirements Engineering*, London, Springer Verlag Series on Applied Computing.

Maiden, N. A. M., Mistry, P. and Sutcliffe, A. G. (1995) *How People Categorise Requirements for Reuse: a natural approach*, Proceedings of the 2nd IEEE Symposium on Requirements Engineering, 148–55.

Mander, R. and Smith, B. (2002) *Web Usability for Dummies*, New York, Hungry Minds.

Millward, L. J. (1995) Focus Groups. In Breakwell, G. M., Hammond, S. and Fife-Shaw, C. (eds), *Research Methods in Psychology*, London, Sage, 303–24.

Preece, J., Rogers, Y., Sharp, H., Benyon, D., Holland, S. and Carey, T. (1994) *Human–Computer Interaction*, Harlow, Addison Wesley.

Rettig, G. (1994) Prototyping for Tiny Fingers, *Communications of the ACM*, **37** (4), 21–7.

Rudd, J., Stern, K. and Isensee, S. (1996) Low vs. High Fidelity Prototyping Debate, *Interactions*, **3** (1), 76–85.

Zaphiris, P. and Kurniawan, S. H. (2001) *Using Card Sorting Technique to Define the Best Web Hierarchy for Seniors*, Proceedings of CHI 2001 Conference on Human Factors in Computing Systems, ACM Press.

6

Managing portal services

Stephen Emmott

Introduction

During the mid- to late-1990s, portals were public websites: the first page displayed when connecting to the internet. They were simple and the same for all users. Typically, they represented the front page of search engines or the default home page automatically set by ISPs (internet service providers) for their subscribers. Portals were in effect gateways to a subset of websites selected from the world wide web as a whole. In this sense, the metaphors of 'portal' or 'gateway' were apt and readily understood.

Today, portals are private websites: personalized interaction between individuals and organizations. They are complex and customized to the individual user. This complexity is evident in the myriad portal services that have been established using numerous portal systems. The quantity and variation is now such that portals can be classified into various types, as identified by Ovum in their taxonomy of portals: Specialized Portals, Public Web Portals, Enterprise Portals, Workspace Portals and Knowledge Portals (Winkler, 2005).

This maturation reflects a progression from serving *audiences* to serving *individuals*. In focusing upon the individual – the customer – the concept of a portal has developed from being a gateway *through which* information services located elsewhere are accessed, to being an environment *within which* information services are consumed, whether located elsewhere or not. In this way, the portal is recognized as a destination in its own right and no longer strictly a gateway through which other services are accessed. In effect, the terms portal and intranet have become largely synonymous in many cases.

For those managing a portal service, the focus needs to be on the word 'service' rather than 'portal'. The aim of a portal service can be expressed as 'meeting the information needs of customers in pursuit of the organization's objectives'. It follows that while a portal service is dependent upon the systems (i.e. technologies) that underpin it, it is the organization's stakeholders who are the manager's primary concern. Specifically, this concern should be focused at the intersection of the customers', suppliers' and organization's interests. This is where a portal service is differentiated from the systems underpinning it. To be effective, the manager needs to maintain a certain distance from each of the three interests and, in particular, the underlying systems.

The goal of this chapter is to provide a pragmatic insight into the portal manager's task with a view to serving the practitioner rather than the theorist. Necessarily, the focus here is on the main issues that face practitioners and how these should be approached rather than addressed: there are no silver bullets. To introduce and contextualize these issues, core management themes are presented to serve as an induction.

Management themes

Five primary themes apply in relation to managing portal services:

1 scope of the management task
2 the management task
3 communication
4 culture
5 change.

The first two – scope of the management task and the management task – are core themes that tie together the remaining three – culture, communication and change. The coverage of each is brief and further reading is recommended: these themes capture salience; depth is available in the relevant literature as signposted.

Scope of the management task

The scope of the management task (Riley, 1997, section 2) is usefully summarized using a simple model with three parts: systems, processes and people (see Figure 6.1).

This model is deceptively simple and easily dismissed. Used in context, it provides – like any good management model – a powerful means of extracting sense and order from the complex layers of daily practice. Models such as these should be treated like a compass or watch – a simple instrument serving as the basis for action.

The model represents the bulk of what a manager has control of or influence over. For instance, uPortal is a system; authentication is a process; the customer is a person. Alternatively, an espresso machine is a system; making espresso is a process; the operator of the espresso machine is a person. Products and services – a cup of espresso, a portal service – result from the interplay of systems,

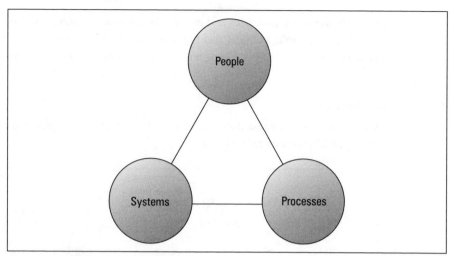

Figure 6.1 Scope of the management task
Reprinted from *Understanding Business Process Management*, Lewis, G., p.16,
Copyright (1997), with permission from Elsevier.

processes and people, i.e. they are the output. Products and services, in turn, are 'consumed' by customers.

Implicitly, products and services are managed by managing the systems, processes and people from which they result. Put another way, products and services are managed indirectly. Recognizing this 'distance' is critical as it reinforces the fact that the modern manager operates primarily through influence rather than control. Managing systems often means working with an individual or group elsewhere in the organization. Managing people requires ongoing negotiation to elicit the best from the complex mesh of strengths, weaknesses and variations in personal style. Managing processes requires consultation to foster inter-departmental harmony. The manager is more diplomat than dictator.

Unlike products, services typically expose – to a greater or lesser extent – the systems, processes and people underlying them. The delivery of a service is directly dependent upon its underlying systems, processes and people at the point of consumption: faults can immediately reveal themselves and curb delivery. For instance, a telephone-based service fails if the CRM (customer relation management) system used by the telephonist is 'down'. With many services, a fault with systems can rarely be compensated for by people and processes. Contrast this with products which once created are independent of the systems, processes and people used to produce them. Provided the product is created to the appropriate level of quality, consumption will not be affected.

A fundamental characteristic of portal services – and many web-based services in general – is that the service is often perceived by its consumers to be synonymous with the systems underpinning it: consuming the service equates to using the systems. This illusion is not unique to customers: it can affect both the portal's suppliers and the organization it represents. As systems embody processes and can run autonomously, processes and people can become invisible. It is therefore helpful to delineate people, systems and processes regularly to achieve a clear perspective of what is being managed. Doing so reveals the scope of the management task.

The management task

Given the scope, the task itself can be expressed in terms of a planning cycle (Dixon, 1997, ch.2) (see Figure 6.2).

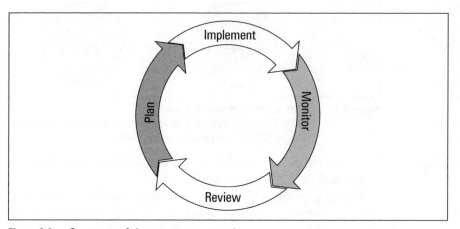

Figure 6.2   Summary of the management task
Reprinted from *The Management Task*, Dixon, R., p.29, Copyright (1997) with permission from Elsevier.

This model illustrates that planning is followed by implementation. This is then monitored and reviewed. The review may result in recommendations which lead to planning and implementation. If not, monitoring continues. The subject of the cycle could be the portal service or indeed the individual systems, processes or people that give rise to it. Inevitably, this results in myriad cycles running in parallel and possibly asynchronously. In relation to portal services, there are many subjects within the scope of the management task. Examples include regular surveys of customer satisfaction (people); three-year replacement cycles for servers (systems); monthly analysis of access logs (processes); and so on.

For the manager, the commonly used metaphor of spinning plates is particularly apt: many plates representing the cycle of the management task and each with their own rate of spin. Following the mantra of 'do the right things right' (ten Have and ten Have, 2003), the art is in judging which plates to spin, when to spin them, and how quickly to spin them. Too few cycles can lead to complacency and a service that fails to change in pace with the needs of its customers and organization; too many cycles can sap resources and lead to dissociation from the primary purpose, i.e. the relationship between the portal service and the interests of stakeholders. Determining the number of plates to spin essentially boils down to the resources available, but this shouldn't stem the aspiration to spin more plates in pursuit of an improved service.

Communication

Communication is the means by which one person effects, or changes, the knowledge of another. In this way, themes and ideas can be propagated between people. As the effects can vary, successful communication can be viewed as the intentional changing of knowledge: changes that are in accordance with goals.

As knowledge is an intrinsic quality of a person, it can be expressed but not 'exported'. Expressing knowledge is achieved through messages which are encoded, transmitted and decoded (see Figure 6.3).

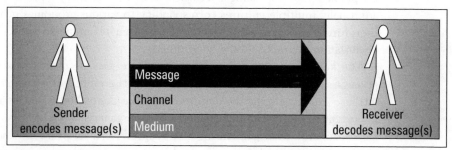

Figure 6.3 Communication

Transmission takes place through various channels (e.g. a television or radio programme, a publication, a website, a weekly meeting, etc.) within various mediums (e.g. television, radio, print, WWW, face to face, etc.).

Understanding communication and practising it effectively requires the sender to be concerned not only with encoding and transmitting messages, but also the receipt and decoding of those messages by the receiver (Lake, 1997, section 1). Communication is not successful until the messages have affected the knowledge of receivers as intended. As this is the purpose of communication, attention should be given to ensuring that the message gets through. As such, communication requires:

- **Planning**: deciding who to affect; the effect intended and hence the messages to transmit; the channels/mediums to be used; and the timing
- **Implementing**: encoding messages and transmitting them through the appropriate channel(s)/medium(s)
- **Monitoring**: observing the effect of the messages
- **Reviewing**: assessing the effect of the messages.

This process reflects the management task earlier and illustrates the cyclical, iterative nature of communication.

Culture

Culture refers to the shared attitudes, practices and values that are typical of an organization and its people. This is often expressed succinctly as 'the way we do things around here' (University of Luton, 2004). It is essential to be clear that people – see Scope of the management task – exist within the wider context of organizational culture. Rather than managing the culture of an organization, the emphasis is upon being able to manage within the culture of an organization.

With reference to organizations – specifically those which are large and within the public sector – speaking of a single culture is often inappropriate because there are usually multiple cultures corresponding to various groupings of people. It is therefore important to appreciate that when referring to the culture of an organization, plurality should be assumed.

The keyword is 'shared'. Although culture may be shaped by systems and processes, it is embodied within people and is therefore – as with knowledge – an intrinsic quality. Implicitly, culture cannot be controlled. For this reason, it is important to work within the culture of an organization rather than in spite, or ignorance, of it. Management must be adapted for the culture in which it applies in order for it to be effective. To do this requires some level of intimacy with the culture – knowing it and understanding its characteristics. This means being a part of, and participating within, the organization's people networks. Liaison and networking is essential.

Within the context of higher education specifically, McNay (1995) provides a simple yet expressive model for identifying and describing an organization's culture. He presents four types of culture differentiated from one another by the extent to which policy is defined and implementation controlled (see Figure 6.4). Although the names are reasonably suggestive of the cultures they represent, McNay attributes a number of characteristics to each of the four types of culture. The most relevant are summarized in Table 6.1.

The extent to which this model is applicable to institutions other than those in higher education is facilitated by McNay. He maps his model to the more widely known, and generically applicable, work of Harrison/Handy (see Figure 6.5).

Although the types are clearly delineated from one another, a culture can span more than one quadrant but typically reveals a bias towards one. Working within and knowing an organization helps to clarify which type(s) apply by matching the organization against the characteristics. A subjective assessment from personal experience correlated with the outcomes of similar assessments by colleagues can help to identify the culture of an organization. For a more thorough analysis, there are various tools and techniques available, e.g. Culture Audit Tool (University of Luton, 2004).

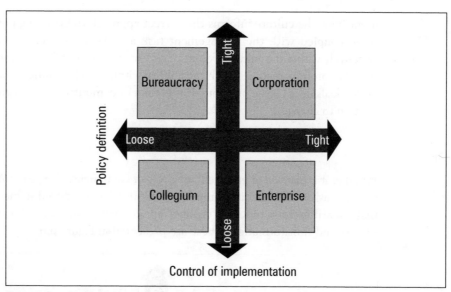

Figure 6.4 McNay's matrix

Table 6.1 Characteristics of cultures

	Collegium	Bureaucracy	Corporation	Enterprise
Dominant value	Freedom	Equity	Loyalty	Competence
Role of central authorities	Permissive	Regulatory	Directive	Supportive
Dominant unit	Department/individual	Faculty/committees	Institution/senior management team	Sub-unit/project teams
Decision arenas	Informal groups networks	Committees and administrative briefings	Working parties and senior management team	Project teams

McNay	Harrison/Handy
Collegium	Person
Bureaucracy	Role
Corporation	Power
Enterprise	Task

Figure 6.5 Comparison of cultures

The material on this page is derived from McNay, I. (1995) From Collegial Academy to Corporate Enterprise: the changing culture of universities. In Schuller, T. (1995), *The Changing University?*, Open University, pp.106, 109.

Identifying the culture informs the correct approach to managing portal services when coupled with the management task and its scope, i.e. tailored to work effectively within the culture. For instance, the approaches taken to communication must be carefully matched with the culture within which communication is taking place: deals over coffee or minuted meetings of committees. The same applies in relation to change.

Change

Whether it is planned or emergent, episodic or continuous, change is both inevitable and pervasive. The Audit Commission (2001) has produced a succinct model that identifies four types of change: operational gains, evolutionary learning, surgery and transformation. These are presented in Figure 6.6.

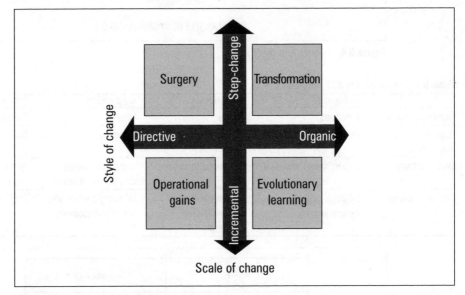

Figure 6.6   Four types of change

Change can be explained in terms of style versus scale. Style refers to the way in which change progresses, expressed as directive versus organic. Scale refers to the pace of change, expressed as incremental versus step change. The following examples illustrate:

- **Operational gains**: upgrading the web server used by a portal service
- **Evolutionary learning**: refining navigation in response to customer feedback
- **Surgery**: migrating portal systems to a new platform
- **Transformation**: many departments contributing applications to portal service over a short period of time.

Change and culture are interlinked. Knowing the culture of an organization can be used to facilitate change within that organization. It can assist both in terms of understanding change that is taking place and in choosing the right approach to enabling change.

Summary of themes

The five themes (the scope of the management task, the management task, communication, culture and change) assist in clarifying the correct approach, or approaches, to managing portal services. This is achieved by:

- identifying the systems, processes and people relevant to the portal service
- addressing relevant systems, processes and people through cycles of plan, implement, monitor and review
- identifying the culture to which stakeholders belong
- identifying the type of change that best fits the culture
- establishing effective communication with and between stakeholders.

Crucially, realizing and remembering that people are not only within the scope of the management task but its primary subject is key to effective management.

Issues

Many issues are encountered when managing portal services. Some are more commonly encountered than others and many stem from underlying issues. Although not definitive, seven of these issues are presented:

1 the portal concept
2 prioritizing objectives
3 customer satisfaction
4 organizational knowledge
5 supporting customers
6 buy, build or customize
7 managing identity.

It is not argued that these are unique to portal services, nor applicable to all portal services. The rationale for presenting them is to illustrate the management of portal services and thereby to serve as guidance for the practitioner, i.e. most or all will be encountered in one form or another. Resolution will require different solutions in different contexts but the themes presented above provide a set of approaches for resolving these issues and others that will be encountered.

The portal concept

As highlighted at the beginning of this chapter, what is meant by portal has changed substantially in a short space of time. Moreover, the perceptions of customers, suppliers and those representing the organization give rise to varying assumptions and expectations.

A lack of consensus on the concept of a portal potentially leads to development and/or deployment problems for suppliers, needs left unmet for customers, and a service that is not fit for purpose for the organization. It is important to resolve this issue by clarifying what is actually meant by portal and to ensure that this concept is then shared by stakeholders. This should not be a philosophical exercise: it should directly address the interests of stakeholders. This might be tackled before or during the portal's project, or later during the portal's operation. Either way, the concept, captured in the context of a valid business case, must be established and maintained.

Communication is the central theme with the aim being to facilitate dialogue, which can then be distilled down into a ratified document, ideally a business case.

Prioritizing objectives

An aim provides direction, but an objective provides a destination. Objectives are clear statements of outcome that should be specific, measurable, achievable, relevant and time based, i.e. SMART. Although aims can give rise to objectives, summarize objectives and/or serve to facilitate progress before objectives have been established, they should be treated with caution. Aims signal a need for consultation, analysis and further discussion whereas objectives signal a need for action. Although it is possible for managers to receive sound objectives, it is typically the exception rather than the norm. Instead, the manager should constantly 'pursue objectives', with both senses of this phrase being equally valid.

When managing a portal service, it is normal to identify many and varied objectives. Some objectives relate to the portal service directly whereas others relate to the systems, processes, and people underpinning it. Inevitably, having too many and/or varied objectives reduces the effectiveness and efficiency of suppliers and thereby impairs the service for customers at the expense of the organization. It is essential to utilize the available resources effectively and this requires prioritization.

Objectives are prioritized by determining importance and urgency. Importance is usefully expressed using the MoSCoW model: Must do, Should do, Could do, Won't do. Fitting objectives under these headings is not necessarily straightforward. If an objective is not immediately a 'Must do' (e.g. an objective relating to legal compliance), then it is helpful to look at the needs of customers and match these against objectives to determine whether it is a 'Should do' or a 'Could do'. Urgency can be more simply stated in terms of whether immediate or scheduled action is required. Prioritized objectives will be subject to constant change, which is where the MoSCoW model can help when used in conjunction with urgency. Although difficult, 'Won't do' is an effective way of keeping the list realistic so this category should be used wherever possible. Even so, prioritizing objectives can only be achieved effectively through negotiation with stakeholders: nobody likes rejection especially if it is poorly handled.

The management task is the central theme with the aim being to maintain a list of objectives (or an operational plan).

Customer satisfaction

The users of a portal service should be viewed as customers consuming a service. The portal's customers may be the organization's customers, internal customers or a combination of the two. Despite best efforts, their satisfaction with the service will vary. Inevitably, there will be a proportion who will be dissatisfied with the service and the size of this proportion will vary over time.

For the organization, dissatisfied customers represent a service that is no longer fit for purpose. Dissatisfied customers may use alternative means to meet their information needs and/or complain. For the suppliers of the portal service, this can often mean being pulled into a reactive rather than proactive position. In this position, customers' immediate complaints – or worse, the organization's interpretation of these complaints – steers the prioritization of objectives. Such a steer can easily result in a vicious circle of dissatisfaction feeding dissatisfaction thereby jeopardizing the portal service in the medium to long term.

Monitoring the information needs of customers as well as their satisfaction with the extent to which the portal service meets their information needs is important. Not only does this indicate which information needs the portal service should meet but it also facilitates managing customers' expectations. Two effective methods for achieving this are regular surveys and face-to-face contact through a variety of methods including user testing, focus groups and interviews. Surveys should be simple, containing only a handful of well chosen questions: responding should be quick and simple. Face-to-face contact should be linked to surveys and other operational activities. For example, user testing should be an integral part of developing the underlying systems.

Change is the central theme with the aim being to make changes in the portal service that are relevant to its customers.

Organizational knowledge

An effective portal service is part of the organization providing it and often cuts across many areas if not the organization as a whole. This pan-organization remit requires that the suppliers of the portal service are familiar with both the breadth and depth of the organization in terms of people, processes and systems, as well as their myriad interactions. Knowing the organization and how it operates is essential. A lack of organizational knowledge on behalf of a portal service's suppliers limits the extent to which the service can be embedded within the organization and therefore its relevance to customers. Worse still, it can lead to significant operational problems for stakeholders if the portal service does not effectively coalesce with or replace pre-existing operations.

Specifications and other documents can assist as a conduit for knowledge and clearly they have their place. They are, however, rarely a substitute for networking and liaison. Wherever possible, it is essential to foster familiarity and appropriate dialogue between suppliers. Secondments, meetings and presentations are all examples of facilitating interaction between suppliers and encouraging familiarity with relevant people, processes and systems as well as with the issues associated with them.

Culture is the central theme with the aim being to develop what is in effect a 'learning circle' among suppliers.

Supporting customers

As revealed earlier, a mix of suppliers is required to provide a portal service. Customers using the portal service will encounter a variety of issues during use which require resolution through support. The issues arising will relate to systems, processes and people. It is therefore necessary to ensure that a call for support is routed to the appropriate supplier so that the issue can be resolved effectively. This is as important for the supplier as it is for the customer.

Routing a call for support to the wrong supplier can lead to dissatisfaction for the customer and operational problems for suppliers, especially if large volumes of customers encounter the same problem. For instance, erroneous instructions in a booking facility can lead to customers seeking support from the suppliers of the underlying system(s) rather than the person or office responsible for the processes (e.g. handling bookings).

Processes need to be established to effectively manage requests for support. This starts with facilitating self-help which if necessary leads to a request for help being routed automatically to the appropriate supplier. Routing is based upon the information submitted by the customer, including indirect information such as the context of the request (e.g. browser and platform, part of the portal service where a need for support was encountered, etc.). Establishing the processes for supporting customers requires buy-in from the suppliers involved but more importantly clarification of responsibilities and remits with the respect to the operational aspects of the portal service.

The scope of the management task is the central theme with the aim being to establish processes that match the gamut of support with appropriate suppliers.

Buy, build or customize

The systems underlying a portal service can be purchased ready made, built through bespoke development (either in-house and/or by a third party), or part built using ready made components that can be customized and/or be brought together to form a customized system (again either in-house and/or by a third party).

Deciding which approach to take can be as crucial to the outcome as the work itself. Taking the wrong approach can doom a portal service to failure from the outset. Not only should the systems be fit for purpose, they need to be sustainable in the medium to long term. The approach to take is largely determined by two factors: the presence, competence and capacity of internal suppliers; and the available budget. At least for the systems underlying portal services, a rule of thumb is to assume by default that purchasing ready made systems is the correct approach. Opting for one of the other two approaches should be justified against this. Arguably, software development is best left to commercial suppliers and/or individuals/collectives (i.e. open source). Accepting this leads to one decision and that is the extent to which procured systems are customized and it is here that the efforts of internal suppliers (assuming they exist) should be focused. Even so, it is essential to minimize customization and constrain this by adhering to standards.

Change is the central theme here with the aim being to undertake change that is appropriate for the culture.

Managing identity

Management of authorization and access is central to the operation of a portal service. The provision of service is grounded in the identification of customers and from this defining what the portal service offers them and how.

As with the issue of organizational knowledge, the absence of effective management of identity limits the extent to which the portal service can be embedded within its organization and therefore its relevance to the organization's customers. Ideally, identity is already being managed within the organization and in such a way that this can be reused for the purposes of the portal service. If not, there is the danger of reinventing the wheel and worse still managing identity in a way that is not relevant to organizational practice.

An effective approach is to attribute access rights and other preferences to roles that are defined within the context of the portal, and to then assign these roles to identified individuals using pre-existing organizational registers for authorization. Successful management of identity reflects the operational reality of the organization with analysis of the culture as the focus.

Culture is the central theme, with the aim being to represent organizational culture accurately through the way in which identity is managed.

Conclusions

A portal service is managed by managing the systems, processes and people that underlie it. This is achieved by subjecting the relevant systems, processes and people to a cycle of planning, implementing, monitoring and reviewing. Given numerous cycles running concurrently, the manager needs to utilize their knowledge and experience of communication, culture and change to ensure that their actions result in a portal service that meets the information needs of customers in pursuit of the organization's objectives. Neither the information needs of customers nor the organization's objectives will be available for the taking. They will be elusive and must be continually pursued as they provide not only the rationale for the portal service, but the criteria by which its success will be assessed.

Bibliography

Audit Commission (2001) *Change Here*,
     http://ww2.audit-commission.gov.uk/changehere/content/intro.htm.
Dixon, R. (1997) *The Management Task*, Oxford, Butterworth Heinemann.
Lake, C. (1997) *Communication*, Oxford, Institute of Management Foundation.
McNay, I. (1995) From the Collegial Academy to the Corporate Enterprise: the changing cultures of universities. In Schuller, T. (ed.), *The Changing University?*, Milton Keynes, Open University Press.
Lewis, G. (1997) *Understanding Business Process Management*, Oxford, Pergamon Flexible Learning.
ten Have, S. and ten Have, W. (2003) *Key Management Models*, London, Pearson Education Ltd.
University of Luton (2004) *Effecting Change in Higher Education – HEFCE Good Management Practice Project (GMP 201)*, University of Luton www.effectingchange.luton.ac.uk/types_of_change/.
Winkler, R. (2005) *Portals – The All-in-one Web Supersites: features, functions, definitions*, Taxonomy, Ovum, www.sapdesignguild.org/editions/edition3/portal_definition.asp.

Section 2

The library and the portal

The activities of information professionals that are related to portals are:

- Guiding users to find the best portal to meet their information need, and also using subject portals in information inquiry work themselves.
- Organizing information sources for information service users, through web directory websites – in effect portals – encompassing both free internet services and library subscriptions to web resources.
- Contributing content to organizational portals, e.g. news streams, and input to the design of the portal from the information perspective (e.g. designing taxonomies).
- Involvement in building major public portals on the open web.

The chapters in this section explore aspects of these themes. Winship looks outwards from the organization at web portals, web subject portals and search engines exploring trends in the aggregation of functions and tools, partly as a guide to help information professionals in their information inquiry work, also with a view to informing organizations about what functions they will find it useful to develop in their own portals. This reflects the sense that organizations are constantly learning from – or, more frankly, being pushed along by – the great sandbox that is the web. MacColl's chapter beautifully captures the evolution of one library's response to the need to organize the expanding universe of web-based information sources for its users. In itself this experience tells us much about the evolution of the portal concept in general. Davies's chapter explores the development of specialist library portal software.

It may be useful in the context of the volume as a whole to reflect further on the character of library portals as a concept. As ever with the word portal there is a certain haziness in the library portal idea. The core function of the commercial products sometimes referred to as library portals comprises tools to cross-search multiple databases from one search string, generally using Z39.50 as a search protocol (Library of Congress, 2005). Such products are also sometimes referred to as meta-search, distributed or federated search tools, because of this core function. Because they integrate data from multiple sources they are truly portals in the strong sense of JISC's definition. The cross-search tool is effectively also a common interface allowing the user to search many databases from a familiar environment. Library portals also offer a searchable and browsable directory of resources (generally organized by subject and including many resources that cannot be cross-searched, often some that are not searchable at all on the web). The search function also handles authentication to the various sources to be searched, providing a degree of simplified sign-on. On top of the cross-searching tool, open URL resolvers/databases such as SFX offer to help the user move forward from the search results to finding the full text, be it in the library or online. Given the range of affordances they offer as a package the name meta-search may seem a little limited, and library portal reasonably appropriate.

Yet 'library portal' may be a slight misnomer. Such a portal is unlikely to replace the library OPAC as the core access point to the main library collections. The OPAC itself is quite likely also to offer a route to electronic versions of journals. The portal does not even replace the library website, for the open web is so flexible it is still likely to be used for news, information about the library, and so forth. Actually with increasing investment in digitized collections of materials and in 'institutional repositories' of academics' published papers, each with its own web interface, there is no sign of there being a unified access point to the academic library on the net as such; rather the number of library services on the web is proliferating. Certainly the library portal is not even the portal to all that the library has on the web. Figure S2.1 suggests some of this complexity. Using the phrase 'library portal' may be perceived by some as a presumptuous claim for this library service to be a gateway to the whole organization's resources. Some library management system suppliers have even tried to sell it as such. This is likely to create political trouble.

For all that, it seems pretty clear that library portals do increase usage of licensed resources. The experience of Loughborough (Hamblin and Stubbings, 2003) of very large increases in usage – even of databases that cannot be cross-searched – is widely cited. The question is, why did this occur? It may have been as much about proxying authentication and presenting the resources more clearly as about cross-searching. This points to the difficulty librarians have had of presenting all that is available clearly on library websites. To date there does not seem to have been a full study of the ways users search with such tools, either by observation (though see Tallent, 2004; Awre and Ingram, 2005) or usage statistics. McCaskie's (2004) masters thesis, based on interviewing and surveying librarians, suggests some more problematic aspects. There were some indications from her study that users understood the results of broadcast searches less well because of the lack of context. Although it is recommended to go to the native interface after a broadcast search, there was evidence that this was not happening. There was evidence that

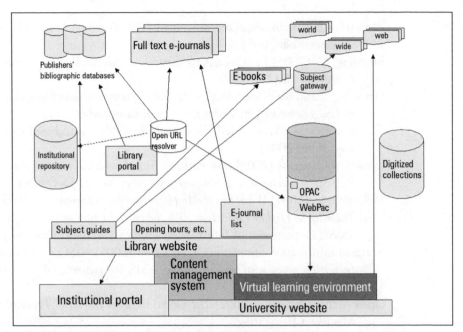

Figure S2.1 Fragmentation in the library webspace

users educated in search syntax by Google – rather than the hard-pressed library staff – did not adjust their search strategies to the tools.

Quite apart from how they are used, library portals are far from perfect. Although they may increase gross usage of databases users still constantly encounter failures of connections and false results. The work of NISO metasearch initiative will hopefully improve this (NISO, 2005). The library portal is undoubtedly better than nothing.

At a more fundamental level Breeding (2005) makes the point that distributed searching is inherently less fast and efficient than searches based on harvested data or pre-indexing as underlies Google. Of course, there are limits to how far this model can be reproduced in the library field, because of the nature of ownership of bibliographic data, but the Discover search on the People's Network (www.peoplesnetwork.gov.uk/) is an example of a library application which uses such an approach, based on the open archives metadata harvesing protocol, OAI-PMH (OAI, 2002).

What is clear from this and from the chapters in this section is that the notion of the library portal is an evolving concept.

References

Awre, C. and Ingram, C. (2005) *CREE Feasibility Study on Presenting Communication and Collaboration Tools within Different Contexts,* www.hull.ac.uk/esig/cree/downloads/CREEcommsresults.pdf [accessed 21 December 2005].

Breeding, M. (2005) Plotting a New Course for Metasearch, *Computers in Libraries*, **25** (25), 27–30.

Hamblin, Y. and Stubbings, R. (2003) *The Implementation of MetaLib and SFX at Loughborough University Library: a case study*, www.jisc.ac.uk/uploaded_documents/Metalibcasestudy.pdf [accessed 21 December 2005].

Library of Congress (2005) *International Standard Maintenance Agency Z39.50*, www.loc.gov/z3950/agency/ [accessed 21 December 2005].

McCaskie, L. (2004) *What are the Implications for Information Literacy Training in Higher Education with the Introduction of Federated Search Tools?*, Department of Information Studies, Sheffield University.

National Information Standards Organization (2005) *NISO MetaSearch Initiative*, www.niso.org/committees/MS_initiative.html [accessed 21 December 2005].

Open Archive Initiative (2002) *The Open Archives Initiative Protocol for Metadata Harvesting*, www.openarchives.org/OAI/openarchivesprotocol.html [accessed 21 December 2005].

Tallent, E. (2004) Metasearching in Boston College Libraries – a case study of user reactions, *New Library World*, **105** (1–2), 69–75.

7

Ready to use: consumer, subject and other public portals

Ian Winship

Introduction

This volume is concerned primarily with portals that are designed for particular institutions. This chapter differs in considering portals – loosely defined – that are general purpose or subject related and available to all through the open web. Broadly these can be divided into two groups: general consumer portals like Yahoo! and more targeted services – often librarian created – such as the academically related UK Resource Discovery Network (RDN).

There are two reasons for including this chapter in the book: first to help information professionals identify suitable portals for reference work, and second to assist them in prospecting web portals as potential models or sources for local services. Librarians may wish to encourage users to personalize one of these sites as a home page or point them to the best starting points. Librarians will continue to want to incorporate appropriate services in their own portal or website and public services staff might want to develop a MyPage as a home page to support reference and enquiry work, or indeed any staff member might wish to use one as a personal home page. Since public libraries may get enquiries on any topic, portals can be useful starting points because of the range of sources covered, though perhaps most libraries now have their own pages pointing to important content.

The notes on content provided in this chapter are intended to permit the reader to disassemble a portal to identify the features they might want to incorporate locally and to compare particular features, e.g. business news, against other independent sources. The notes on the use of partners should help in seeing which sources are perhaps already familiar, but which might be enhanced in the portal compared with the service's own site.

The portals considered are chosen as important examples of the type and their content is analysed in some detail as it is often not clear from a brief inspection what sort of features there are. Of course, it is inevitable there will be changes by the time you read this. We shall be looking at the value of portals to libraries and their users as more than just a site or a search engine referencing: range of content, how they aggregate resources together, what sort of searching or cross-searching of resources there is, what sort of personalization is offered and, to a lesser extent, if there are any transactional facilities.

The sites discussed below should not be seen as perfect examples of portal design. Though they aggregate many services, interfaces for consumer portals are often poor, usually either being complex with links everywhere and hard to navigate or, like Google, being over-simple considering the wealth of services provided. Some will have advertising, animation or perhaps lists of most popular searches that could be seen as just obscuring the real information. A sitemap or A–Z list of services may be a better essential starting point than the default page.

The use of RSS feeds is a common aspect of portals, either through them providing a reader like Google and My Yahoo! or offering news or other feeds to read in a MyPage service or separate reader. These services should be promoted to library users. It is also possible to incorporate them into local pages, perhaps using something like FeedSweep (www.howdev.com/services/feedsweep/) to gather from various sources.

Cross-searching – often assumed by libraries to be important – is not widely used, other than in EEVL Xtra and parts of ChemWeb and the NLH. Google does more of a sequential search in that you can do one type of search, then click on another search tab and it is run automatically there, though Scholar is not included. Use of some of these examples of cross-searching might benefit libraries not able to develop or purchase their own facility. Saving searches is possible in Yahoo! and AOL – another reason to encourage users to look beyond Google for their searching.

Personalization is quite common to deal with news, feeds or alerts, though personalized pages do not always offer searching. They give some guidance as what content might be included in any local personal pages. Such pages, of course, will require a login process.

Consumer portals

These are those portals that have grown from being a single service to encompass a wider range of tools, such as Yahoo! – initially a directory of web resources – and Google – a search service – or, like AOL, the home site for an internet service provider. Content tends to be more personal and recreational, but still includes serious material libraries should find of value for their users. Generally in this chapter the UK version of these is assessed, though sometimes the US version is examined for additional features as well. Some of these sites also have versions for other countries, with a slant to that country in news, finance, etc. However, such variants are never very consistent in content and not all features are available in all versions.

Yahoo! UK and Ireland (http://uk.yahoo.com)

Yahoo! began in 1994 as an early (though not the first) directory of web resources and through development and acquisition has grown to have an extensive range of services. The directory is seen as less important and is located low on the page. However, it is still a prime source to identify sites of general interest. Yahoo! is probably the most comprehensive portal of its type, though Google is developing fast.

It is not the intention to discuss all the types of content, only to highlight those of major interest to libraries. The 'All Y! Services' link from the first page gives an overview of topics. This list is valuable as the navigation is not too intuitive otherwise.

Searching (http://uk.search.yahoo.com)

Yahoo!'s web search service was revamped last year and now is usually seen as second to Google in terms of general effectiveness. The Shortcuts link explains the syntax to find factual information like sports scores or definitions. The Services and tools link at the bottom of the page explains the various search services. (Note that the links from the US search pages are not the same.) Other types of search are for images, video and news. In addition, for images Yahoo! has a photo-sharing service – limited to registered users – and owns the similar Flickr (www.flickr.com/) service, though there seems to be no link to it. A subscription search of services like Factiva and LexisNexis is available from the advanced search page. Recently added is a Business finder for companies and organizations in partnership with Thomson Directories. In beta use – i.e. a service still under development – is a Podcasting search (http://podcasts.yahoo.com) for books, politics, speeches, sport, etc. A shopping search is run in conjunction with Kelkoo (www.kelkoo.co.uk/). A search for blogs/webfeeds is planned.

Web directory (http://uk.dir.yahoo.com)

The web directory is probably familiar to most readers: with its browsable categories, supplemented by a search function. The directory on the UK Yahoo! site is international in coverage, but browsing and searching can be limited to the UK or to Ireland.

News (http://uk.news.yahoo.com)

There is a wide range of news grouped in categories such as Top Stories, World, Business, Entertainment, Technology, Science, Health and drawing from sources such as Reuters, ITN, Press Association, AFP, Sky News, *The Scotsman*, *The Register*, vnunet, *New Scientist*, politics.co.uk and more. The search option covers the last month's stories and the news search on the US site also includes blog entries. For regular updating in particular areas an RSS feed can be set up after doing a news search.

Finance (http://uk.finance.yahoo.com)

Information on corporate finance includes FTSE 100, UK, World, US etc. indices, currency rates, company information and stock market activity. For personal finance there is advice on insurance, mortgages, loans, credit cards, savings accounts and the like with comparisons and best buys as can be found on various other sites. There is also a section on student finance, part of a broader section for students.

Business (http://uk.smallbusiness.yahoo.com)

The Yahoo! Small Business section deals with business orientated finance, such as mortgages, loans, insurance, leasing and other aspects of business like office supplies through Viking Direct and document translation from a number of partners. Online quotations are available for many services.

Cars (http://uk.cars.yahoo.com)

This contains reviews, test reports and maps and routes in conjunction with Map24 (www.map24.co.uk/).

Travel (http://uk.travel.yahoo.com)

Yahoo! has a typical service to book holidays, hotels, flights, car hire, etc. as well as having information on tourist destinations. User reviews are included.

My Web

This service – in beta at the time of writing – allows users to save a copy of pages viewed and a link, so moving beyond bookmarks. Pages can be categorized, searched and shared via e-mail, IM and RSS. Access is from anywhere, not just a particular computer. There is clearly potential here for libraries to create useful resources for staff for enquiry work.

My Yahoo! (http://uk.my.yahoo.com)

This is the personalization option generating a personal Yahoo! page – perhaps as a home page – with whatever content you choose from Yahoo!'s services (see Figure 7.1). The search services are standard and you can add Yahoo! e-mail, a calendar and events list, news including RSS feeds, address book or, indeed, whatever you

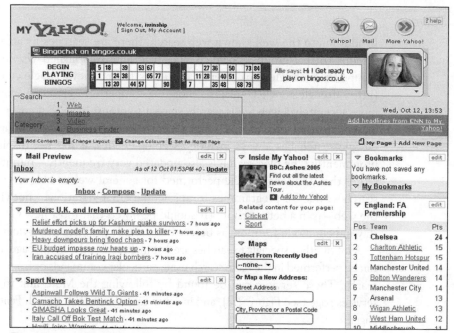

Figure 7.1 My Yahoo! page

© 2006 Yahoo! Inc. YAHOO! and the YAHOO! logo are trademarks of Yahoo! Inc.

choose. Again there could be potential for libraries here, though most would want something branded for their organization and with a wider range of services beyond those from Yahoo!.

Book content

Yahoo! is a partner in the Open Content Alliance (www.opencontentalliance.org/) together with the UK National Archives, University of California and others. OCA will digitize public domain and copyright permitted print and multimedia and make it available through Yahoo! and its own site.

Google (www.google.co.uk)

Google started as a search engine in 1998 and, as well as extending its range of search services, it has moved into other areas, particularly since its flotation as a public company when it acquired huge amounts of money for development. Its remit remains 'to organize the world's information and make it universally accessible and useful'. Its collection of services makes it something of a portal, though based on searching rather than presenting organized content like some of Yahoo!'s services. Its layout and organization are not always helpful – the familiar simple search page becomes limiting when you want to use other features.

Search

In addition to the well known web search, there are searches for images, Google Groups (http://groups.google.co.uk) – the long established Usenet discussion groups that Google took over – and news (http://news.google.co.uk). Froogle (http://froogle.google.co.uk) is a shopping comparison service. A blog search – or more accurately a web feeds search, since it's not just blogs, but covers other types of services that offer feeds – has recently been introduced. Though the main Google search has always included weblog entries, it has not displayed results prominently. The blog search is also updated very frequently – minute by minute rather than the longer cycle performed for general web search services. A video search service for programmes from selected US TV stations – not video clips on the web – is in a beta version. (It should be noted that most new Google services stay in beta mode for months before being made permanent services.)

A lot of other specialist searches are not included in the home page, though some can be performed in the basic search using particular commands or from the advanced search. These services can be found by following the More link to the Google services page (see Figure 7.2), and in some cases from Web Search Features on that page:

- Book Search (Google Print) – Google Print is Google's controversial scheme to digitize various library book collections. Links to those books appear under Book Results at the top of a search results page. There are links to a bookstore selling the printed book online.
- Calculator – Can solve maths problems involving basic arithmetic, more complicated maths, units of measure and conversions, and physical constants. No special syntax is needed.
- Definitions – Searches for glossary definitions gathered from various online sources.
- Films – Finds reviews and showtimes for films or films related to a specific actor, director or plot detail.
- Local Search – Searches for local businesses and services in the UK, USA and Canada. Gives addresses and a location map.
- PhoneBook – Looks up US street address and phone number information – business and residential.
- Q&A – Get answers to fact-based questions or queries, such as birthplaces, population.
- Search By Number – Accesses US package tracking information (UPS, FedEx), US patents, UPC codes and other US numeric databases.
- Stock Quotes – US share information using NYSE, NASDAQ, AMEX or mutual fund ticker symbols.
- Street Maps – US street maps.

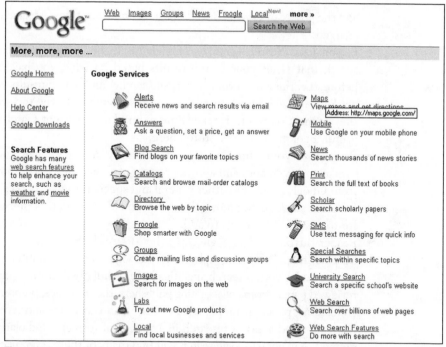

Figure 7.2 Google's services list, www.google.co.uk/help/features.html

- Travel Information – Checks the status of an airline flight in the USA or views airport delays and weather conditions worldwide.
- Weather – Current weather conditions and forecasts for any location in the US.
- Who Links To You? – Finds pages that point to a specific URL.

Other features and services from Google (some hidden under the Labs link and some requiring you to login) are:

- Alerts – E-mail updates of the latest relevant Google results (web, news, etc.) based on your choice of query or topic.
- Answers (http://answers.google.com) – 'More than 500 carefully screened Researchers are ready to answer your question for as little as $2.50 – usually within 24 hours.' Another part of the competition that libraries face.
- Directory (http://directory.google.com) – The Google directory of websites is based on the Open Directory (http://dmoz.org/) and is enhanced using Google's own technology. Search or browse the categories.
- Maps and satellite images (http://maps.google.co.uk/) – Use these to find a location, check for a business or service, or get a detailed route between towns. Google Earth (http://earth.google.com) (which needs special software – Win2000, XP only) is an additional service combining satellite imagery, maps

and the power of Google Search. Basic services are free – advanced services are charged.

- Personalized Search (beta) – This claims to be an improvement to Google search that ranks your search results based on what you have searched for before. 'Learning from your history of searches and search results you've clicked on, Personalized Search brings certain results closer to the top when it's clear they're most relevant.' It takes time to build up sufficient search history to be useful. Bookmarks can be stored here.
- Personalize your home page (currently only at www.google.com) – This is similar to My Yahoo! and allows preview of Gmail messages, shows headlines from Google News and other general and specialist news sources, has weather forecasts, stock quotes, movie showtimes and lifestyle sources. You can also search for topics and RSS feeds to add.
- Reader (http://reader.google.com) (beta) – An RSS reader.
- Scholar (http://scholar.google.com) – Google Scholar (another service still in beta) enables you to search specifically for scholarly literature, including peer-reviewed papers from collaborating publishers, theses, books, preprints from major collections, papers from personal websites, and abstracts and technical reports from all broad areas of research in a variety of formats. 'Scholarly' is not well defined. A general Google search will find many of these references, but usually not prominently. Author and journal title searching is possible, though this does not always work correctly. Content is often much less than on the publisher's own site, and more fields, like publisher, would be helpful. A citation searching option is included. Problems include: multiple sources of the same paper; multiple versions (e.g. preprint, published paper); often only the abstract is available; payment may be requested if a library doesn't subscribe to the journal. Linking to full text with a link resolver may be possible. It is not clear how often the database is updated or, indeed, exactly what is the content being searched, but Scholar has value as a simple multidisciplinary source, though subscription databases will be better. For a fuller evaluation, see Jacso (2005).

The outlines of Yahoo! and Google have given a fairly detailed idea of the sort of services to be found in these types of portal, so the following summaries are briefer.

AOL (www.aol.co.uk)

AOL is a well established ISP, claiming to have 34 million users worldwide. The UK portal has a limited range of features. The basic searches of the web and of images are provided by Google, with an audio and video search from Singingfish (www.singingfish.com). There is a shopping comparison search using http://uk.shopping.com with paid links from Overture, a Yahoo! company (http://searchmarketing.yahoo.com/). A weather search is provided by The Weather

Channel (http://uk.weather.com), from where, if you wish, you can search the web with Yahoo!. News is from the Press Association and is grouped as Top Stories, World, Sport, Entertainment, Technology, etc. There is no news search (see Figure 7.3). There is also a login to AOL e-mail.

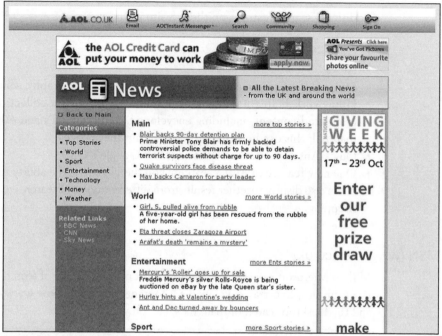

Figure 7.3 AOL's news page

The US site (www.aol.com) – from the AOL International link on the UK home page – has a more extensive range of features, many of value to a non-US audience. These include:

- Movies (http://movies.aol.com) – reviews, features, trailers
- Research & Learn (http://reference.aol.com) – homework, genealogy, science, history, space
- Health (http://health.aol.com), from WebMD (www.webmd.com/) – diseases, drugs, diet, fitness
- News (http://news.aol.com) – an extensive coverage with the usual range of categories
- Small Business (http://aol.entrepreneur.com) – starting, managing businesses
- Travel (http://travel.aol.com) – airfares, hotels, etc.
- Maps and directions – from Mapquest (www.mapquest.com); the basic link is to US information, but a further link covers the UK and other countries
- Yellow pages (www.yellowpages.com/)

- White pages – address, phone number, e-mail – from Infospace (www.infospace .com)
- Government guide (www.governmentguide.com) – has US federal, state and local services and resources. It is rather well hidden.

Additional search features on the US site include:

- Local – businesses, events
- News
- Music (http://music.aol.com/) – artists, including biography, songs, albums
- Homework help (http://homeworkhelp.aol.com/) – a collection of school-orientated content, including encyclopedias, dictionaries and other reference material; this can be searched from within these pages
- Quick Answers – factual questions like Google's Q&A
- One new feature of AOL's searching on the US site is the ability to save results. It can also display together results from different types of search, e.g. web, images, shopping.

MSN (www.msn.co.uk)

MSN is Microsoft's portal (see Figure 7.4). It offers a variety of search options: web, news, images, Encarta encyclopedia, shopping (using Kelkoo – www.kelkoo.co.uk) and the Desktop search of mail, files, etc. on your PC.

Figure 7.4 MSN home page (Microsoft product screen shot reprinted with permission from Microsoft Corporation)

Other major features are:

- Computing & tech – reviews, news, virus and security information, etc.
- Health, including for travel, using Netdoctor (www.netdoctor.co.uk) and other partners
- Money (http://money.msn.co.uk) – insurance, mortgages, investing
- News & Weather – from Reuters, Sky News videos, articles from Newsweek and other news at MSNBC; as with Yahoo! you can save a news search as an RSS feed to get regular updates
- Property – sale, rent, mortgages
- Shopping – browse or search for products
- Travel – a simple link to the Expedia (www.expedia.co.uk) site.

Also included are:

- Encarta Online Learning – homework, reference books
- Currency Converter
- Financial Advisers – searchable directory of IFA members
- Maps & Directions – using Microsoft MapPoint.

There is a link to Hotmail and a search box for eBay. MSN Groups (http://groups.msn.com) – comprises discussion forums, sometimes with additional documents. Topics include business, computers, health, money and investing, news and politics. MSN Spaces is a weblog facility for all.

The personalization option is predictably called MyMSN. You can choose content, such as local news, weather, sports, etc. from MSN or the web in general. There is a link to Hotmail and the colours, design, etc. can be varied.

MSN is also developing a test portal Start (www.start.com) that may or may not be around when you read this, since they say it is 'an incubation experiment and doesn't represent any particular strategy or policy'.

Lycos (www.lycos.co.uk)

Lycos was once a major search engine, but has since developed into more of a portal with a directory and many other features. There is a variety of searches. The Web Search uses Looksmart (http://search.looksmart.com/) and Yahoo! and has simple and advanced options. There is also a picture (image) search. A local search for businesses and organizations uses the TouchLocal directories (www.touchlocal.com/). In this context 'local' means companies, etc. anywhere in the UK, not just where the user lives. The web directory can be browsed and searched. Note that this includes paid entries. A shopping search (http://shopping.lycos.co.uk/) has the usual product comparison features – categories can also be browsed. A domain search is available for anyone wanting to purchase a domain name.

Other major features include:

- News (http://news.lycos.co.uk/) – appears to be all from the AFP agency and is divided into a few categories; there is no search facility. RSS feeds from news sources are available, but only to users of Lycos mail
- Travel section – booking facilities and information from a variety of partners, including Cheapflights (www.cheapflights.co.uk) and WordTravels (www.wordtravels.com/)
- Money section (http://money.lycos.co.uk/) – deals with personal finance – loans, credit cards, mortgages, etc. – and is largely provided by Interactive Investor (www.iii.co.uk/) .

Lycos also has an 'adult' section – not described here! This is an interesting addition when you expect the audience for an ISP's home page to be all ages, though the inclusion of chat and online dating features suggests the target audience is perhaps largely young people.

The US Lycos site (www.lycos.com) has similar features, together with more US orientated ones like white and yellow pages searches. It also has a very useful discussion search (http://discussion.lycos.com/) that searches many web discussion forums – but not Google Groups – including from the UK (see Figure 7.5). It does, however, seem to pick up things that merely include words like 'discussion forum' in the text.

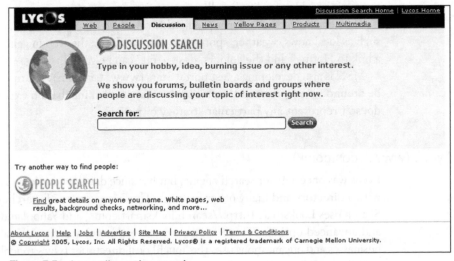

Figure 7.5   Lycos discussion search

There is also a My Lycos feature (http://my.lycos.com/), similar to other personalized home pages.

Subject and other portals

This section looks at subject-focused portals – some portalized more than others. These tend to be mainly for an academic or professional audience.

Resource Discovery Network – RDN (www.rdn.ac.uk)

The RDN is the collection of eight subject hubs (or gateways) that have developed over the last ten years or so from various JISC-funded projects. Primarily these comprise collections of high-quality, reviewed websites from around the world, particularly of academic value. The hubs have developed individually, with different features; for a number of years there was no real co-ordination, with significant gaps in subject coverage. In recent years coverage has become more comprehensive. Accordingly the simple search of the combined collections available from the RDN home page now has some value as a multi-disciplinary search, though effective searching needs the additional features available at individual hubs – e.g. restriction by subject category or type of resource, or the ability to use Boolean operators. The RDN page also offers RDN Behind the Headlines – selected RDN resources offering background information related to the latest news headlines.

The hubs are not true portals but, like the consumer ones, do have added features and resources beyond their collections of sites. The RDN has developed the RDN Virtual Training Suite (VTS) – a set of free online subject tutorials designed to help students, lecturers and researchers improve their internet information literacy and IT skills. The VTS is linked from the RDN page and hubs will link to the tutorials in their subject area. Most hubs have some sort of regular listing of recent items added to their directory and often have news in their subject area. RSS feeds may be available for these two activities.

Other notable features of particular hubs are:

- Artifact (www.artifact.ac.uk) – arts and creative industries: cross-searching of collections and exhibitions and of image banks
- EEVL (www.eevl.ac.uk) – engineering, maths, computing: Recent Advances in Manufacturing (RAM) database; Ejournal Search Engine (EESE); OneStep Jobs and OneStep News services that aggregate from many sources
- GEsource (www.gesource.ac.uk) – geography, environment: geological timelines, a natural hazards collection, country guides with articles, maps data, etc.
- HUMBUL (www.humbul.ac.uk) – humanities: links to free electronic journals
- SOSIG (www.sosig.ac.uk) – social sciences: the Grapevine conference and events listing; social science search engine that searches selected social science websites
- PSIgate (www.psigate.ac.uk) – physical sciences: chemistry and electronics tutorials; chemistry data tables; cross-searching of Institute of Physics and Royal Society of Chemistry journals and the Royal Society of Chemistry Library catalogue; searching of free databases on spectroscopy, chemical compounds, patents, safety data and related topics (see Figure 7.6).

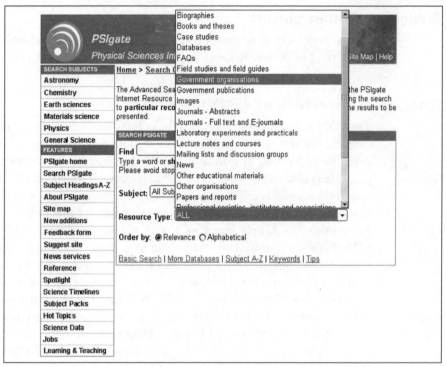

Figure 7.6 PSIgate search page

These additional features do suggest that hubs could be developed into portals, and that was, indeed, intended as part of the JISC Subject Portals Project (www.portal.ac.uk/spp/). The stated objectives were to deliver:

- an aggregated cross-search tool searching across both JISC-supported and non-JISC information resources specially selected by the hubs themselves
- a streamlined account management system which acts as a trusted broker between the user and an authentication service such as Athens on behalf of resource providers
- a store of user profiling data
- a tailored e-mail alerting service
- a range of additional services, such as aggregated newsfeed, conference information, etc.

Open source software was to be developed and tested in some of the hubs, and though this happened, despite what was expected in a recent article (Guy, 2005), a roll-out as a service has not occurred. This is likely to be because JISC has decided it is too costly to implement.

However, the EEVL hub – always innovative in extending beyond the basic collection of sites – has introduced EEVL Xtra (www.eevlxtra.ac.uk/) to take forward some of the ideas, funded by Heriot Watt University which hosts EEVL.

EEVL Xtra cross-searches over 20 different collections relevant to engineering, mathematics and computing, including content from over 50 publishers and providers (see Figure 7.7). The content includes, among other things:

- publishers – Emerald, IoP Electronic Journals, Inderscience
- databases – RAM, Citeseer
- eprint archives – arXiv, ePrints UK
- library catalogues – Copac
- newsletters and magazines – *The Register*, vnunet.com, *PC Magazine*, *New Scientist*
- technical reports – NACA technical reports, NASA technical reports
- engineering news – OneStep Industry News
- jobs – OneStep Jobs, Jobs.ac.uk
- learning material – SearchLT Engineering.

There are also links straight through to the collections, which can be searched separately when preferred.

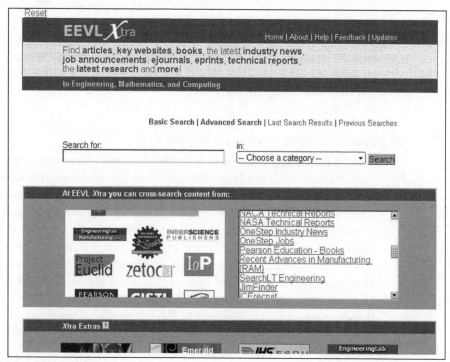

Figure 7.7   EEVL Xtra

In many cases, the full text of items should be freely available, e.g. from arXiv, CiteSeer, EEVL Ejournal Search Engine, ePrints UK, but in some cases the full items are just details of books or websites, e.g. from Copac, EEVL, Pearson Education, SearchLT Engineering, so users need to click through to the website, or find a library which holds the book. Full text of journal articles is available only if the user's library has a subscription or a copy of the article is purchased. (Clicking directly through to the full text will be possible for some databases if the institution has a link resolver.)

The background information on the site makes it clear that subscription databases, especially with a cross-searching facility, may well produce better results than EEVL Xtra, but points out that EEVL Xtra has some information not usually available through library sources.

There are several 'Xtra Extras' featured on the home page, familiar from EEVL itself, including those noted above and others, such as Hot Topics – reports on topical issues, from CSA; Design Data – validated engineering design data, from ESDU; and Offshore Engineering – information on publications and meetings in offshore engineering.

EEVL Xtra might offer a model for other hubs, if funding can be found, since it searches a wide variety of types of resource easily, and thus would be attractive to users, since most rarely use more than a handful of different resources.

Some other interesting portals

It is not proposed to look at other subject portals in any great detail, but merely to draw attention to a few that might be of value and which show how portal principles are being applied.

National Library for Health (www.library.nhs.uk/)

The NLH is being developed from the National Electronic Library for Health (www.nelh.nhs.uk). NeLH had the aim to 'provide clinicians with access to the best current know-how and knowledge to support healthcare-related decisions'. NLH is more ambitious and plans to bringing together 'all NHS library and information services, and working with other service providers . . . to deliver the best health library service to all NHS staff, students, patients and carers'.

Currently features include a cross-searching facility of various sources (either all or particular ones that are specified), such as Health Technology Assessment Database, NLH Protocols & Care Pathways, Bandolier and Cochrane Database of Systematic Reviews (see Figure 7.8). Search profiles of the required databases can be set up by users with NHS Athens accounts, who can access further databases, journals and other resources directly.

Medical news headlines are available from a number or sources, all with RSS feeds. A few other sources of publications, projects, etc. with feeds are listed.

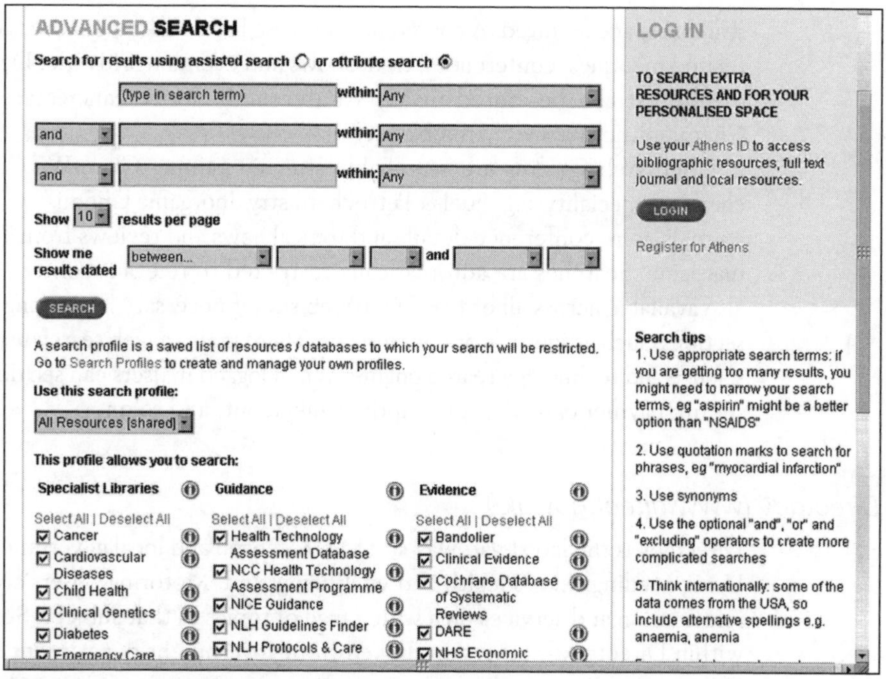

Figure 7.8 National Library for Health cross-search

The Primary Care Question Answering Service is a pilot service created to help members of the primary care teams of England get answers to their clinical questions. The service team uses various databases to supply answers and the cumulated questions and answers can be searched, or browsed, by speciality.

ChemWeb (www.chemweb.com)

ChemWeb is a specialist site run by Elsevier for chemists. Some features are freely available, others only to registered members. Journals ChemWeb has around 350 full-text, chemistry-related journals from several scientific publishers. Tables of contents and article abstracts can be searched free of charge. Full text articles from Elsevier Science journals are available to ScienceDirect subscribers. There is an alerting service for the contents of new issues.

The Chemistry Preprint Server (CPS) was launched in August 2000 and is a freely available and permanent web archive and distribution medium for research articles. Submission to, and use of, the CPS is open to all. A small number of databases is also offered, such as ChemWeb.com Free Abstract Search and ACD/Labs Spectroscopy Databases. There is software used online rather than locally, such as ACD/Labs IUPAC Name generation.

News is provided from *The Alchemist* magazine, which also has weekly features and highlighted hot papers, plus profiles, reviews and conference reports. It is fully searchable and archived. A conference database has details of hundreds of chemistry-related meetings, conferences, tradeshows and events worldwide. Details of those of interest can be stored in My Conferences. Job vacancies are offered via Chemjobs.net (www.chemjobs.net)

ChemWeb Forums are searchable sites containing ChemWeb content for a chemical speciality, e.g. Fuel & Petrochemistry, Inorganic Chemistry. This includes journals, jobs, conference details and topical news and reviews from *The Alchemist* magazine. Searches are automatically restricted to relevant content. Searching is also available across all of the ChemWeb site, if necessary restricting to particular sections, such as journals or conferences. There is also a web search using the Scirus science and technology search engine. When logged in users can see details of alerts set up, payments made, subscriptions taken out, and so on.

Directgov (www.direct.gov.uk/)

Directgov is the latest gateway site to UK central and local government resources. Using headings like 'Health and well-being' and 'Motoring', users are directed to information and services on a wide range of topics in that subject. Some pages are within Directgov – others are linked from government department sites, such as Customs and Revenue. There seems to be some repetition of content between them as Directgov tries to summarize topics, with links to other sites for fuller details.

Browsing in this way may not lead most easily to the required information and a site search facility is offered. This unhelpfully and, these days, unusually uses an implied OR in the searching so giving large numbers of references if users do not realize this and is just for the Directgov site, so does not cover the related ones. There are simple and advanced searches, though the latter is hidden at the end of the search results list. There is an A–Z of topics, but this seems limited in content and not especially helpful for many purposes.

As the Government is pushing electronic delivery of services from local and national government, with targets for getting services completely online, there is naturally a listing of services available online (see Figure 7.9). Thus, you can find information – local schools; apply for items – a driving licence; buy services – a TV licence; and complete forms – tax returns. Activity like this doesn't extend to local services, so you can find your council tax band, but not pay the tax. There are directories of government departments and agencies, local authorities, and public sector, charity and voluntary organizations in the UK if you want to go direct to any of them.

Conclusion

Librarians, especially in public libraries, answer a vast variety of queries, and many of the portals discussed in this chapter are useful in locating answers or links to sites with answers. The RDN offers a very useful access point to the open web organized

Figure 7.9 Directgov list of online services

on disciplinary lines. It also offers streams of information that can be built into local websites and portals. EEVL in particular seems to offer some examples of innovative ideas that might also work locally. Surprisingly the consumer portals seem to be in many ways examples of poor design, especially in basic navigation.

Bibliography

Guy, M. (2005) Lessons and Outcomes from the Subject Portals Project, *Vine*, **35** (1), 2005, 58–63.

Jacso, P. (2005) Google Scholar (redux), *Peter's Digital Reference Shelf*, June, www.galegroup.com/reference/archive/200506/google.html.

Lossau, N. (2004) Search Engine Technology and Digital Libraries: libraries need to discover the academic internet, *D-Lib Magazine*, **10** (6), June, www.dlib.org/dlib/june04/lossau/06lossau.html.

Miller, P. (2003) Towards a Typology for Portals, *Ariadne*, 37, [online], www.ariadne.ac.uk/issue37/miller

Plosker, G. (2005) Do You Really Know Yahoo? *Online*, **29** (5), Sept./Oct., 51–3.

SearchEngineWatch blog, http://blog.searchenginewatch.com/blog, for news on the consumer portals.

8

Portals and university libraries

John A. MacColl

The promise of libraries

Libraries are places of contradiction. The library many of us still think of when we use the word – the building or place filled with mostly printed material – invites its users to find or ask for an item of recorded knowledge by which they may be informed for their improvement or their harmless entertainment. The invitation has behind it a thrilling and inspiring assumption: that the work of humankind should be freely available for all to share, and that the places for sharing it should be found within every town or city, and essentially within every place of learning. Nevertheless, this free use of our collective intellectual resource is not really free at all. As contributors to our societies, we pay for the service through taxation and, in doing so, we pay for a service based on a distribution ratio of one resource to many users. The use of the resource is therefore constrained by demand, and time-limited. If we breach that condition, we pay a fine, or a replacement item charge. And if we want an item which is not held by our local library, we may well have to pay a charge for the administrative effort of using our library as a user of some larger library somewhere else. The assumption behind the existence of libraries is thrilling and inspiring indeed, but the reality of service is inevitably compromised so that the freedom which they deliver is of course only a limited freedom.

Nonetheless, people love libraries because they are witness to something generous in our collective spirit: like free health care and free basic education, they acknowledge our duty to each other. What sets them apart from health care and education, and other social services, indeed, is that their usage is optional. Alongside museums and galleries, they belong to the category of use we call 'culture'. They exist in their purest form as public libraries. The libraries we are concerned about here, academic libraries, are less pure because their use is mandated for the students, researchers and staff they serve for which they provide a collective resource pool. Nonetheless, they still behave with the altruism we are used to from using public libraries: they treat requests for material seriously, and they rarely say 'no' to a request. They also function as back-up libraries for the use of the public, and the current political climate in the UK encourages them to respond positively to this broader role, as universities themselves open their doors more widely to the general public, transforming their role as symbols of learning within communities into one which is genuinely functional.

University libraries now, like all publicly funded libraries, need to consider their users as sets arranged in concentric rings. Their duty lies in serving their immediate circle of users – staff and students of the institution – first and foremost. Once that need is met, however, they also need to provide ways to serve the users in the further rings, albeit with more restricted services, or with charges applied for service. Often, however, libraries must say 'wait', and the solemn act of waiting may seem an appropriate act of homage to the privileged act of learning from great minds. Users in the inner circle should have the least waiting to do, since their need of access to great minds is the most urgent, as recognized by their membership of the university.

So libraries promise fullness and freedom, but have to deliver on that promise within the constraints of time, place, limited resource and user prioritization. Now libraries are going digital, which is a leap forward in many ways, not least because it is much more frequently the case that they can say 'yes' rather than 'wait'. For users, digitally available equivalents of the material requested – book chapters, journal articles, exam papers, music recordings, etc. – are a gem because they can be used immediately without the need to go to the library premises to fetch them, or (worse) to find that they are currently unavailable, and waiting is required. This allows the digital manifestations of works to promote Ranganathan's Fourth Law of Library Science: 'Save the time of the user.'[1] Of course, not all library users are satisfied with using resources on-screen from their own study bedrooms or homes. Many, particularly in the arts and social sciences, hold firmly to the positive value of browsing and serendipity. One of the tasks, indeed, for the digital library, is the simulation of browsing books on a shelf.

The success of e-journals, however, has propelled the development of the digital library more than any other type of content. The acceptance of the e-journal on university campuses has spread now to most disciplines, and the rejoicing which has recently come from the academic community over Google Scholar[2] has been largely due to their preference for instant access to an e-journal over a wait of a few days for a paper version to arrive from the interlibrary loan department. Digital content, in this area at least, is now highly valued, and needs its libraries just as much as did content in any previous format, and librarians have now accepted that the day has come and gone when they might have seen the use of the digital medium somehow constrained to material which was not relevant to their roles. All library services therefore now need to develop digital libraries, and a world of wonderful possibilities has opened up. Digital and communications technologies offer the prospect of overcoming some of the frustrating limits of library services based upon physical objects: time, speed, distance and cost. But even as they do, they bring in frustrations of their own: lock-out, system crashes, data obsolescence and loss, vendor reliance and cost.

The arrival of portals

Portals are a familiar landmark in the digital world. Like the shopping mall, or the superstore or the multiplex cinema, they offer a themed multiplicity of content. They attract people, encourage them to feel hungry, and offer a range of goods to satisfy appetites. They have hooks designed to draw users in, and to bring them back again. To be effective, a library portal – like any other – will have to present a variety of options designed to meet the desires of different types of user all within a small area of screen real estate. They must satisfy users seeking to do serious research, users seeking quick reference information, users seeking basic service information, users looking for visually appealing content, and users wishing to make contact with the organization behind the portal. And, common to every option which the portal must satisfy, are some basic quality indicators: a fast, responsive service; good, clear navigation; accessible language; and design for usability and for the desires and expectations of the primary user group.

The portal has to reassure users that they have come to the right place. It should give some instant recognition and relief, and some enjoyable content to a user on a journey from an idea of what they seek to the end-point of their enquiry. A portal is an orientation space, a place where a user metaphorically sits down for a few moments to take a breather, scan some notices, and plan what to do next; a place where resolution may occur, halfway between a decision already made and a decision which they could be persuaded to accept. In the physical world, the portal is much more like the foyer of a museum than that of most libraries. Museums have been better at giving their visitors orientation spaces than have libraries. Museums greet their visitors with cafés; they give them visually appealing tasters, guides to collections and details of tour schedules. Libraries have rather assumed a seriousness of purpose from the point of entry to the building, with the idea perhaps that users are so intent on pursuing their quest that they are uninterested in taking a breather and orienting themselves. What distinguishes a library from a museum is the depth of its content, and the private way in which that content is to be consumed and enjoyed – either within the walls of the library, or by being taken away and used by readers in their own time. Are portals perhaps too frivolous for organizations with such serious aims to pursue?

The answer, of course, is 'no'. Libraries need portals in the same way that their buildings need foyers. It may be inappropriate for academic libraries to seek to appeal for portal users using popular entertainment 'hooks' – celebrity pics and gossip, half-price sale offers and online gaming – but they are now liberated by digitization to dangle images of their most precious manuscripts or to assemble online exhibitions based on themes or authors in which they are strong. Lorcan Dempsey considers this parallel between the physical and the virtual library portal:

So, interestingly, as collections and services move to the network, we see a renewed emphasis on the library place as 'agora', as a social assembly space. Developments include major new building work which focuses on this social aspect and on the symbolic aspect of the library, a growing interest in the exhibition and display of special collections and rare materials, on redeveloping space for social learning and interaction, on the library as a neutral 'third place', and on information and research commons activities.[3]

Making a portal instantly gratifying is of course only going to go so far, especially for academic libraries. What is more important is the one-stop shop function, what we might consider the depth to the service by which it delivers convenience, which is arguably what distinguishes a library portal from a simple library website. Any site can of course call itself a portal, and the presence of even a single link makes the argument. But for our purposes it is helpful to think of portals as richly integrated and comprehensively representative resources which provide convenience, and save the time of the user. Portals must have both depth and breadth, to justify their claim on the title.

University library portals: historical development

Library portals have had a different evolution from the portals of most organizations, because an online library presence, certainly in the case of academic libraries, has been a reality since the early 1980s for most. That was the time when OPACs (online public access catalogues) made their mark, and they were presented to users via terminals in the public areas of library buildings. When the web came along, and in time the idea that every organization should have a website, libraries initially created sites which were little more than lists of library services, with links out to services which had web or telnet interfaces. Thus, to draw on the experience of my own library, see Figure 8.1 for how the website looked at Edinburgh University Library in July 1996.

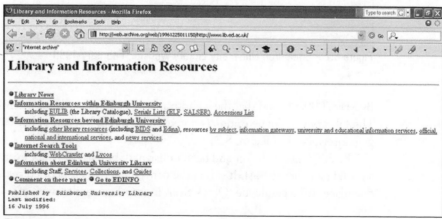

Figure 8.1 Edinburgh University Library website, July 1996

In this presentation, the Library catalogue (EULIB) is just one among several services available via links. Clicking on the link opened a telnet session in a separate window. For most of the promised content, there is, in other words, no integration from one service to another beyond the presentation of meta-information. This is therefore simply a directory-style web page. What prevents it justifying any claim to be a portal is that its convenience value claim – the collocation of links – is negated by the reality of following up on them. A collection of heterogeneous sites, with different interfaces, authentication demands and search vocabularies, represents a succession of barriers to the user.

Eighteen months later, the website is presented slightly less crudely, with more resources available. Again, however, the library catalogue is not integrated, and the Library website's purpose is to point to other useful resources, rather than itself to be one (see Figure 8.2).

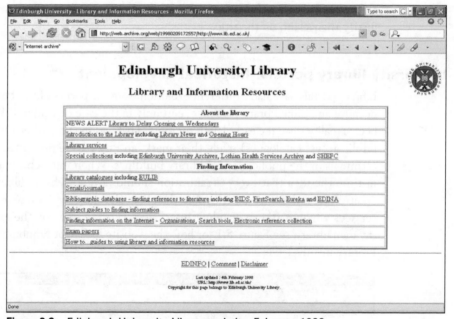

Figure 8.2   Edinburgh University Library website, February 1998

By May 2000, we find that the website at last begins to pay some attention to design. The Library Catalogue option is not yet integrated, but it is at least available via a web interface (see Figure 8.3).

The 2005 site is slicker and better designed, but arguably not even yet properly a portal (see Figure 8.4). It offers the convenience of embedded searching in only one place, for a catalogue 'Quick Search' (see Figure 8.5 overleaf).

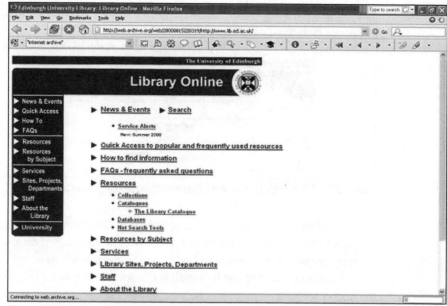

Figure 8.3 Edinburgh University Library website, May 2000

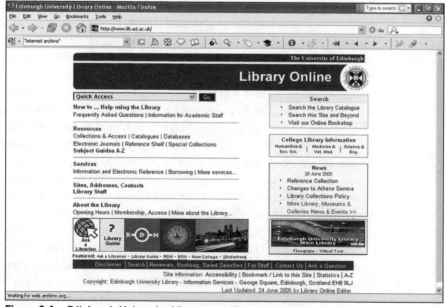

Figure 8.4 Edinburgh University Library website, June 2005

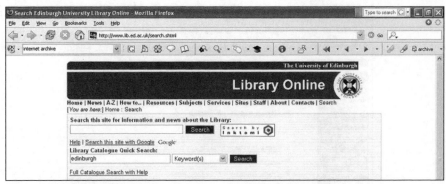

Figure 8.5   Edinburgh University Library catalogue quick search

Edinburgh University Library, like many, has spent a lot of time considering the merits of introducing a separate library portal. Given the fact that most users of library websites are in a tearing hurry to find a resource as quickly as possible, it has been argued that a portal may not be worth the investment. Once a user finds a site via the library website – whether it be a publisher's server, an open access repository, an online index or any other service – and is happy with that site, their usual behaviour is to bookmark it so that they can find it the next time they need it, within the shortest possible timescale. On the other hand, we should not be too quick to presume that all users behave in the same way, and we do also need to present our services comprehensively for first-time or occasional users. At Edinburgh, for instance, we have continued with the development of our library website, but have been hesitant about calling it a portal.

Recently there has been a real impetus to portal development, however, as a new generation of search tools has appeared from library system vendors, based around the technologies of metasearch or harvesting, and in some cases providing a mix of both. These tools are designed to provide discovery functionality across the range of digital resources provided by libraries – both those held locally and those purchased under licence and held remotely by publishers or other aggregators. At the present time, the best known of these products is Metalib by Ex Libris,[4] ENCompass by Endeavor,[5] Sirsi's SingleSearch[6] and Innovative's Metafind.[7] Once installed, these tools are configured to work with their library's particular range of databases, and their whole objective is to offer one-stop-shop searching in order to save users time spent in discovering and aggregating results database by database, in learning different search interfaces, and in negotiating a succession of authentication and authorization credential challenges. They are in effect portal creation toolkits, designed to fit the content provided by the digital library.

If libraries adopt these solutions, they are presented with a dilemma, because normally they will have a website running separately, and will initially link to the metasearch service from the 'main' website. Nevertheless, it soon becomes clear that the new service has in effect stolen a lot of the business of the website, which had previously provided links to the range of services now capable of being metasearched. Should the website now discard these links? Surely it would be better to rebuild the library website around the metasearch portal? In short, we have arrived at a new juncture in the architectural development of academic digital libraries, which is akin to the one we reached when we built our first library websites and linked out to our separate telnet OPAC services.

A few leading libraries have understood the implications of this, and have already made the transition to a fully fledged library portal, with a metasearch tool at its core (incorporating the OPAC). The University of Pittsburgh provides an example of this (see Figure 8.6).

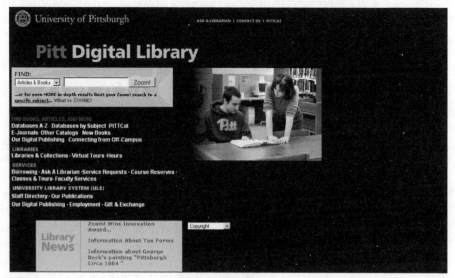

Figure 8.6   University of Pittsburgh Library portal

With a proper library portal now functioning, the digital library has arrived at the equivalent of the central campus library building, concentrating a range of services into a single point, and standing ready to serve all comers.

Yet, as with the central library building, what libraries have found almost at the same moment is that the 'centralized' portal is not enough for its user community. Academic staff love to have their own departmental libraries just down the corridor. They value having their own dedicated, specialist library staff. They like to be able to send their research assistants along to pick up their interlibrary loan photocopies, or to borrow books in their name. They want a key which will let them into the library in the middle of the night if, during an experiment, they have an urgent need to check back to a paper published some time ago. What they want, in fact, is a bespoke library, customized around their own needs. They do not want the authoritarian attitude of the central library, with its stern rules about not borrowing journals, its fixed opening and closing times, and its unfamiliar staff who are ignorant of their disciplines. It may offer an impressive range of services, but they need only two or three of them, provided they are of top quality. The central library is still very important – for the undergraduate community in particular – at least as long as most learning materials are still physical objects, and as a back-up facility for the entire service. But researchers find that their time is more effectively used with specialist library satellites.

Undergraduates, too, are increasingly liberated from the pressure to study on the library premises through the wide use of virtual learning environments (VLEs). As elements of those environments are unbundled and presented within a portal which represents their own experience of the university, so the library is similarly pressured to deliver content to a single customizable portal at the campus level.

Customizable portals

It is for that reason that the customizable portal which is now appearing on university campuses may fit the requirements of many library users better than either the centralized portal or its predecessors. Portals which can be personalized to the range of campus services relevant to or desired by individual members of the university are now being developed through systems like JA-SIG's uPortal.[8] They offer a default set of services which are either native to the portal, or channelled in from other parts of the campus web architecture, including, of course, the library. These channelled services together compose the bespoke portal, and are known as 'portlets'. Users can choose which channels to retain and which to discard. The technology of the personalized portal is still somewhat clunky and imprecise, and the organizational arrangements on campuses to build them and maintain them are having to be developed on the ground, with a great deal of difficult liaison effort.

The University of Edinburgh recently released its customizable portal, MyEd, which incorporates a library channel (see Figure 8.7).

The library channel is not yet ideal, offering a selective subset of services and functions which are determined more by what is technically possible than by what is ideal for delivery to personalized portal users. Again, this stage of development is reminiscent of library websites of ten years ago, which provided links to other services on the internet on the basis of what was available rather than what was desirable. Its presentation, at the time of writing, requires the user to scroll down through three screens, as shown in Figure 8.8.

It is also clear that this portal does not yet offer maximum convenience: most of its services are not truly integrated. The majority of them need to be launched from the portal, which is simply a way of providing links to them. True portalized integration brings the search functionality into the portal, allowing the user to remain in the portal while having their various needs met. MyEd's library pages achieve this at the present time only for the Find Resources service.

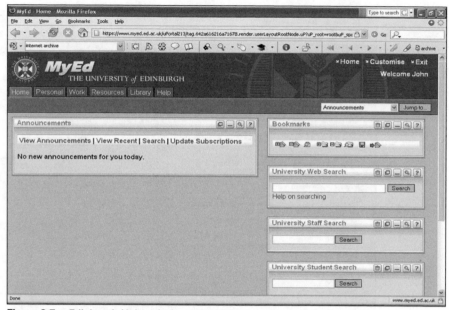

Figure 8.7 Edinburgh University's customizable portal

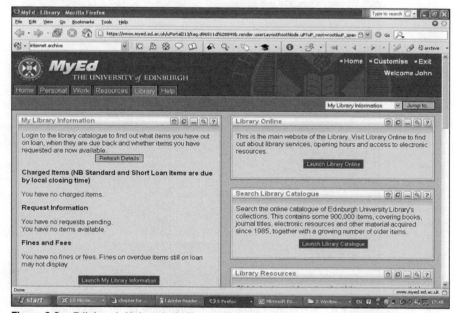

Figure 8.8 Edinburgh University's library channel

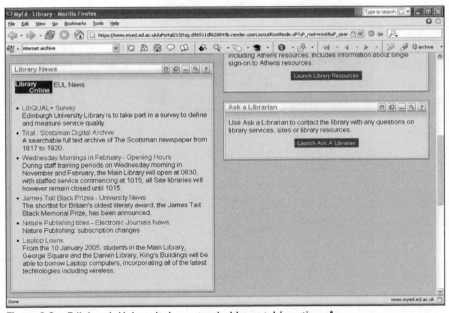

Figure 8.8   Edinburgh University's customizable portal (*continued*)

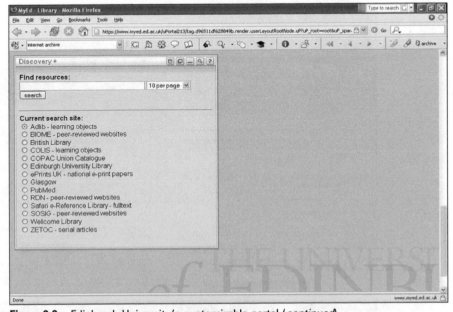

Figure 8.8   Edinburgh University's customizable portal (*continued*)

Integration and portals

In his article on library portalization, Lorcan Dempsey discusses integration in terms of shallowness and depth:

> In the first case, a resource is made available at, say, a web page. The intended consumer is a human, so it is oriented towards reading and navigation. Integration of resource content needs to be provided by the user. Think of the user who successively looks at several catalogs: typically, he or she will have to manually integrate, sift, manipulate or merge. Most of our information services are now made available in this way. Think of the library 'portal' which provides organized lists of internet resources. The user may be guided to resources of interest, but once they commit to looking at a particular resource, they leave the 'portal' environment and are delivered to the door of the remote resource. Think of lists of e-journals, or of abstracting and indexing databases: again, the user may be guided, may have a personalized list of resources presented to them, but is then delivered to the front door of the desired resource. Once they go through the door of the desired resource, the user is in that remote resource environment, and needs to behave appropriately. The desired resource sits on the network behind its own user interface. Integration is shallow.[9]

Many such portals at the present time deliver the experience of 'integration failure'. It can be difficult to spot unintegrated portal services, because portals by definition make bold claims of integration for themselves. Seeking to provide 'sticky content'[10] they wish to take credit for integration when often all they are providing is collocation. As users become more savvy, however, they will not be fooled, and both libraries and their institutions need to be careful not to oversell their portal offerings. Savvy users, once disappointed, will often not return.

Some sites have already developed reasonably advanced integration, such as the University of Nottingham's portal, which is also based on the uPortal platform (see Figure 8.9 overleaf).

Here, the integration is almost complete, though the eLibrary Gateway remains a challenge. Such integration is achieved by the machinery of the portal, rather than by a simple collocation of links which remove the user to remote environments. Dempsey considers that this level of integration makes a portal into a 'broker':

> A broker provides a deeper level of integration. Here are examples of what broker applications do:
>
> • hide difference and the mechanics of interaction from users, so as to save time and simplify procedures. An example here would be a cross-searching application which creates a federated resource from several others. Of course, such applications raise various complications in implementation.

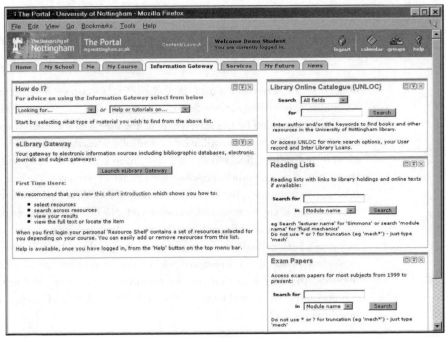

Figure 8.9   University of Nottingham's portal

- facilitate flow of data between applications so as to automate processes. This includes inter-application integration. An example here would be a resource sharing application which mediates searching, ILL, resolution, and document delivery transactions, perhaps interfacing with billing or other applications.
- aggregate resources for further use. An example here would be an OAI-PMH-based harvester which takes data from several sources and makes it available at a machine or a user interface. The Open Archives Initative Protocol for Metadata Harvesting is a technique for sharing metadata between services. One service – a data provider in OAI terms – makes metadata available in an agreed way; another service comes and 'harvests' it. The latter service – a service provider in OAI terms – may harvest from multiple 'data providers' and in turn may provide access to the metadata it collects in this way.[11]

Conclusion

The degree of brokerage which Dempsey describes is hard to find on university portal sites, whether library portals or institution-wide portals, either personalizable or not. But there is progress towards it. The library channel in the MyEd Edinburgh portal described above deploys harvesting, for example, and our ability to deliver search results from different types of database – OPACs, databases of exam papers or of reading lists – is growing, as we convert data structures to XML and build web services into our sites. We have some distance to go to achieve the sort of portalization technology which makes the top commercial services on the web, such as Amazon, so successful, and of course we have lacked the commercial imperatives to develop our portals to that extent.

Nevertheless, we do need to do this development. Academic libraries feel threatened almost to the point of paranoia. There can seem to be so many challenges to our business that we are not sure who to be most threatened by, and whose threat is the greatest. Google and Amazon are threats from outwith the university; institutional portals can seem like threats from within it. But the only real threat comes from services which provide pseudo results – references and documents – which are not based on good retrieval algorithms and which provide easy material, or material which has a hidden agenda (such as linkage to advertisements), rather than quality-controlled content. A library, as Ross Atkinson noted in an article published in *The Library Quarterly* in 1996, is a controlled environment (what he calls a 'control zone').[12] While its content, now digital or with digital proxies in the form of metadata, may be and should be 'unbundlable' and resurfaceable, in portlet form, within other portals such as those which present the whole campus experience, there is still a strong reason to keep it also bundled and assembled, to provide a full picture of the quality-controlled content which represents the sum of its collections, designed around its various user groups. The only comprehensive way to do that now is to do it digitally, and so the development of an effective, fully integrated academic library portal is a task of the utmost importance. Though its buildings and its physical objects are still essential, the library portal is now the only means now available to represent the library in its entirety. Building it well and ensuring that it meets the needs of our users is one of the highest priorities for academic libraries at the present time.

Notes

1   Ranganathan, S. R., (1931) *The Five Laws of Library Science*, London, Madras Library Association.

2   See http://scholar.google.com/.

3   Dempsey, L. (2003) The Recombinant Library: portals and people. Co-published simultaneously in *Journal of Library Administration*, **39** (4), 103–36, and in *Improved Access to Information: portals, content selection, and digital information*, ed. Sul H. Lee, Binghamton, NY, Haworth. Available online at www.oclc.org/research/staff/dempsey/recombinant_library/.

4   See www.exlibrisgroup.com/metalib.htm.

5   See http://encompass.endinfosys.com/.

6   See www.sirsi.com/Solutions/Prodserv/Products/singlesearch.html.

7   See www.iii.com/mill/digital.shtml#metafind.

8   See www.uportal.org/.

9   Dempsey (2003) The Recombinant Library (see Note 3).

10 'Sticky content' is a phrase which has been around since the late 1990s. See a definition at www.realdictionary.com/computer/Computer/sticky-content.asp.
11 Dempsey (2003) The Recombinant Library (see Note 3).
12 Atkinson, R. (1996) Library Functions, Scholarly Communication, and the Foundation of the Digital Library: laying claim to the Control Zone, *Library Quarterly*, **66** (3), 239–65.

9

Library portals

Ron Davies

Introduction

All portals seek to integrate information access within a single framework, but different types of portals focus on different information resources, different types of services or different groups of users with varying needs and areas of interest. Within any one organization, there may be a need for several portal-type applications in order to address the full range of user needs. Even an organization that has successfully implemented a corporate or enterprise information portal providing broad, horizontal services to a wide range of corporate, financial, personnel, customer and administrative information may still require 'a specialized application-specific vertical portal' (Gourley, 2003) to provide richer and more focused services in the areas of bibliographic and library information. These specific and specialized needs are those that the library portal seeks to address.

Various formal definitions of a library portal have been put forward by different groups (Library of Congress, 2003; European Library Automation Group, 2002; ARL Scholars' Portal Working Group, 2001; Cox and Yeates, 2003, in a report for JISC). Ignoring differences in perspective and emphasis, these different definitions can be summarized as follows:

> A library portal is a web-based service that allows end users to discover relevant information resources, use a common interface to search one or more resources simultaneously, and then make use of the content of those resources as directly as possible. It offers customization, personalization and authentication services to make the end user's experience as simple and effective as possible.

Services offered by a library portal

In functional terms a library portal can be expected to provide all of the following services.

Resource discovery

A library portal helps users to discover resources such as electronic catalogues, citation databases, abstracting and indexing services, collections of journal articles or other digital collections that are relevant to their needs and interests. Specifically, users may browse lists of these information resources in alphabetical order or categorized by topic; they may also search metadata descriptions by title, subject or keyword, retrieving only the resources that are likely to be most useful to them.

Common search interface

Many of the information resources available online are searchable via a search interface supplied by the publisher, using specific screens, commands, displays and metadata formats. A library portal uses software 'connectors' to translate between each of these different database-specific syntaxes and formats into a single, common portal-specific way of searching. This helps by allowing the user to search many different resources using the same user interface – the interface of the portal itself – so that the user has to learn only one way of searching.

Federated search

While a common search interface allows users to search different resources using the same interface, federated searching (also called metasearching) allows users to select and search a number of different databases simultaneously. There is no need to retype search strategies over and over again for each information resource. When the search returns, the user will see an integrated set of results, which can be merged and sorted as a single consolidated list of bibliographic references.

Direct access to content

Dynamic, context-sensitive link resolvers are commonly marketed separately from library portals, but practically speaking they are an essential part of a portal. A link resolver service based on the OpenURL protocol allows users to go from citation to electronic full text with a couple of mouse clicks. With a library portal, even search results from resources that are not OpenURL-aware can have OpenURL links embedded in them as those search results pass through the portal.

Authentication to information resources

Commercial information resources require authentication of users before they are authorized to use the resource. A library portal authenticates users to these resources transparently so that the user does not need to log in to each of those resources or to remember different usernames and passwords. If licensing terms allow, users should be able to authenticate whether they are at their organization's site (such as business office or university campus) or whether they are at some other location (such as at home, in a hotel room or in an internet café).

Customization and personalization

Portals can be customized to allow selections of information resources to be presented to different categories of users, based on their interests, departments or work function: chemists in a pharmaceutical firm will see a different view of resources in the portal than marketing staff. Personalization provides an even finer degree of tailoring, allowing individuals to select and group specific resources that they personally judge most useful. Individuals can also save citations and previous searches, and have past searches rerun automatically with new search results sent by e-mail, providing them with a personalized current awareness service.

Development of library portals

While library portals have been available only since 2001, in fact many of these portal functions have roots in services that libraries and commercial information vendors have provided for some time. Resource discovery was first supported in the mid- to late 1990s by libraries that developed subject gateways, that is to say, large catalogues of internet-accessible websites that allow users to discover the best sites available in a certain subject area. Federated searching or metasearching initiatives are even older: the online service Dialog implemented a cross-database search facility in 1987 (Basch, 1997) and the ANSI Z39.50 Search and Retrieval protocol as developed in the early 1990s offered the ability to broadcast searches to disparate databases using a common software client. In numerous recent projects, Dublin Core has provided a simple universal structure into which different metadata formats can be translated. As to full-text access, many library catalogue records have for a number of years carried hypertext links to the electronic full text in the 856 field of a MARC record, though these fixed links tend to 'break' at alarming rates as target sites are reorganized or documents are removed to make way for newer content. Many academic libraries have also extensive experience using proxy servers to authenticate users to external information suppliers without the user having to know or supply additional usernames and passwords. The rapidity with which libraries have taken up the library portal concept since the first portals appeared is undoubtedly due to positive experiences and general user satisfaction with these portal precursor services.

Within four years of the first appearance of library portals, there were already some 15 or 20 different portal solutions on the market. Commercial vendors of integrated library systems currently dominate the marketplace, though a number of firms that specialize in more general search solutions also offer portal-type solutions that may appeal to libraries. Perhaps surprisingly, there have been few concerted efforts to develop a broad-based open source library portal product, though there are several components based on Z39.50 search capability that might serve as a starting point for an institution to develop a portal solution. The burden of maintaining connectors to external databases may be one factor limiting interest in open source development of a library portal.

The speed with which these portal products have appeared and the number of library systems vendors that have come out with portal products is due to a number of factors. The most important is undoubtedly end-user demand for simple, effective ways to make use of the electronic resources that take up a larger and larger part of library acquisition budgets. However, on the technical side, these developments also owe something to system vendors licensing the 'connector' technology (the software component that links the search technology to a particular database) from specialized companies such as WebFeat or MuseGlobal; this means that the system development life cycle can be drastically reduced. The rapid development of library portal software also reflects an attempt on the part of vendors of library software to protect market share: they hope to pre-empt existing clients from buying software from a competing vendor since this may impact future sales and upgrades of their core product, their integrated library system (ILS). This marketing imperative has led to some surprising offers, with at least one vendor providing a time-limited, hosted version of its portal product to existing ILS customers at virtually no charge, presumably to allow the company time to catch up with the market leaders in terms of overall functionality and perceived market share.

Universities have been the sector that has embraced library portals most enthusiastically. Looking at the history of library automation, this is not surprising. Innovations and new developments often come out of the higher education community, where user populations are large, research is an essential part of the institutional mandate and computing support is often fairly cheaply and easily obtainable. Integrated library automation systems, for example, developed first in large academic institutions and national libraries, and only later spread to smaller colleges, public libraries and corporate libraries and information centres. However, even now, portals are not exclusively part of the academic scene. Organizations that have considered or implemented library portals (in some cases in conjunction with corporate portals) include large scientific research organizations such as the Commonwealth Scientific and Industrial Research Organization (CSIRO) in Australia (Girke, Porter and Westwood, 2003) or the Consultative Group for International Agricultural Research (CGIAR); large public or multi-library consortia such as the Alberta Library in Canada (http://talonline.ca/searchalberta/index.jsp) or the London Libraries Development Agency (www.londonlibraries.org.uk/will/); and public and government organizations such as the Bristol NHS Trust in the UK and UK Trade and Investment.

While the trend to increased implementation outside academia is likely to continue, particularly as costs for portal software continue to fall, there are issues in terms of licensing and models that need to be addressed before portals will become as ubiquitous as integrated library systems. Library portal vendors frequently base their pricing models in the academic sector on a total number of potential users, such as the number of full-time equivalent (FTE) students. It is not always easy in a non-academic organization to find an equivalent to this figure that fairly represents the overall expected usage. Public organizations also may seek to offer portal access to freely available resources to members of the public, not just their own employees; they may even wish to provide some kind of controlled or semi-public access to commercial information resources. These approaches do not fit well with some standard licensing and pricing models and as a result it may be more difficult to negotiate software contracts. Flexibility on the part of vendors may be required to achieve real penetration of these non-academic markets.

Challenges and outcomes of implementing portals

In practice, implementing portals has not been without challenges, in terms of management, technical and usage issues. The integration of a library portal with an enterprise or institutional portal sometimes poses problems for library managers. First, use of the word 'portal' to describe both corporate and library portals often suggests to senior administrators that having two applications represents needless duplication, despite the high degree of specialization in library portals and the different types of resources, formats and protocols involved. This problem might have been mitigated if some word other than portal had been used to characterize the library service (Miller, 2003, suggested among other options 'thingummy'), but 'library portal' now seems inevitably fixed in common parlance. (Some projects have had success with branding their portal service as a 'virtual library' or a 'virtual information centre', but this in turn may lead to other kinds of misunderstanding, such as the assumption that the library portal replaces the need for all other library services.) Second, the opportunity to develop corporate and library portals may give rise to power struggles as IT and library managers compete for limited budgets and leading roles in terms of providing information access. Third, technical issues arise such as consistent 'look-and-feel' and authentication of portal users against institution-wide authentication services where co-operation is required between IT and library departments. While integrating corporate and library portal services has been successfully achieved in a significant number of organizations, these management issues are not likely to disappear in the near future for organizations considering a library portal.

In terms of technical issues, the time required to configure, implement and test a connection to a particular data source can be considerable even with standard kinds of connections, such as using the Z39.50 search and retrieval protocol. One of the ways that vendors can distinguish themselves is to offer preconfigured software connectors for the most popular information sources. The difficulty of maintaining connectors to external information resources, which may break after even a relatively trivial change to a vendor's service, has led to considerable frustration on the part of some early adopters. Connectors that depend on non-standard syntax, such as proprietary XML formats or even parsing HTML pages of search results, are particularly prone to this kind of problem. It is now recognized by both vendors and implementers that a high level of ongoing maintenance is generally required for a library portal to remain operational. This is paralleled by the need to maintain the information stored in an OpenURL link resolver to keep it current with changing content offerings and subscription options offered by journal publishers and electronic serial aggregators. Library systems vendors now have to think about delivering ongoing services, rather than the simple sale-and-maintenance cycle as has been common with integrated library systems in the past.

In terms of portal use, some institutions have found the user interface lacking in user-friendliness. Though portals are sold on the basis of simplifying access to electronic resources, they offer such a rich array of services that users have sometimes considered library portal interfaces too complex and have required training before becoming comfortable and effective using this tool. In addition, since portal managers inevitably want to change the interface to brand it for their own local institution, vendors may have felt that investing a lot of effort in terms of designing the user interface was not justified. This attitude has definitely changed. Leading vendors now seem convinced of the necessity to apply formal usability testing in their portal development process and, since 2004, several have either re-designed their portal product interface or announced future redesigns in order to further simplify and improve user interaction.

However, the most dramatic impact of implementing a library portal has been a positive one: a significant increase in the usage of the electronic resources. Hamblin and Stubbins (2003, 17) reported that at the University of Loughborough use of various databases searchable through the portal's interface increased from 10% to 300%. Where information resources are licensed on a site licence basis for a fixed fee, increasing usage on this scale represents a considerable increase in the library's return on investment for its parent institution, and helps improve the quality of the research being carried out within the institution.

Future developments

Library portals have developed very rapidly in their first few years of existence, and a good range of functionality has now been implemented by a wide range of vendors. We can expect further changes in the future, but probably at a reduced pace. Increased standardization will be one area to watch. In the USA, the NISO Metasearch Initiative (www.lib.ncsu.edu/niso-mi/index.php/Main_Page) is looking into standard formats for search results and standards ways of describing information resources that could result in simplification of portal processing. The wider deployment of the Z39.50 International New Generation protocols, SRU and SRW, may also serve to simplify access to data bibliographic data sources. However, both these developments are likely to take some time before they have a significant effect on the marketplace.

We can also expect to see one or more open source developments seeing the light of day. However, the risks and costs will be high for early adopters, at least until there is a stable community large enough to ensure the maintenance of the potentially hundreds of different connectors. Increasingly portals will be implemented by public bodies, special libraries and corporate information centres; with each new installation, there will be the need to access specialized data resources, particularly document-related internal databases. At the current time it is not easy for organizations to build their own connectors, but demands to do this will grow. As a result, we may see systems vendors providing not just prebuilt or configurable connectors but real software development toolkits which users can build and maintain their own database connectors, perhaps ultimately sharing those connectors with other libraries. Increasing deployment of web services will also allow chunks of library portal functionality to be included as a component in other computer systems such as corporate portals and virtual learning environments, though ensuring a simple user experience of these integrated environments may present challenges.

Over the longer term, improving the quality of cross-database searching via library portals is going to involve mapping subject vocabularies used in one database with the subject vocabularies used in another. This would mean that a search in one database for the subject 'teenagers' is automatically translated into the search term 'adolescents' in another database where that term is the preferred subject descriptor. This mapping between knowledge organization systems is a huge challenge, comparable to that currently being addressed by the world wide web's Semantic Web activities, but it's a task that library and information professionals are going to have to undertake.

Conclusion

Library portals have developed rapidly in response to a strong demand for simple, user-oriented discovery and searching of networked information resources. It is perhaps ironic that while simplifying life for end-users, portals have complicated the lives of library staff. On the one hand, librarians now have to worry about potential changes in the services of external information suppliers over which they have no control, but which may upset users who find their favourite resource no longer works. On the other hand, they have to co-operate more closely with staff responsible for corporate or university-wide systems to ensure that their information systems integrate well into these other environments. Even just the management required of a library portal, quite different from the old and familiar library catalogue and integrated library system, has in some sense changed the professional responsibilities of all librarians, from acquisitions librarians obtaining licences to access electronic resources and cataloguers who describe those resources, to reference librarians who must teach and help users to access these new facilities. However, there is no doubt that while the technology and techniques of library portals may develop and change in the future, there is no putting the genie back in the bottle: the functionality that library portals provide will be an essential part of our information environment for many years to come.

References

ARL Scholars' Portal Working Group (2001) *Report*,
www.arl.org/access/scholarsportal/may01rept.html.

Basch, R. (1997) Twenty Years of Headline News, *Online*,
www.onlinemag.net/JanOL97/headlines.html.

Cox, A. and Yeates, R. (2003) *Library-orientated Portal Solutions*, LITC, South Bank University,
www.jisc.ac.uk/index.cfm?name=techwatch_report_0203.

European Library Automation Group (2002). *Report of the Portal Workshop at the European Library Automation Group Meeting*, Rome, 17–19 April 2002, www.ifnet.it/elag2002/ws_paper/ws2_post.html.

Girke, T., Porter, J. and Westwood, R. (2003) The One-stop Shop: a single end-user interface for search and discovery across digital library collections, *Online Information*,
http://conferences.alia.org.au/online2003/papers/girke.html.

Gourley, D. (2003) *Library Portals in a Shibboleth Federation*,
http://shibboleth.internet2.edu/docs/gourley-shibboleth-library-portals-200310.html.

Hamblin, Y. and Stubbings, R. (2003) *The Implementation of MetaLib and SFX at Loughborough University Library: a case study*, Loughborough University, www.jisc.ac.uk/project_portal_casestudies.html.

Library of Congress Portals Applications Issues Group (2003) *List of Portal Application Functionalities for the Library of Congress: first draft for public comment, July 15, 2003*,
www.loc.gov/catdir/lcpaig/portalfunctionalitieslist4publiccomment1st7-22-03revcomp.pdf.

Miller, P. (2003) Towards a Typology for Portals, *Ariadne*, 37 [online],
www.ariadne.ac.uk/issue37/miller/.

Section 3

The portal in the corporate sector

Much new thinking about portals comes from the corporate sector, e.g. from commentators like Firestone. The most impressive and advanced applications team multinational corporations with market leaders in the technology. Public sector organizations can only dream of having the budget and command-line leadership style to exploit the latest technology in the same way.

However, what is really happening in the corporate sector is often difficult to gauge. We are likely to take the trade literature and sales brochures with a very large pinch of salt. They often do not really seem to come down to specifics (presumably it is that as much as the code one pays for). However, the two chapters in this section go some way to explore the truth behind the flood of white papers. Sugianto and Tojib review much of the existing case-study literature, in itself a useful exercise – but they are realistic about the potential benefits and drawbacks. White's authoritative chapter dissolves much of the hype with a refreshing dose of good sense. Both frame evaluation as a key issue.

Section 3

The portal in the corporate sector

10

Information at your fingertips: B2E portal as a strategic tool for today's workforce

Ly Fie Sugianto and Dewi Rooslani Tojib

Introduction

One prominent aspect of globalization is the voluminous flow of information. Many organizations today deploy internet and mobile devices as they believe that their workforce needs to be empowered with multiple tools to work and access information to be efficient and effective. Partly as a consequence it has become increasingly difficult to navigate the resulting rich information environment and find the right information.

A solution that has emerged in the last decade is the corporate portal or business-to-employee (B2E) portal. B2E portals represent a customized, personalized, constantly changing mix of news, resources, applications and e-commerce options intended to be the desktop destination for everyone in the organization and a primary vehicle through which people do their work (Ransdell, 2000). Accessed from the desktop, or using notebooks or even personal digital assistants (PDAs), such portals link employees to a range of internal and external information and connect them with other employees. The portal provides not only general corporate information for employees, but also some applications aimed at assisting employees with work-related and specific tasks, such as managing benefits, insurance and payroll cheque. The portals also provide employees with the personal information they need in the form of web links such as to stocks and shares information, weather forecasts, travel sites or even shopping services. Using B2E portals, employees can manage their work as well as personal matters without the intervention of other administrative staff.

Plumtree Software (2002a) has identified the main drivers for B2E portals (see Figure 10.1). The promised benefits include (Forrester Research, 2001):

- **Streamlined information access** – to improve communications by aggregating information and making relevant sections accessible based on users' roles. This reduces time spent publishing, distributing and searching for information.

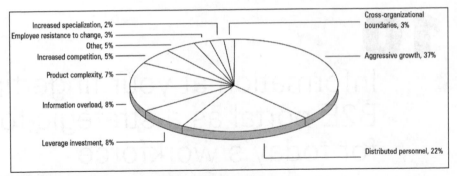

Figure 10.1 Driving factors for B2E portal application
Source: Plumtree (2002a)

- **Reduced effort to supply customer support** – the portal technology supports a 'self-service model'. Employees are encouraged to find out for themselves about policies, procedures and information they need to perform a particular task, as well as in relation to their personal needs.
- **Business intelligence resulting in improved decision-making processes** – the business intelligence component allows dynamic report generation. Further, the portal can compile a log of frequently retrieved information. This could result in efficient web-based customer service.
- **Enhanced collaboration resulting in growth of intellectual capital** – employees can identify colleagues working in similar areas. Access to expertise and intellectual capital, such as patents, methodologies and data warehouse, can be centralized and stored securely. Employees can share resources, collaborate in their work and avoid duplication of effort.

Considering the enormous potential benefits B2E portal can deliver to organizations, this chapter presents a general overview of B2E portals: the market, the benefits, the drawbacks and the trends.

Portal market

Portal software vendors, who have been aggressively promoting portal technology to help organizations manage their interactions with suppliers, business partners and customers, are now recommending that they should turn their attention to improve their relationships with employees. Both large and small portal software vendors offer in-house customized packages and standard packages. They either sell the entire software package or host the system for a monthly fee. The large vendors address many aspects beyond B2E portals and add sophisticated functions to their portal software. Plumtree Software, Viador, SAP Portals, Hummingbird, Oracle, Vignette and PeopleSoft represent the large portal vendors. Small vendors include such companies as Workscape and ProAct technologies. They tend to specialize only in B2E software products.

Table 10.1 lists a number of case studies which have documented different problems faced by companies and how the portal can fit in as a solution. The results and benefits gained by deploying the portal were also reported in the case studies.

Table 10.1 List of case studies reporting companies' experience in deploying B2E portal

Vendor/portal solution	Company	Report
Plumtree Software	Boeing	(Plumtree, 2002b)
CITRIX Systems	Radisson Edwardian Hotels	(Citrix, 2002)
Corechange	Philips Electronics	(Corechange, 2002)
	BroadVision	(Corechange, 2002)
	UnumProvident	(Corechange, 2003)
Hummingbird	Aird & Berlis LLP Dickstein	(Hummingbird, 2003)
	Shapiro	(Hummingbird, 2003)
Microsoft Corporation/ Share Point Portal Server	Nucor Corporation	(Extreme Logic, 2003)
Autonomy Inc.	Barclays Bank	(Hall, 2000)
	Shell International	(Hall, 2000)
Viador Inc.	Charles Schwab	(Hall, 2000)
	Cisco Systems	(Hall, 2000)
Glyphica	First American	(Hall, 2000)
	Wells Fargo Bank	(Hall, 2000)
Brio Technology	State University of New York	(Hall, 2000)
MineShare Inc.	Union Bank of California	(Hall, 2000)

A study by Tojib (2003) found that B2E portals have been implemented in many industries: health care services, aerospace, automobile, education, energy utilities, financial services, high technology, manufacturing, media telecommunications, professional services, the public sector and retailing (see Table 10.2). This study suggested that improving internal communications through portals is one of the most important benefits.

Table 10.2 The use of B2E portals in various industrial sectors

Industry Company	Portal solution	Vendor
Aerospace		
America West Airlines	COMPASS	Computer Assoc. Int. Inc.
American Airlines	JetNet	Plumtree Software Inc.
Boeing Co.	Boeing Employee Portal	Plumtree Software Inc.
Pratt & Whitney		Plumtree Software Inc.
British Airways	ESS Portal	In-house development

Continued on next page

Table 10.2 *Continued*

Industry Company	Portal solution	Vendor
Automotive		
Daimler Chrysler		DC e-Life
Ford Motor Company	my.ford.com	Plumtree Software Inc.
General Motor	Socrates	Workscape
Banking & Finance		
ABN Amro		In-house development
Bank of America		Broad Vision, Inc.
USB AG		Viador, Inc.
Visa	Visa Employee Portal	Abilizer Solutions, Inc.
Energy utilities		
Cinergy		Plumtree Software Inc.
Shell		SAP Enterprise Portal
Enbridge Inc.		Plumtree Software Inc.
Pioneer Natural Resources		Plumtree Software Inc.
Syncrude Canada		Plumtree Software Inc.
Food manufacturing		
Maple Leaf Foods	myMapleLeaf	Plumtree Software Inc.
Government		
DfES (UK)		Plumtree Software Inc.
Health care/pharmaceutical		
Clarion Healthcare Network		ATG Portal
GlaxoSmithKline	myGSK	Plumtree Software Inc.
VHA	@Work	Plumtree Software Inc.
Insurance		
Aetna Life Insurance		Viador Inc
Media telecommunications		
BBC		SAP Enterprise Portal
Comcast	MyComcast	Plumtree Software Inc.
Ericsson	Zoops Global Network	
MTV Networks	Rufus	Plumtree Software Inc.
Spanish Telefonica		
Public relations		
Ketchum Public Relations	myKGN	Plumtree Software Inc.
Retail		
Best Buy	TagZone	Plumtree Software Inc.
Guess	GUESS Express	Plumtree Software Inc.
Hy-Vee	The Hy-Vee Net	Plumtree Software Inc.
Technology		
Hewlett Packard	@HP	Hewlett Packard
Sun Microsystem		Abilizer Solutions, Inc.
Consumer package goods		
Pulmuone		Plumtree Software Inc.

B2E portal characteristics

As different B2E portals have different uses and different target users, they have some distinct characteristics that are not fundamental for other type of portals. One of them is that each user has their own single point of entry (Intisar, 2000). Each user needs to enter their username and password only once to gain access to all information sources and applications in the entire portal. As B2E portals act as a gateway to a large number of information sources (of both numeric and non-numeric data) as well as a knowledge-sharing point for employees, these portals must be supported with business intelligence (BI) tools and knowledge management (KM) tools.

BI and KM tools enable employees to search and retrieve specific information. The main difference is that BI tools mostly focus on numeric data. They provide the ability to analyse the data as well as identify trends and patterns in retrieved information. These tools are important for employees who would like, for example, to retrieve sales information and predict the sales trends in the future. On the other hand, KM tools collect all available information, then separate them into several categories and subcategories to make the search and retrieval process for requested information easier and quicker. To enhance knowledge sharing among employees, collaboration tools must also be integrated into a portal. Groupware applications such as e-mail, chat tools, discussion threads, and the group calendar enable employees to collaborate with their colleagues.

Moreover, as internet shopping is becoming more common, many portal vendors have incorporated e-commerce options within their product package. The idea is to offer employees discounts on a wide range of consumer goods. For example, Boeing is currently working with Bensussen Deutsch & Associates, a merchandise agency, to market products to employees (Schwartz, 2000).

Another significant characteristic of B2E portals is the integration of employee self-service (ESS) and manager self-service (MSS). These two self-service applications enable employees and managers to perform their work-related tasks online. Currently, mobile readiness is the most advanced characteristic of B2E portals. This offers real-time remote access to mobile workers so they can access information and data from the portals through mobile devices, such as PDAs, cell phones and handheld computers (Adhanda Enterprises, 2003b).

Benefits and drawbacks

Although B2E portals may not be the most glamorous of IT applications, when it comes to the bottom line they are valuable and consistently valuable (Cochrane, 2003). Figure 10.2 shows the proposed relative benefits of B2E portals from the perspective of organizations and their employees. The following section outlines both the benefits and the drawbacks of such portals implementation as discussed in Tojib (2003).

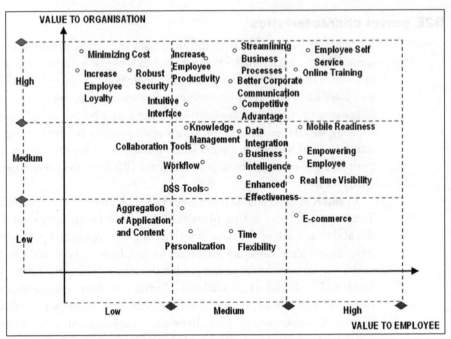

Figure 10.2 A map of organization's vs employee's benefits
Source: Tojib (2003, 24)

Benefits to organizations

B2E portals are a medium through which organizations can keep their employees informed and disseminate important messages and corporate announcements. Hewlett Packard employees have been experiencing these benefits since the implementation of @HP B2E portals. With the integration of 'Collaboration Central' into @HP, employees are able to arrange meetings and conferences virtually, access messaging tools such as e-mail and instant messaging and calendaring services, which allows any HP employee or contract worker to schedule a meeting with other staff around the world and across time zones. Additionally, employees can instantly receive critical news so that they can take action quickly and stay aligned with the organizational goals. The timely and accurate information they receive helps them to make better forecasts and to improve decision making. Hence, each employee can better contribute to the company's overall competitive advantage. The online training application integrated in Toshiba's B2E portals helps salespeople and service representatives to be authorized to sell new models of Toshiba products up to two weeks faster than anyone else, it is claimed (Voth, 2002). So it clearly increases their competitiveness.

Furthermore, B2E portals help organizations reduce the time delay in processing business tasks caused by the difficulty in contacting the relevant individuals. For instance, TransAlta B2E portal is designed to improve the way its mechanics and maintenance planners work, and is adjusted to route reports and work orders directly to the appropriate workers when the employees sign on (Roberts-Witt, 2002). After the implementation, the organization realized that the biggest benefit it experienced was time saved which, in turn, led to an increase in employee productivity.

Probably the main appeal to organizations of implementing B2E portals is their ability to reduce organizational costs. First, portals can potentially eliminate redundant hardware and software and consolidate a large number of websites to a few. According to a Broad Vision White Paper (2001), organizations could easily realize a 30% saving on website administration and development costs through portal implementation in this way. Second, B2E portals allow employees to access information electronically. This reduces the number of paper-based documents flowing within the organization. As a result, the cost of printing paper and distributing printed document is reduced, or even eliminated. Ford claims that putting pay-cheque histories in its portal reduced printing and mailing bills by million of dollars per year (Plumtree, 2003). This is also supported by a recent report from Killen & Associates which states that organizations can save 50% or more per employee by modifying internal processes from paper-based documents to online documents (Adhanda Enterprises, 2003a). Third, by offering employees online access to training from the B2E portals, organizations can reduce not only travel costs but also employee travel time. IBM has estimated annual savings of more than US$120 million using B2E training method (Sun Media Corporation, 2002). Finally, moving most internal processes online requires certain business functions to be reorganized behind the portal implementation. Self-service applications allow employees to perform tasks previously performed by HR staff. As previously discussed, portal implementation requires less supervision by IT staff because fewer hardware and software tools have to be supported than before. Consequently, fewer employees may be needed, which in turn reduces labour costs.

Benefits to employees

The implementation of B2E portals provides benefits for all employees in general and specifically for managers, HR staff and IT staff. The automation of internal processes simplifies and helps organize the daily routine of employees. Consequently, employees have more opportunities to control their own lives because they can perform their tasks in the office, at home or even when they are on a business trip. Providing them with such freedom may increase their morale and loyalty to the organization. B2E portals offer personalized and role-based content to employees whereby the portal only displays relevant information to the employees based on their roles within the organization. The portal also allows employees to choose information they would like to see in their portal. As a result, employees may spend less time when searching for information because they are no longer overloaded with different sources and items of news. This could increase employee productivity.

The integration of manager self-service applications allows managers to review performance appraisals, compensation plans and other administrative tasks at their own convenience as these types of information are available electronically. Thus, managers can spend more time with customers and on other strategic concerns. Similar to HR staff, the use of HR self-service reduces helpdesk calls so that HR staff can focus on other responsibilities. As for IT staff, the use of portal technology replaces multiple websites (Broad Vision Inc., 2001). Hence a portal environment requires less maintenance by IT.

Drawbacks

Although B2E portal implementation may give substantial benefits to organizations and their employees, some obstacles and issues should also be considered.

The cost of B2E portal installation tends to be high and may even reach US$5 million (Bannan, 2002). This high cost suggests that B2E portal implementation may be limited to medium to large companies. Since the portal installation cost is high, it is understandable that organizations implementing B2E portals want to see their investments reaping benefits. In other words, such investment is intended to make their employees satisfied with the portal so that they are actively using it to perform their tasks. However, introducing a new system to employees who are used to the old one is always quite challenging. Certain employees may resist accessing the portal for several reasons. B2E portals are designed to provide almost everything that employees need to perform their tasks at their own convenience, whether at the office, at home or during break time at their own pace. Employees may suspect that the organization demands higher commitments from them in return for the freedom the portal provides. Additionally, putting forms online requires employees to work directly from their personal computers. Employees who are used to a paper-based culture may be reluctant to use the portal because they will have less time to meet and have a chat with their colleagues in person. These issues pose a real challenge for organizations, especially those with deeply entrenched cultures as it is very hard for them to accept change.

Furthermore, most portal solutions try to foster employee-initiated knowledge sharing. Unfortunately, employees often feel that their value and job security is higher if they do not share what they know with others. Organizations need to create compelling reasons for users to participate in knowledge sharing and may need to create incentives, such as recognizing employees that share the most knowledge in some way or providing bonuses or financial incentives. Moreover, through having online systems, employees may become suspicious about what happens to any personal information when asked for it online: for example, if their attendance sheets are put online. Employees may suspect that they are being watched more closely. When employees register themselves for an online training system, they may worry about the implications of admitting the weaknesses they have. Finally, the integration of employee self-service into the portals obviously reduces bureaucratic activity and allows HR staff to do more challenging tasks. In some cases, however, companies may reduce the number of their HR staff. Accordingly, some managers and HR professionals may see B2E portal as a threat to their jobs.

Another issue that should be carefully thought through prior to B2E portal implementation is the security bridge. Portals should be able to provide each employee with secure access to a diverse range of resources with compatible security controls (Benbya, Passiante and Belbaly, 2004). Furthermore, employee portals should also be designed to assure users that any information submitted online will remain confidential. One of the reasons organizations should pay attention to this issue is the risk of data theft, which is in danger of increasing with the growing number of organizations storing their personnel files electronically (Anon., 2002). This risk will be even greater if the data could be accessed anytime anywhere through internet or mobile devices from various remote locations (e.g. home or public places) as information can easily be stolen from these places (Anon., 2002). Thus, it is crucial for organizations to ensure that their portal sites are highly secure.

Trends in B2E portals

An increasing number of organizations have started to realize that employees are their most valuable assets (Maza, 2001). Building a more committed work force has become a business necessity. Tojib and Sugianto (2005) stated that a web-based intranet has been widely adopted by many organizations as their employee support system. However, since the introduction of portal technology, many organizations are switching to portals because of their superior performance over a simple intranet. Precisely how the portal is used as an employee relationship management tool is also changing overtime. This is shown in Figure 10.3, which describes the different types of employee support systems and their proposed evolution in the market place.

As can be seen in Figure 10.3, simple and basic web-based staff portals may only have ESS or MSS applications – hence, they are categorized as human resources (HR) portals (Tojib and Sugianto, 2005). Most HR related tasks, such as maintaining personal contact information, requesting leave, processing new-hire applications, managing and reviewing performance appraisals, and approving expenses claims, support the self-service model. Along with the implementation of HR portals, more applications are added into the portals to accommodate other needs. Employees could access their e-mail, search for company news and information, access an employee directory, and collaborate with other colleagues through groupware applications. They could even create links to internet resources such as weather forecasts, stocks and shares information, a daily newspaper and even e-commerce websites. Hence, HR portals are gradually elaborated into B2E portals.

As employees become more geographically distributed and mobile, portal users have begun to demand functionality to help them stay connected with colleagues and retain their sense of community. Employees cannot rely solely on internet access

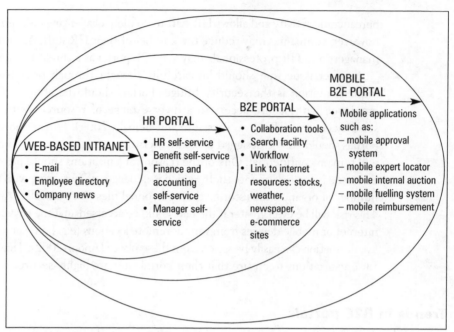

Figure 10.3 The evolution of employee support systems
Source: Tojib and Sugianto (2005)

through desktop PCs or notebook computers. Thus, aggregating mobile technology to B2E portals is becoming more viable, adding pervasiveness to portal use. Consequently, the trend is now to move to the implementation of mobile (or wireless) B2E portals. Such portals enable employees to connect and configure a personalized menu of options for accessing content any time, anywhere from WAP-enabled mobile phones and PDAs. Table 10.3 provides a comparison of common features available in web-based and mobile B2E portals.

As there are more mobile applications in the current market, it is likely that there is an opportunity for some future trends in mobile applications to be integrated into the portal, such as mobile approval systems, mobile expert locators, mobile internal auction systems, mobile fuelling systems and mobile reimbursement systems (see Tojib, 2003 for detail). Even though mobile B2E portals have not been widely implemented due to their associated costs and technology limitations, such as unreliable connection speed and the different screen capabilities of mobile devices, some portal vendors are optimistic that there will be an increasing demand for a mobile portal market to develop (Adhanda Enterprises, 2003b).

Table 10.3 A comparison of features between web-based and mobile B2E portals

Function(s)	Web-based B2E portals	Wireless/Mobile B2E portals
General information		
Company news	✓	✓
Employees' directory	✓	✓
Weather	✓	✓
National and world news	✓	✓
General applications		
E-mail	✓	✓
Groupware application	✓	–
Search facility	✓	✓
Link to internal application	✓	–
Link to external websites	✓	✓
ESS and MSS		
HR self-service	✓	✓
Finance self-service	✓	–
Benefit self-service	✓	–
Manager self-service	✓	–
Mobile applications		
Mobile instant messaging	–	✓
Mobile unified messaging	–	✓
Mobile CRM	–	✓
Mobile locator	–	✓
Other applications		
CRM tools	✓	–
Project management tools	✓	–
E-commerce	✓	–

Concluding remarks

Enterprises and organizations seem to be moving towards more distributed workplaces with telecommuting, teleworking and other novel office arrangements. Such dynamic business environments often lead to a lack of communication between organizations and their employees (McNay, 2000) and inhibit employees from collaborating with their partners and colleagues. One possible approach that is increasingly adopted by many organizations is for them to maintain communication with their employees and to build a sense of community through the development and implementation of B2E portal technology. This chapter is an attempt to further the understanding of the use of such B2E portals by identifying the benefits they can bring to organizations, and also the potential drawbacks if the deployment is not aligned with the needs of the organizations and the employees. This chapter also provides insights for management of potential adopters on how the portal technology can enhance work productivity and reduce costs by promoting the self-service model. Finally, the chapter has presented some trends in B2E applications that are made possible by the convergence of web and wireless technology.

References

Adhanda Enterprises (2003a) B2E: instant ROI, *Portals Community*, www.PortalsCommunity.com/news/article.cfm?oid=C963D890-5A6E-475E-BC1F957B73FC6DAE. [accessed 20 April 2003].

Adhanda Enterprises (2003b) Portal for the Mobile Workforce: an overview, *Portals Community*, www.PortalsCommunity.com/news/article.cfm?oid=6E2F7F29-05BB-4941-9A1FEFBE9A97113F [accessed 20 April 2003].

Anonymous (2002) How to Combat Growing Risk of HRIS Data Theft, *Managing Human Resources Information Systems*, **6**, 6.

Bannan, K. J. (2002) If You Build It (Right) They Will Come, *EContent*, www.econtentmag.com/Articles/ArticleReader.aspx?ArticleID=774&IssueId=121 [accessed 2 May 2003].

Benbya, H., Passiante, G. and Belbaly, N. (2004) Corporate Portal: a tool for knowledge management synchronisation, *International Journal of Information Management*, **24**, 201–20.

Broad Vision Inc. (2001) *Employee Portal: creating the collaborative workplace* (White Paper), California: Broad Vision.

Citrix (2002) *Case Studies*, www.citrix.com/press/news/profiles/radisson.pdf [accessed 15 April 2002].

Cochrane, N. (2003) Central Intelligence, *The Age Newspaper*, 9 December.

Corechange (2002) *Customer Stories*, www.corechange.com/documents/case_studies/2001.11-Phillips_CS.pdf [accessed 15 April 2002].

Corechange (2003) *UnumProvident Streamlines Information Management*, www.portalscommunity.com/library/case_studies.cfm [accessed 11 May 2003].

Extreme Logic (2003) *Nucor Corporation Uses SharePoint Portal Server to Break Free of Organizational Boundaries and Share Information*, www.portalscommunity.com/library/case_studies.cfm [accessed 11 May 2003].

Forrester Research (2001) *Making Enterprise Portals Pay*, 15 August, www.forrester.com/home/0,6092,1-0,FF.html [accessed 15 April 2002].

Hall, C. (2000) *Enterprise Information Portals: hot air or hot technology?*, Arlington, MA, Cutter Information Corp.

Hummingbird (2003) *Collateral – success stories*, www.hummingbird.com/collateral/index.html [accessed 11 May 2003].

Intisar, N. S. (2000) *Business-to-employee Model (B2E): portals for the people*, DCS Solutions Ltd, www.smehome.com/b2e.htm [accessed 20 April 2003].

Maza, J. (2001) Corporate Portals: the value to your enterprise, *DM Review*, www.dmreview.com/master.cfm?NavID=198&EdID=3047 [accessed 2 May 2003].

McNay, H. E. (2000) *Corporate Intranets: building communities with data*, Proceedings of 2000 Joint IEEE International and 18th Annual Conference on Computer Documentation (IPCC/SIGDOC 2000), 24–27 September, 197–201.

Plumtree (2002a) *Corporate Portals: a simple view of a complex world*, www.portalscommunity.com/library/fundamentals.cfm [accessed on 25 March 2002].

Plumtree (2002b) *Customer: Boeing*, www.plumtree.com/customers/industries/manufacturing_consumer_gds/boeing.htm [accessed 25 March 2002].

Plumtree (2003) *Plumtree Portal Solution for Employee Services*, California, http://img.plumtree.com/pdf/Employee_Services_Datasheet.pdf [accessed 28 April 2003].

Ransdell, E. (2000) *Portals for the People*, www.fastcompany.com/magazine/34/ideazone.html [accessed 20 April 2003].

Roberts-Witt, S. L. (2002) The @HP Way, *Portals Magazine*, www.portalsmag.com/articles/default.asp?ArticleID=4101&KeyWords=employee++AND+portal [accessed 15 March 2003].

Schwartz, E. (2000) *The Selling of the Intranet – co-marketing deals drive B2E model*, www.findarticles.com/cf_dls/m01FW/19_22/61946485/p2/article.jhtml?term=employee+portal+and+business+to+employee [accessed 28 April 2003].

Sun Media Corporation (2002) Brace for Second Wave of Internet Revolution, *London Free Press*, (24 June), 10.

Tojib, D. R. (2003) The Use of Business to Employee (B2E) Portal in Workplace: a preliminary investigation, Bachelor of Business Systems Honours Thesis, Monash University, Victoria, Australia.

Tojib, D. R. and Sugianto, L. (2005) *Facilitating Employees with B2E Portal*, Proceedings of the 7th International Research Conference on Quality, Innovation and Knowledge Management, 16–18 February.

Voth, D. (2002) Why Enterprise Portals are the Next Big Thing, *E-learning*, **3** (9), 24–9.

11

Enterprise information portals

Martin White

Introduction

This chapter describes the functionality and use of enterprise information portals (EIPs). These are applications which integrate structured and unstructured information onto a desktop that can be customized by each user. The concept of EIPs dates back to the late 1990s, but there are now virtually no stand-alone EIP server applications because the EIP vendors that survived the dot.com crash have now been acquired. Although in theory the concept of an enterprise portal providing integrated access to a range of disparate applications is one of considerable utility, in reality EIPs have failed to deliver the anticipated benefits. Nevertheless, individual features of EIPs do have value, but these are now being delivered through broader-based enterprise platforms. There is some encouraging development in portal standards through JSR 168 and WSRP (see below).

Integrating structured and unstructured information

Until the mid-1980s investments in computer power were justified on the basis of providing better access to large structured databases of information. The metric for intellectual property of a company was the size of the computer room sitting behind glass screens in an air-conditioned paradise. Then came the PC! Only people older than about 40 can remember offices where desks were full of paper but there was hardly a computer in sight. Access to corporate computing power was over dumb terminals used by people who did little else all day except enter and retrieve data.

Over the last two decades the volume and scale of unstructured data has increased enormously as everyone becomes their own typist, and the default method of communication seems to have become e-mail. As a result, the general rule of thumb is that 85% of the information in an organization is now unstructured text, e-mail and external business information. Gaining access to this information is a considerable challenge, but an even greater one is the need to gain simultaneous access to both unstructured and structured information through a single user interface and with a standard set of tools.

Faced with this volume of information the typical user asks why they cannot have rapid and effective access to just the information that they need, rather than have to work through the entire corporate repository. A salesperson in the south of England wants to be able to see what their customers have bought, and review the last set of visit reports and e-mail communications without having to work through a list of all UK customers. The concept of personalization is a familiar one through the way in which services such as MyYahoo! have developed, and it is difficult to explain to people why such a facility cannot be added on top of the current applications.

It is the plurality of applications that presents users with the next set of problems. The 15% of information that is contained in databases seems to be randomly distributed between a dozen or more applications, some of which date back many years. One UK university was quite surprised to find that over 70 different databases were being maintained by either the central IT department or by individual departments, and this excluded specialized research databases. Building up a picture of an individual student involved a nightmare journey through many different databases, each with its own coding structure, screen display and password/log-on sequence.

Another problem that is starting to affect organizations is that of multiple intranets. The capital cost of an intranet is usually close to zero because the organization already has suitable web server and page authoring software, and so it is not long before every department starts up an intranet that meets its specific needs. Once this starts intranets seem to grow exponentially, and it is not unusual to find that large multinational companies have stopped counting the number of intranets they have as the figure exceeds 500, and may well be in excess of 1000.

As a result the holy grail of IT directors, especially in the corporate sector, has been to find some technology that integrates all these applications onto a single consistent desktop. The solution seems to be to implement portal software, so that the technology does all the work and users have a scalable universal interface to all existing and future applications. The reality is different.

The birthday of EIP

It is probably unique that the birth of a specific software application can be pinned down to a date, but that is the case with enterprise information portals. The date is 16 November 1998, when Merrill Lynch published a report on EIP technology written by Christopher Shilakes and Julie Tylman. This report catalysed the growth of an industry, and by 2000 there were probably more than 200 companies claiming to provide EIP software.

In their report, Shilakes and Tylam identified three forces driving the development of EIP applications:

1 Corporate realization of the gold mine of data currently stored, and not readily accessible in enterprise systems
2 The emergence of 'packaged' information applications
3 The availability of affordable, ubiquitous distribution channels such as the internet and intranets.

Their view of an EIP was an application that enabled companies to unlock internally and externally stored information and provide users with a single gateway to personalized information needed to make informed business decisions. They predicted that EIP systems would provide companies with an excellent return on investment and would not only cut costs but also generate revenues. As a result the authors of the report felt that a forecast of $4.4 billion for 1998 sales growing at 36% CAGR (compound annual growth rate) over the next few years to be a $14 billion market by 2002 was probably a conservative forecast.

At a time when the software business was struggling, numbers like this brought joy to the heart of the venture capital community, especially in California, and before long the list of companies offering EIP functionality was increasing at a dramatic rate. However, a careful look at the addresses of these companies showed that they often had no more than a suite of rooms in a managed office block. Writing an EIP application is not difficult but getting it to work is a substantially different problem. From the 200 or more companies that were in business in 2000 there are now no more than a handful that specialize in EIP software. The story of what went wrong is an important one to understand.

EIP functionality

The basic objective of an EIP is to provide a user with personalized access to a range of internal and external applications through a configurable web browser desktop presentation layer. Although there are some variations between vendors the core functionalities are the following:

- **Single sign-on** – This enables the user to access all the applications that they have permission to use without needing to remember multiple passwords.
- **Personalization** – There are two aspects of personalization. The first should enable users to decide what information they need to have access to, either pushed to the desktop or available through search and enquiry routines. The second is the ability to manage the appearance of the desktop so that, for example, only the latest ten e-mails received are displayed.

- **Application integration** – The EIP should provide access to both internal and external information resources so that the user gains a balanced view of the organization within its business environment.
- **Collaboration** – Portals are increasingly being seen as knowledge management platforms supporting collaborative preparation of documents, instant messaging and the ability to build specialized applications that support the requirements of specific communities of practice.
- **Search** – Because of the range of applications a powerful search function is essential, and this is where some technical issues arise at present. Running a query against a SQL database and presenting the results back through a business reporting application is rather different from searching through possibly thousands of documents looking for a specific paragraph about the outcomes of a project.
- **Content management** – Only recently have portal vendors jumped onto the content management bandwagon and realized that there is a need to add information to a portal. The content management functionality of most EIP applications is still relatively weak compared with a fully featured content management system (CMS).

EIP standards

One of the issues that has probably impeded the market adoption of EIP applications is that of interoperability. The basic concept of an EIP is that it uses small application programs, often called portlets or widgets, to access an application and render the information in an appropriate format on the desktop. A portlet is a Java technology-based web component, managed by a portlet container, that processes requests and generates dynamic content.

Not only are these portlets highly proprietary; they are not interoperable. There are now important moves to standardize the logical separation of portal applications from portal servers. The typical scenario has been that the portlets run on the same J2EE application server as the portal server. This makes it difficult to scale up the application by transferring the portal to a different server, and also inhibits individual departments from building their own portlets. Currently two standards are being developed:

- Java Specification Request (JSR) 168, www.jcp.org/aboutJava/communityprocess/final/jsr168/
- Web Services for Remote Portlets (WSRP), www.oasis-open.org/committees/tc_home.php?wg_abbrev=wsrp from OASIS.

Without going into the details of the two standards there is currently no immediate prospect of making any particular portlet compatible with both standards, mainly because the objectives of the organizations supporting these two standards are different. The WSRP language is much broader in concept than JSR 168, but the way in which extensions are implemented within WSPR may well vary between vendors.

EIP vendors

There are three basic approaches to the provision of portal functionality. A number of vendors provide a tightly integrated approach in which the application server, the portal and integration functionality are combined into a single platform. Examples of this approach include:

- BEA WebLogic, www.bea.com
- IBM Websphere, www-306.ibm.com/software/websphere/
- Microsoft SharePoint, www.microsoft.com/sharepoint/
- OracleAS Portal 10g, www.oracle.com/solutions/enterprise_portals/index.html
- Sun Portal Server, www.sun.com.

A more open approach that is less platform-dependent is offered by Hummingbird, Vignette and Plumtree, all of whom come out of the original EIP business, albeit in the case of Vignette through the purchase of EIP vendor Epicentric. From the outset these companies had to offer solutions to businesses that already had well entrenched relationships with the leading IT vendors:

- Hummingbird, www.hummingbird.com
- Plumtree, www.plumtree.com
- Vignette, www.vignette.com.

A number of other companies provide portal solutions based on enterprise resource planning (ERP) applications, such as Sun, J. D. Edwards and PeopleSoft (now acquired by Oracle). Open source portal software, such as Metadot (www.metadot.com), is becoming increasingly popular. A survey of the relative popularity of the various vendors, based on a poll of subscribers, can be found at http://portlets.blogspot.com, published by Punit Pandey.

All that glistens is not gold

In theory EIP applications seem to meet all user requirements, so what are the problems? One of the issues seems to be that portal implementation has been IT led, rather than user led. This is especially the case in larger companies where there is a strongly entrenched IT vendor keen to gain more licence revenue. There have been many successful implementations, and those are the ones that appear in the press releases, but there are also many that have failed to meet the expectations of the users. In many cases this seems to be a result of the IT department working on the basis that since the interface is totally user-configurable there is no need to do anything more than provide access to the server and undertake some basic training.

However, most users, faced with the apparently unlimited functionality of an EIP, do not know where to start, or if they have been given a start are concerned about how to develop their desktop any further. The same holds true for web portals such as myYahoo! At first the ability to select certain towns for weather information, or topics for a news feed, is welcomed. But, before long the profiles get optimized at increasingly extended periods of time.

This is especially the case with a corporate intranet. The applications that people use on a frequent basis are the staff directory, corporate policy documents, expense and other HR forms and applications such as room booking. In a well designed intranet each of these may take less than a minute to accomplish. The benefits of adding a portal on top of the intranet are not at all clear, even when the aim is to provide enterprise-wide access to information. This can also be accomplished by a good enterprise search application supported by good metadata. Although the basic premise of parallel access to structured and unstructured information is good in theory, in practice access to structured database information is usually by a small group of users who need this information on a regular basis. By comparison, unstructured information is required by every employee at every desktop.

Putting structure to unstructured information is where content management software applications come into their own, often using XML-based standards to provide the database environment. An emerging issue for portal vendors is the extent to which they provide integrated content management applications (and Plumtree and Oracle are both going down this route) or support CMS applications as one of many other applications. Currently Microsoft SharePoint really needs to be integrated with Microsoft Content Server to provide a full range of CMS functions, though this will almost certainly change in the course of 2006 with the launch of the Vista platform.

One pharmaceutical company failed to recognize the amount of information that was being added to the intranet because the volume was not visible to the IT department. The result was that employees found that it was taking 15–20 minutes to add a document to the portal, compared with five minutes at the most with the original FrontPage-based intranet. A year of development work and a lot of money were wasted as the portal was abandoned.

In most organizations the day-to-day activities of many employees involves e-mail communications, developing PowerPoint presentations, updating Excel spreadsheets and writing reports and other documents in Word or another document management system. To do this users need to close down any portal application and use the full screen. As a result all the investment in providing customization and personalization is lost until the user remembers that they have minimized the portal onto the tool bar!

At present there is increasing understanding of the value of usability in the design of web desktops. The benefits in terms of productivity and speed of access to reliable information are well documented. In the case of a portal the problem is how to ensure that the basic elements of usability are not lost by users with insufficient skills constantly changing the appearance of the desktop. If the loss of productivity through managing the complexity of this process is to be overcome with role-based desktops that have some degree of consistency across a number of employees then one of the fundamental benefits of a portal is lost.

Making the business case for an EIP

The preceding section may seem rather negative about the benefits of an EIP. However, there can be some significant business benefits in certain information environments.

Identifying the information requirements will take time and effort even before the process of selecting the portal software begins. Increasingly the benefits of using personas to understand the way in which employees actually use information are being recognized. Personas are especially important in portal development as they will assist in identifying users from perhaps different departments and nominal roles who have common information-based task and information requirements. Rather than allow personalization at an individual level the benefits may well be in enabling a core group of users to develop a customized desktop that can be changed to meet business needs.

In general portal applications are well suited to users who need to access both structured and unstructured information, rather than those who only comparatively rarely need to access structured data. Business reporting tools are complex in their own right without adding to the user's problems. As a result staff in sales and customer relationship roles find real benefits in portal applications when they are at the basis of their day-to-day work.

Portals can also play an important role in supporting collaborative working, though implementing a portal will not in itself create a collaborative environment. Indeed it may illustrate the converse rather too well for comfort. Understanding how groups of people work together is often very difficult, if only because there may be some informal collaboration routes that staff may not wish their managers to become aware off. This is where the emerging technique of social network analysis can have some significant benefits.

Implementation

One of the most important decisions is whether the EIP is implemented on an enterprise-wide basis or on department/location basis. The general view now is that a staged implementation is the preferred route, enabling the required level of application development, testing and training.

As a result the full benefits of the portal implementation may not be gained for some time, perhaps two or three years, and this is why considerable care needs to be taking in the specification stage. A view will need to be taken on what the business needs over this period of time, so that the organization does not find itself using applications that were developed five years ago.

One of the key implications of the lack of standards at the present time is that if the organization is planning, or even anticipates, acquiring other companies over the next few years then the risks in not being able to integrate the acquired business (which may be an HEI) through an inability to merge either two portals or a range of different applications into the current portal needs to be taken very seriously indeed. As with content management systems, migrating legacy data from one system to another can be a very time-consuming task, and prone to error and project overrun. In the meantime users are not getting the best from the investment.

In conclusion

The benefits of EIP applications, just like CMS applications, are almost too self-evident. The dangers lie in the detail, and in particular understanding how staff actually make use of information in their daily tasks, rather than making some blind assumptions based on mainly anecdotal information.

Almost certainly the total cost of implementation will be significantly higher than the licence costs because of the development time taken to write the individual portlets for each application and then test them individually and in combination. The more effort that is put in to preparing a sound business case, the more likely the EIP will be to meet the expectations of the organization. The work does not stop when the portal is deployed. An EIP will have an impact on every desktop in the organization once fully deployed and, as business requirements change, and new or enhanced applications are implemented, then the portal itself will need to be upgraded.

The sign above the gate to Hades in Dante's *Inferno* reads 'Abandon hope all ye that enter here'. That should not be the epitaph for an EIP, but all too often it is!

Resources
Books

Collins, H. (2001) *Corporate Portals*, New York, Amacom, www.amacombooks.org.

Cross, R. and Parker, A. (2004) *The Hidden Power of Social Networks*, Boston, Harvard Business School Press, www.hbspress.org.

Firestone, J. M. (2003) *Enterprise Information Portals and Knowledge Management*, New York, Butterworth Heinemann, www.bh.com.

Terra, J. C. and Gordon, C. (2003) *Realizing the Promise of Corporate Portals*, New York, Butterworth Heinemann, www.bh.com.

Note – a report on Enterprise Portals is planned to be released in 2006 by CMS Watch (www.cmswatch.com) but this could not be confirmed at the date of writing this chapter.

Websites

Apache Pluto, http://portals.apache.org/pluto/.

CMS Watch, www.cmswatch.com.

CMS Watch Enterprise Portals Channel, www.cmswatch.com/Portal/.

IT Toolbox – Enterprise Portals, http://knowledgemanagement.ittoolbox.com/nav/t.asp?t=322&p=322&h1=322.

Yahoo! Group on WSRP, http://groups.yahoo.com/group/wsrp/.

Blogs

JSR 168, WSRP, Portlets and Enterprise Portals, http://portlets.blogspot.com/.

Section 4

Portals in the public sector

The present UK government's commitment to digital access underlies a significant level of portal activity across the public sector. In the first chapter in this section, Musgrave makes some fundamental points that are surely relevant to portal development in most sectors. He points to the many cultural divides between the agencies involved in creating portals as far more important than purely technical issues. He distinguishes between top-down and bottom-up portal developments, asking how they will get joined up.

Given the culture of publication in universities and the responsibility to share outputs from publicly funded work, it is not surprising that many chapters in this volume have already reflected a perspective strongly influenced by the HE experience. Most of Franklin's comments in Chapter 3 use the university as an example, though doubtless the technologies he is discussing apply as much in other sectors. In Chapter 6 Emmott is writing from an academic perspective – though again he makes an effort to generalize. The fact is that very few can draw from deep cross-sectoral experience. Hopefully this book will stimulate a little more cross-sector thinking.

In this section two further chapters draw on university experiences, but surely their conclusions are relevant in many other contexts. Schelleman's beautifully honest account of portal development at one institution gives us a valuable insight into the forces at work in such a complex, far-reaching project. As in Musgrave, people issues seem central. The difficulties encountered should not be attributed to bad will, perhaps not even to the cultural differences that Musgrave identifies, but to the requirement made by a portal for many organizational groups to work together at a deep level for the first time and, of course, to contingent events. Technology changes so fast and a portal project is so big that things are likely to take unpredictable turns. The special difficulties of working in uncharted territory are apparent. Klein is primarily concerned with technology. Her chapter is usefully read alongside Franklin's: both stress single sign-on (SSO) as a core aspect of a portal. Her chapter illustrates another vital point: the importance of opportunistic development – portals are often developed not out of some grand vision, but in response to technological opportunity. Both these chapters, then, contribute to the general question of how portals are designed and evolve as well as giving us an idea of how portals are now defined in HE.

We have found space in the volume for just three chapters about the public sector – further examples could be multiplied, but it is worth mentioning two prominent cases that illustrate important points. First, the new People's Network site (www. peoplesnetwork.gov.uk/) includes a 24-hour reference service ('the mortal in the portal'), a research tool searching metadata harvested from the many publicly funded digitization/cataloguing projects across the museum–library–archive sector, and a community-building section based on reading groups. This presentation effectively draws together the whole of a library sector. At the other end of the scale, the National Library for Health (www.library.nhs.uk/) is exploring ways to feed information sources to the user's desktop and embed information into the electronic patient record – in addition to providing a central portal to bibliographic information sources. Both approaches are as much about 'integrating' people and technology, as about simply integrating technology.

Clearly, the portal concept is evolving rapidly in this sector, as in the business world.

12

Community portals and the e-Confluence Zone: where bottom-up meets top-down

Stephen Musgrave

Introduction

Community portals use technology as a presentation medium for community and civic networking. Although the intrinsic properties and functionality of such portals are similar, the generic term 'community portal' as it has evolved over the past decade encompasses two quite distinct types of activity:

- **civic portal** – government sponsored and working top-down
- **civil portal** – organized by activists and working bottom-up.

Community portals have to be considered in the wide perspective of the socio-technological context of citizen–portal relationships. Community portal development has technical, organizational and human aspects: engaging social science, information systems and telematic technology. In the government domain of civic portals the shift towards digital government (e-government) places the portal as a significant 'presentation' gateway component within a wider set of potentially transformative changes, delivering new interactive services for citizens.

During 2000–5 a shift took place in which the topic of community portals migrated from the domain of telematics to the new field of community informatics (Gurstein, 2004), representing the concept as a broader socio-technological endeavour. This links to the newly recognized civil society constituency, given prominence by the processes around the World Summit on the Information Society (WSIS).

Community portals

Schuler (2005) finds that 'technology on its own is not a panacea for citizen access to government services and citizen–citizen interactions', and Mumford

(2003) explains that 'technology is only one piece of a very complex puzzle'; technology is not the only driver. The need to understand portal requirements from a citizen user perspective is essential. The 'people' element, especially the creation of local champions, is a critically important factor in the development, implementation and sustainability of community networks (Gurstein, 2004; Mumford, 2003), and should therefore be a prime driver of community portal development. But, if it is clear that analysis of community portals cannot be based solely on technological determinism, until recently there has been a relative lack of academic research that straddles the domains of telematics and social systems (Bannon and Griffin, 2001; Romm and Taylor, 2000). In particular, there has been a paucity of evaluation of the technical architecture of community portals. According to Bannon and Griffin (2001, 40), commenting on community network projects, 'while there is a wealth of anecdotal material as to the successes and failures of such experiments, there is, unfortunately, a lack of objective evaluation studies'.

These three linking strands of social, technical and information systems are identifiable as being inevitably intertwined in the community portal creating links between people and technology in a socio-technological system. Development of information systems involves a complex interaction between the user and the technology (Buscher and Mogensen, 1997). So the people issues are a significant factor in community/civic/civil network development. This justifies a wider scope for community portal research to consider people issues about users, as well as the 'technology' issues. Developers find a lack of 'joined up people', and further need to 'join up technology'; in particular for systemic links between central and local government portal developers, and the citizens that the portals serve. Community portals are difficult to implement, and the software currently available is still in its relative infancy.

Local authority websites (portals) in the UK as yet possess few online 'transactional' service capabilities. Individual community portals at UK local authority level tend to be insular developments that are not capable of easy replication across government departments or between local authorities. This is not only a UK phenomenon. Case studies (e.g. Blacksburg, Virginia) of portal systems that have been deployed in many parts of the world have had the same findings (Carroll and Rosson, 1996; Cohill and Kavanaugh, 1997; Patterson, 1997; de Cindio, Casapulla and Ripamonti, 2001). Case studies of the city of Milan and Cape Gateway (Cape Town, South Africa) etc. point to people and technology issues of 'citizen engagement' as vitally important to the portal development process.

Analysis of portals in central, regional and local government in the UK has identified the existence of a culture gap between central and local government developers (Musgrave, 2004). Again commentary on global aspects of portal usage (de Cindio, Casapulla and Ripamonti, 2001; Gurstein, 2004; Romm and Taylor, 2000), confirm that this is not specifically a UK issue.

Factors affecting portal development

Technological development such as service-oriented architecture, and use of web services now enable systems to be integrated (joined-up) in ways that were not previously possible, but difficulties in joining up people in different domains, e.g. central government portal developers and local government portal developers, involves cultural differences and the need to bridge cultural gaps. Attempts to create integrating portals have brought into sharp relief the need to build new relationships between existing groupings of people.

Dependencies (and separations) exist between portal developers in:

- local, regional and central government
- local government and local citizens
- citizen–citizen relationships and sub-groupings
- system architects and system implementers.

So cross-cultural factors are a significant issue affecting the process of community portal development. It is difficult to generalize the cross-cultural factors that emerge in the practitioner literature; for instance Curthoys and Crabtree (2003) identify culture difference as a key issue in their iSociety research. The Morino Institute report (1994) identifies the need for a local focus to community network development, and this is supported by more recent literature (Castells, 1996, 2000; Hunter and Beck, 1996; Heeks, 1999).

Although Romm and Taylor (2000) never fully engage with the importance of the use of information technology for community development, use of IT is implicit in their arguments in support of local development; an obvious example being the phenomenon of social relations through online communications facilities. It is important to connect this to the debate concerning local development and citizen participation where lowering the barriers to community networking is to be achieved through community engagement. Deployment of telematic systems to support community network service development (including the community portal) led to early optimism (Gurstein, 1999) that community regeneration could be achieved through the liberating and enabling role of IT in community networking, following the collapse of some traditional industries, e.g. fishing, coal-mining, etc. Bannon and Griffin (2001) find such optimism unfounded and express caution about exaggerating the capability of community portals to have an appreciable impact on regeneration, especially where broadband services are pervasive, as currently is the case in the UK.

Ohmae (1994) is an advocate of the idea that 'cultural convergence' is taking place, arguing that a process of cultural convergence over time will largely eradicate issues of cross-cultural difference. This optimistic view tends to ignore the resilience and embeddedness of culture. So, in the specific case of community networks, acceptance of the existence of national, regional, sub-regional and small group culture makes the notion of convergence seem somewhat simplistic, even facile. Even if local and small group culture can be manipulated, Levinson and Asahi (1995) argue that national culture is more resistant. The deep embeddedness of social factors such as tradition and historical background are, they argue, unique. So the obstacles to portals lying in cultural fragmentation and diversity are not easy to address – they will not simply go away.

The survival of local cultures needs to be anticipated and addressed in the development of community portals. This reinforces a requirement for locally driven initiatives, probably led by local authorities within the UK. To support local development there is also a need for tools and facilities, at sub-community level, to enable local publishing of content pages within the community portal, by individual champions drawn from within the community.

Cultural differences between central government and local government departments lead to gaps in understanding, and lack of collaboration, between officers in local and central government services. The culture of non-cooperation across UK government has been identified by at least one commentator as the most substantial obstacle to sharing services, more significant than legal or IT issues (Kablenet, 2004). Jain (2003) suggests that there is a divide between 'the envisioners who dream about what technology can do, the technologists who understand what technology can do, the funders who have the money but do not necessarily know how best to spend it, and the implementers on the field who know what solutions are needed'. These issues are evident in UK government portal initiatives and account for many of the difficulties encountered in development to date.

Cultural differences that exist between central and local government departments create a gap in understanding, and lack of collaborative development. The UK government aims to bridge this gap through improved dialogue between the Office of the Deputy Prime Minister (ODPM) and the Office of e-Government (OeG) (eGovMonitor, 2004). Some improvement is indeed evident in recent UK initiatives such as the Citizen Relationship Management programme, with its 'Integrated e-Government Delivery Roadmap Framework' (Devin, 2004). This UK national programme is aimed at saving time and resources through the central development of tools, components and best practice standards (www.crmnp.org).

However, examples in Musgrave (2005) show that *centralization* of development and support of community network services at the national government level would be unsustainable, and *distributed* development is essential. To achieve this it is critically important to have joined-up thinking, planning and development between central, regional and local government departments, and this must be cascaded to individual officer level. Joining up at each of the people levels is necessary, ranging from politician (e-champion) to government officer level, government officer to citizen groups, and citizen–citizen interactions.

Leicester (2001) argues for a radical change with new models of service delivery and a new model of politics and organization to match. Outlining a vision for local service delivery based on the concept of the community portal he argues, 'Local

Government should and could be leading this revolution rather than trailing in the wake of Whitehall.'

It may appear naïve that this chapter has so far focused on such basic issues of communication between people and interoperability between technical systems, but a reality is that fundamental people and technology issues need to be resolved and cultural differences acknowledged and circumvented, in order to optimize benefits from community portal development. Vision leaders need to communicate their planned development in detail to people who will be expected to undertake the operational implementation and system development.

The cultural divide in this case is between central government departments and local government departments. Such differences appear to hamper the potential progress in portal development and deployment. Absence of serious dialogue between central and local development teams restricts access to resources, software tools and toolkits that may have been developed centrally for local authority personnel who are unaware of their existence. It also indicates that transfer of global effects into local development will not just be uni-directional in future – i.e. from central to regional/local departments as in a traditional model – but that increasingly examples will show local development influencing the shaping of global structures.

The current state of community (civic) portal UK development reflects a lack of in-house resources in local authorities. There is a need to understand the larger picture and plan long term, because lack of strategic investment is a major factor hampering portal initiatives. Limited availability of in-house development may be remedied by collaborative partnering with an external developer, but such short termism itself creates constraints given the need to continue to evolve and develop the system and its portal functionality. However, the gains appear to outweigh the limitations and drawbacks.

The work of Mumford (1983, 2003) in the information systems (IS) area has been particularly influential in prescribing a socio-technological view. Mumford asserts there is a 'need to understand the bigger picture – the total problem situation – into which the jig-saw piece fits' (in this case a community portal). This is suggestive of the importance of business process change through socio-technological intervention.

Customer First is the programme in the UK local government sector that is currently the umbrella title that the community (civic) portal fits beneath, and this generic programme serves as a process change agent.

People, technology and purpose

The potential for advanced information and communication technologies (ICTs) (in particular service-oriented architecture and web services) to impact on community portal functionality, integration and interoperability is immense. Adoption of advanced ICT, i.e. telematics and informatics, is transforming the process of community networking and portal building, in particular through the availability of middleware for systems integration between the web front-end and the back-office systems. Possibilities now exist to create interactive information channels to facilitate and support online transactions between citizens and government at various levels, along with citizen–citizen interactions.

Technology advances in systems integration have now produced the potential to build interoperable systems and modules that easily plug together. Adoption of common standards, and common components, is necessary (Linthicum, 2004) to simplify interconnectivity of software systems. The existence of plug-compatible software made up of new elements called 'web services' enables connections between disparate systems if they comply with common standards for web service connection. Use of web services for business-to-business transactions is gaining ground in many organizations, and this technology will become the standard by which portal services will be integrated with different applications (Barry, 2003). This is part of a larger transformation in a shift to a service-oriented architecture for systems development (as discussed by Franklin in Chapter 3).

The goals of a service-oriented architecture (Erl, 2004) are use of web services with adoption of common standards (including web services and eXtensible Markup Language (XML)), and use of common components (in particular open source software). In a service-oriented architecture, rather than interconnecting different systems with interfaces at the top portal/presentation level, or alternatively integrating data in a single large database at the bottom level, the new way is to expose the middle tier application logic level as a service (web service). Information (as messages) is then in a format that can be utilized by other applications (Olivier, 2004).

So, in the technical arena, the emergence of a service-oriented architecture, and use of web services, is of significant relevance to portal development.

Existing enterprise portal products in the commercial sector demonstrate the functionality that could be achieved in community/civic portal systems; and research in the e-Science GRID community offers functionality, in particular with log-in authentication to the portal that can be applied as advanced system functions within a community portal.

New IS development approaches are needed for community portals. These must include improved citizen engagement. Existing approaches to community portal development have limitations and give a perception of a false dawn (Musgrave, 2004) in the first-generation portal software that is available. Current limitations reveal issues that need to be taken into account in future developments. Further work is needed to extend software capability, with advanced interfaces to integrate front-office and back-office systems. Citizen engagement is essential to ensure a match between services developed and services needed by citizens.

A centrally developed and supported government portal would not be a panacea, and a distributed system of computer services better fits the needs for community portals in the context of UK government. The UK government is adopting a model where 'intermediaries' (e-Envoy, 2004a) are taking responsibility for individual service development and support within a centrally organized framework. Access to these services from local authority portals can be achieved by embedding a portlet within a local authority's portal that links seamlessly (and invisibly to the user) to the chosen service.

Viewing the process of portal development from the engineering perspective is potentially disastrous as it takes a view of IS development as culturally neutral. As the discussion so far has indicated, political, management and cross-cultural issues for portal developers (and citizens as portal service recipients) are critically important and cannot be addressed by quick-fix solutions. This for example frames a need for a cyclic iterative process to reach a mutual understanding in citizen requirements. Coupling to the potential technology options is needed to support new information channels that are beneficial and valued by citizens.

Key cultural differences that may affect the process of IS development for community networking are mentioned earlier in this chapter. Improved dialogue is needed between local authority developers who may be faced with overwhelming problems that exceed their technical capability, and central government research and development teams who may not possess insight into citizen needs at a sub-community level. To foster and maintain long-term trusted relationships between central government and local/regional government portal developers (or development teams), a process of holistic mutual education should take place.

Gaps between strategic vision and operational realization need to be bridged. Heeks (1999, 2000) asserts that gaps exist between the high-level vision architects of portals and those charged with the operational implementation of the portal system.

Little dialogue generally occurs between portal developers in the civic and civil domains. Only low levels of dialogue are generally found between government sectors in the civic area, and consequently a lack of mutual respect and trust exists between developers in central government and developers in local government, and more generally between developers and citizen users elsewhere. New relationships should be fostered and cultivated. This is particularly the case for central government managers who need to get beneath the surface of development plans, specifications and designs to understand the grass-roots problems facing citizens wishing to engage with government for online interactive service access and transactions. Use of local government departments as an intermediary would give access to citizen groups who are considering the needs for improvement in interactive service provision. Inevitably the relationship between individual citizens, citizen groups and designers is likely to be dynamic, with links forming and reforming between groupings of involved persons.

Improved communication is needed between central government and local government to enable collaboration in project planning, development and implementation. Although there has been emphasis in this chapter on central–local government relationships, it is also the case that internal relations within a local (or central) government department might benefit from similar scrutiny. Lack of internal communication within a government sector can lead to misunderstanding, where the system developers and e-systems team members do not have sufficient insight into the architect vision of the proposed development. Arguments by Heeks (2000), Jain (2003) and Schuler (2005) support this view that busy people at all levels, i.e. vision architects or systems implementers, often fail to communicate, creating gaps in understanding. A potential remedy to this problem is posited by Schuler (2005) who introduces the concept of civic intelligence, and a model for re-examining community networking endeavours where there may be an incoherent core where the mental model of the development is not shared by the principals of the organization.

Absence of the equivalent building-block architecture capability for joined-up people systems highlights a need for citizen participation in the overall portal development process. Wilson (1999) argues that it is the context of participation that is important but, despite the growing number of participatory exercises, little knowledge exists as to their effectiveness in community networking development. Participation needs to be seen to amount to more than a simple listening exercise. In other words, the involvement of local citizens in the portal development planning process must lead to real changes to avoid the risk of raising expectations that are subsequently frustrated by an inability to deliver the anticipated new services and interactive service channels. The need for join-up between the developer and those for whom the systems are being developed (Heeks, 2000; Jain, 2003) is comparable for systems integration in the technology domain.

Portal developers need to understand the types of activity that will be beneficial to citizens, and this can only be achieved through engagement with citizens themselves. Local teams are best placed to be able to understand, interpret and communicate citizen requirements for inclusion in portal specifications. Once trust has been established through face-to-face contact between developer and local citizen, asynchronous online communications can evolve the necessary dialogue in an iterative manner – as effective citizen consultation, either with individuals or groups.

Having considered people issues, and technology issues, the third need is common purpose. People and technology working to a common purpose is a powerful combination (see Figure 12.1).

This chapter challenges the arguments that deploying community portal technology is necessarily associated with improvements in society, or in an individual's experience of their interaction with society at large, and with government in particular. Debates around community portals have gone through at least three discrete stages during the last decade, with the early optimistic accounts of various activist-entrepreneurs such as Schuler (1996, 2005), Gurstein (1997, 2000, 2002), Castells (2000) and Beamish (1995) being questioned by those who doubt the value of communitarian ideals and the effectiveness of online interactive services (Mansell, 2002, 1). Such debates have been linked to wider discussion about the politics of web-enabling communities (Horrocks and Hambley, 1998), inequality in access to web-based services (Lentz et al., 2000), and the social impact of this new connectivity (Doctor and Ankem, 1996).

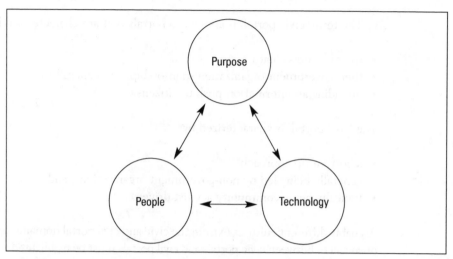

Figure 12.1 Civic/civil portal boundary zone factors

The development of community portal technologies, and their relationship to broader social and political forces, needs to be understood from multiple perspectives. Romm and Taylor (2000) make the point that for some the development of community networks and portals has been viewed as a wholly technical endeavour. However, it is increasingly recognized that the process of establishing and sustaining a community portal contains many sophisticated issues beyond the purely technical. Buscher and Mogensen (1997) point out that information system development involves a complex interaction between the user and the technology. Development of community portals within civic networks is inevitably complex and cannot be left to a technological determinist approach. Development of the community portal in the civic context is necessarily part of the bigger picture of business process change in generation of transformative citizen service interactions. Whether the community civic portal can exist as a separate entity is doubtful. Embedding the development of the portal within the service offered by a local authority gives development a place within the organizational structure, and importantly a budget line for sustainable development funding. The conclusion is that the civic portal will become deeply embedded in the service delivery mechanism of government and its management processes and as such lose its separate identity as online citizen service interaction grows.

Civic portal and civil portal

The generic term 'community portal' applies to technology as a presentation medium for community networking and civic networking. Although the intrinsic properties and functionality of portals are similar, the generic term community portal now segments into two distinct categories of civic portals and civil portals.

The term 'civic portal' is applied to portals that are characterized by:

- their top-down nature
- their government organization sponsorship, and generally associated with
- providing an information-push to citizens.

The 'civil portal' is characterized by:

- a bottom-up approach
- generally being led by non-government organizations, and
- typically being community activist driven.

Arguably different cultures exist in the civic and civil portal domains. Synergies and dissonances between civic portals and civil portals must be highlighted to understand the opportunities for a link between these two distinct portal types. In looking at community networking in the context of community portals cultural difference points to the need for people with Janus qualities to address the duality that exists between culturally different types, e.g. central and local government developers, civic and community portal developers, etc. Brown and Duguid (1998, 2001) hint at the positive effects of 'translators, boundary brokers, and boundary objects' in negotiating epistemic differences among communities that do not share practice.

Influence between the two types, and the actors related to each, are an important issue. Community engagement is a key term in any discussion of both portal types, but what this means may be different, due to the top-down push and the bottom-up pull that is characteristic of each type. Bridging between civic and civil portal types is a challenge, but successful implementation can improve the overall engagement and dissemination of information.

Schuler (2005) identifies a new paradigm of civic intelligence to describe the capability that organizations and society use to find solutions to environmental and other challenges collectively. This combines Putnam's (1995) 'bonding social capital', with civic 'bridging social capital'. Schuler uses the recent experience of the Seattle community network to highlight the 'inertia of inaction' that currently exists, asserting it is time to re-examine the mental model in relation to the original community network and its capacity to act. A change is now happening whereby the technology is empowering the citizen to function in a far more individual manner than was previously possible, with personal access to the internet, personal content creation tools and personal communication tools, giving the ability to interact through technology solutions in a far more individual way.

People issues are arguably more complex than the technology, which in itself is not straightforward. Cross-boundary activities can be encouraged, supported and nurtured across what is typically a cultural divide, as well as a logical boundary of different portal technology solutions.

New dialogue is required to enable routine exchange of information between different portal types – civic and civil – to enrich the overall information available to citizen users. There is a need to reach out across the existing divide between civic and civil portals and thereby extend the functionality and information resource. This may assist in overcoming the philosophical inertia that Schuler (2005) currently claims to exist and enhancing capability in a way that results in more citizens choosing to use the portals that are available to them.

An e-Confluence Zone

We need to investigate activities at the boundary layer where the two portal types of portal – civic and civil – interface with each other. The boundary layer is an interaction zone that metaphorically may be considered as an e-confluence between two portal types – each with a distinctive nature. The concept of an e-Confluence Zone is analogous to the meeting of two water systems (e.g. rivers). Arguably different cultures exist in the civic and civil portal domains, but at this e-confluence boundary zone, where civic-meets-civil, the sharing of information, data and services across this potential union territory requires concord and common consent to bridge-build.

The e-Confluence Zone is depicted in Figure 12.2, identifying culture difference, lack of common standards and technical incompatibility of systems as factors preventing cross-portal sharing of resources.

Bridging between civic and civil portal types is a challenge, particularly with civic portals where different levels of government are active in creating, hosting and developing portals. In the UK the central government portal is Directgov (e-Envoy, 2004b), but individual local authorities fund and support their own separate civic portals. This compounds the complexity for the citizen user, who is presented with more than one portal gateway to access the service channels or information they require.

Evolution from Figure 12.2 (overleaf) could bring us to the gateway access points depicted in Figure 12.3 (page 161). This highlights the further complexity where sub-types in civic portals and the existence of multiple instances of civil portals complicates the landscape for the citizen user. This can be explained by reference to the UK government's development of a central portal, Directgov (www.direct.gov.uk). Lack of technical expertise and resources at local government level in the UK has hampered portal implementation in many local authorities that aspire to develop and host a civic portal. Conversely, central government in the UK has access to technical expertise and the funding resources to support the development. Directgov is now set to become a fully integrated online resource for citizens, bringing together information from a range of government and public services through this single national gateway point of access.

Following the evolution of Directgov from Ukonline, the intention has been to use 'intermediaries' as customer segmented franchise operations (Edwards, 2004), building upon and sustaining the 'brand' of Directgov through improvement of the

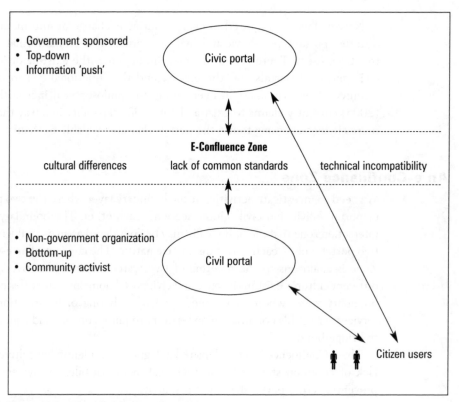

Figure 12.2   The e-Confluence Zone

user experience. Market research was undertaken to identify citizen 'needs' and what citizen services they would 'consume'. The UK Government claims very positive responses to Directgov as a pan-government department site through which there is access to information and online transactions across the full spectrum of central and local government services (Tan, 2005).

Directgov as a central gateway represents a change in approach to the use of the national infrastructure that hosts and supports the distributed computing network. Originally a hierarchical model was envisaged where citizens would access government services via a local authority portal that was geographically closer to their location. In this scenario the citizen would interact with the local authority site to access services that may be delivered from a national online source. The new model is one in which deep-linking portlets are embedded into a local authority website to facilitate links to external services in a way that is robust, reliable, resilient and easily maintained. This inverts the earlier model. Directgov is not seen as a substitute for local authority websites, but it aims to complement their online services and information offerings. In this model operational transaction services, including reporting of abandoned vehicles, fly tipping, requests for street light repair and disposal of bulky household items, is enabled by citizens participating in the online

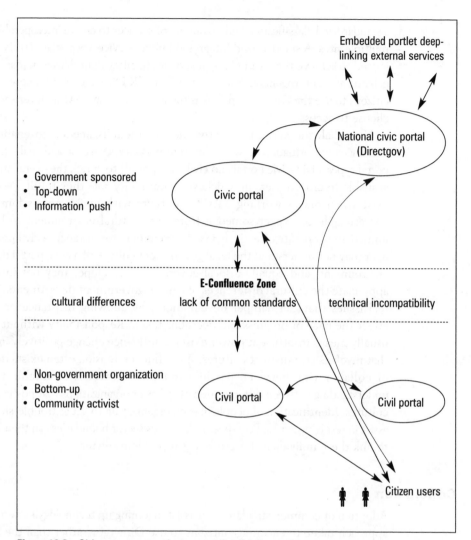

Figure 12.3   Citizen access pathways to civic/civil portals

interactive service transaction once they have made the 'hop' to the local authority website via the Directgov gateway. The UK project that has enabled local authorities to link directly to the Directgov portal, rather that just being redirected to the home page of a local authority website, is called ENCORE. This proof of concept site went live in April 2005 and uses the technology innovation of deep-linking within a website using portlet embedding technology for seamless integration between the local authority website and the remote service provider.

Fundamental to the ability to integrate formerly disparate websites and services in this new way is the adoption of common standards. Through development of the e-Government Interoperability Framework (eGIF), Directgov in the UK is working with the Local Authority Web Sites (LAWS) National Project to ensure a standardized classification and taxonomy of services to create interoperability across multiple sites. A standardized Integrated Public Service Vocabulary (IPSV) language is used to achieve the interlinking of services to allow data sharing across a formerly eclectic and heterogeneous mix of sites. The UK Directgov model now encourages citizens to use the Directgov portal as the initial gateway to whichever services they choose to access.

New dialogue and collaborative development is needed to enable routine exchange of information between different portal types – civic and civil – (and within portal types, civic–civic portal and civil–civil portal) to enrich the overall information available to citizen users in whichever community role they fulfill. People issues exist when one is working outside contexts with which one is familiar. It is unreasonable to expect someone from one cultural environment to be able to immediately operate effectively in a different one; for instance, a civil portal developer may not understand the local government culture of a civic portal developer's environment, and equally a local government developer may not immediately appreciate the cultural differences of central government departments. These are real issues that can hamper development, by allowing resistance or inertia to affect the pace of progress and decisions taken. Responsibility without authority usually means insufficient power exists to influence change positively in a project that involves two distinct cultures. E-confluence tension often exists due to lack of collaboration between parties, and this is often attributable to lack of understanding between different departments or organizations that possess different cultures. Identification of people in each organization to act as trouble-shooters can assist in resolving issues. Peer–peer links across sector boundaries can then be created to link these individuals for cross-sector problem solving.

Conclusion

Adoption of common standards can assist in joining up technology systems, but the approach taken to encourage citizens to use Directgov rather than the local civic portal is no universal panacea. The UK Directgov development leaves lack of support at community level for online content development tools that enable citizens to both publish and consume information content, as well as use the interactive service channels that are characteristic of the Directgov approach.

Bridging the existing divide between civic and civil portal development would extend the functionality and information resource. This may assist in overcoming the philosophical inertia that Schuler (2005) claims to exist currently and enhancing capability in a way that results in more citizens choosing to use the portals that are available to them.

This chapter identifies the limitations and relatively primitive nature of this first generation of civic and civil portal software, compared with the existing enterprise portal applications of the commercial sector. Second-generation products may emerge to provide further functionality and remedy, in particular, the lack of systems integration with back-office existing business applications, but it is forecast that in the civic portal context they may lose their discrete identity, becoming embedded in the core business systems for the e-administration of government in the UK. Through this shift towards the core civic portal services are likely to become sustainable. Civil portals comprise similar technology, but their bottom-up nature is typically problematic, with inadequate resources (both physical resources and skilled people) making sustainability difficult.

Linking top-down civic portals with bottom-up civil portals will give emergent properties and increased effectiveness. The need for joined-up people systems, joined-up technology solutions and common purpose is identified as a critical need for portal development.

The present limitations of generic community portal systems will undoubtedly be overcome through technology advances in the next few years. The need is to focus on the joining-up people issues through common goals, long-term planning and anticipation that the technology tools will be in place by the time the people systems are ready to utilize them in a transformative manner. In this sense effort needs to be invested in the design of people systems, shared purpose and new interactive service channels to deliver transformative citizen services.

References

Bannon, J. and Griffin, L. (2001) New Technology, Communities, and Networking: problems and prospects for orchestrating change, *Telematics and Informatics*, **18**, 35–49.

Barry, D. K. (2003) *Web Services and Service-oriented Architectures*, San Francisco, Morgan Kaufmann.

Beamish, A. (1995) Communities On-line: community-based computer networks. Masters thesis in city planning, Department of Urban Studies and Planning, Massachusetts Institute of Technology, Cambridge, MA, http://sap.mit.edu/anneb/cn-thesis.

Brown, J. S. and Duguid, P. (1998) Organising Knowledge, *California Management Review*, **40**, 90–111.

Brown, J. S. and Duguid, P. (2001) Knowledge and Organization: a social-practice perspective, *Organization Science*, **12**, 198–213.

Buscher, M. and Mogensen, P. H. (1997) Mediating Change: translation and mediation in the context of bricolage. In McMaster, T. and Mumford, E. (eds), *Facilitating Technology Transfer through Partnership Learning from Practice and Research*, IFIP TC8 WG8.6, International Working Conference on Diffusion, Adoption and Implementation of Information Technology, New York, Chapman & Hall.

Carroll, J. M. and Rosson, M. B. (1996) Developing the Blacksburg Electronic Village, *Communications of the ACM*, **39** (12), 69–74.

Castells, M. (1996) *The Information Age: economy, society and culture*, Volume 1: The Rise of the Network Society, London, Blackwell.

Castells, M. (2000) *The Information Age: economy, society and culture*, Volume 1: The Rise of the Network Society, 2nd edn, London, Blackwell.

Cohill, A. M. and Kavanaugh, A. L. (1997) Community Networks: lessons from Blacksburg, Virginia, Artech House, *Communications of the ACM*, **39** (12), 69–75.

Curthoys, N. and Crabtree, J. (2003) *SmartGov – renewing electronic government for improved service delivery*, ISociety Report (July 2003), London, Work Foundation, www.theworkfoundation.com.

de Cindio, F., Casapulla, G. and Ripamonti, L. (2001) Community Networks and Access for All in the Era of the Free Internet. In Keeble, L. and Loader, B., *Community Informatics: shaping computer-mediated social relations*, London, Routledge.

Devin, A. (2004) Roadmap for Local Government Peace, *Government IT*, **34**, February, GovNet Communications, www.govnet.co.uk.

Doctor, R. D. and Ankem, K. (1996) *An Information Needs and Services Taxonomy: for evaluating computerised community information systems*, Community Networking '96 conference papers, www.laplaza.org/about_lap/archives/cn96/doctor1.html.

Edwards, W. (2004) *Delivering High Take-up of E-services – Directgov, a case study*, Keynote address at Kablenet Conference Manchester (UK), 23 September, www.kablenet.com/ip2004.

e-Envoy (2004a) *Intermediaries*, Annual Report 2003, www.e-envoy.gov.uk.

e-Envoy (2004b) Press release, *Office of the e-Envoy Unveils New Online Service – Directgov*, 1 March, www.e-envoy.gov.uk/MediaCentre/Current PressReleaseArticle/fs/en?CONTENT_I.

eGovMonitor (2004) No. 115 – Monday 8th March 2004, Knowledge Asset Management Ltd, www.egovmonitor.com/links?115r [accessed 11 February 2006].

Erl, T. (2004) *Service-oriented Architecture: a field guide to integrating XML and web services*, New Jersey, Pearson Education, Prentice Hall PTR.

Gurstein, M. (1997) Information and Communications Technology and Local Economic Development. In MacIntyre, G. A. (ed.), *Perspectives on Communities: a community economic development round table*, Sydney, Nova Scotia, UCCB Press, 159–81.

Gurstein, M. (1999) Flexible Networking, Information and Communications Technology and Local Economic Development, *First Monday*, **4** (2).

Gurstein, M. (2000) *Community Informatics: enabling communities with information and communications technologies*, London, Idea Group.

Gurstein, M. (2002) A Community Innovation System: research and development in a remote and rural community. In Wolfe, D. and

Holbrook, A. (eds), *Knowledge, Clusters and Regional Information Systems*, Kingston, McGill-Queen's University Press.

Gurstein, M. (2004) *Community Innovation and Community Informatics: building national innovation capability from the bottom up*, Community Informatics Research Network (CIRN), www.ciresearch.net [accessed 11 February 2006].

Heeks, R. (1999) *Reinventing Government in the Information Age: international practice in IT-enabled public sector reform*, Routledge Research in Information Technology and Society, London, Routledge Press.

Heeks, R. (2000) *Lessons for Development from the 'New Economy'*, Institute for Development, Policy and Management, University of Manchester, http://idpm.man.ac.uk/idpm/isps_wp.10.htm [accessed 11 February 2006].

Horrocks, I. and Hambley. J. (1998) The Webbing of British Local Government, *Public Money and Management*, April–June, 39–44.

Hunter, M. and Beck, J. (1996) A Cross-cultural Comparison of Excellent Systems Analysts, *Information Systems Journal*, **6**, 261–81.

Jain, R. (2003) *Tech Talk: transforming rural India: a wider view*, www.emergic.org/archives/indi/004833.php [accessed 20 July 2004].

Kablenet (2004) Kablereport White Paper, *What Do They Mean by 'Yes'? Shared services and the Gershon agenda*, www.kablenet/kablereport/.

Leicester, G. (ed.) (2001) *The Community Portal: democracy, technology and the future for local governance: a report of the joint working group of the Scottish Council Foundation and the New Local Government Network*, www.scottishdicgnet.org.uk/scf/publications/paper14/contents/shtml [accessed 11 February 2006].

Lentz, B., Straubhaar, J., LaPastina, A., Main, S. and Taylor, J. (2000) *Structuring Access: the role of public access centres in the 'digital divide'*, University of Texas at Austin, Telecommunications and Information Policy Institute.

Levinson, N. and Asahi, M. (1995) Cross National Alliances and Inter-Organisational Learning, *Organisational Dynamics*, **24** (2), 65–78.

Linthicum, D. S. (2004) *Next Generation Application Integration: from simple information to web services*, New Jersey, Addison-Wesley.

Mansell, R. (2002) *Inside the Communication Revolution: evolving patterns of social and technical interaction*, Oxford, Oxford University Press.

Morino Institute (1994) *Assessment and Evolution of Community Networking*. Presented at the Ties that Bind Apple Computer/Morino Institute Conference on Building Community Computer Networks, Cupertino, CA, 5 May.

Mumford, E. (1983) *Designing Human Systems – the ETHICS method*, Manchester, Manchester Business School.

Mumford, E. (2003) *Redesigning Human Systems*, Information Science Publishing, London, IRM Press, Idea Group Inc.

Musgrave, S. J. (2004) Community Portals – Is there a technology barrier for local authorities?, *Telematics and Informatics*, **21**, 261–72.

Musgrave, S. J. (2005) Community Portals – the UK experience: a false dawn over the field of dreams?, *Journal of Community Informatics*, **1** (2), 32–44.

Ohmae, K. (1994) *The Borderless World*, London, Sage.

Olivier, W. (2004) *Application & Tool Component Frameworks*, CETIS, www.cetis.ac.uk.

Patterson, S. (1997) Evaluating the Blacksburg Electronic Village. In Cohill, A. and Kavanaugh, A. (eds), *Community Networks: lessons from Blacksburg*, Norwood, MA: Artech House.

Putnam, R. (1995) Bowling Alone: America's declining social capital, *Journal of Democracy*, (January), 65–78.

Romm, C. and Taylor, W. (2000) Community Informatics: the next frontier. In *Proceedings of the Information Resources Management Association Conference*, Anchorage, IRMA.

Schuler, D. (1996) *New Community Networks: wired for change*, Reading, MA, Addison-Wesley.

Schuler, D. (2005) *Community Networks and the Evolution of Civic Intelligence*, Springer-Verlag, AI & Society.

Tan, A. (2005) In at the Deep End, *Government Computing*, March.

Wilson, D. (1999) Exploring the Limits of Public Participation in Local Government, *Parliamentary Affairs*, **52** (2), 246–59.

13
Portal implementation in UK higher education institutions: a comparative analysis

Yvonne Klein

Introduction

At the height of the dot.com bubble, portal technology was hailed as the transformational force that would change higher education institutions (HEIs) forever. In streamlining business information processes and offering members of the university a one-stop-shop experience, it was claimed that the institutional portal would act as the catalyst catapulting institutions into the new millennium. Consequently, universities worldwide have started to form collaborations and networks to explore and develop this technology and specifically plan to make it a key institutional platform.

The research reported in this chapter investigates the implementation of portal systems in UK HEIs between December 2003 and June 2004. It covers 45 universities[1] and two university sector colleges[2] in the UK for a comprehensive representation of the sector. It establishes a practical and realistic overview of the real progress of portal development and integration at British universities. How far has the much promised seamless integration of different software into one big network with a single sign-on facility been accomplished? What kind of problems or obstacles and also advantages have been identified? What does the pattern of past progress suggest about how future development will proceed?

Methodology

Methodologically, the research draws on previous work in the area of portal development and integration in large organizations and on organizational theory (Katz, 2002; Strauss, 2002), as well as of principles and types of information portals and managed learning environments in general (Britain and Liber, 1999; Davydov, 2001; JISC, 2001) and in specialized portal solutions specifically (Cox and Yeates, 2002).

Empirical research for this study involved the evaluation and analysis of the development of institution-wide portal systems, acting as an umbrella structure for the underlying information system configuration of the university. The research addresses a debate over the stage of portal integration in higher education and the progress they have made, using ethnographic observation strategies, as well as semi-structured and unstructured interview techniques. The research also took a comparative approach, involving the systematic comparison of different university systems to understand their similarities and differences and how they interrelate to each other and are integrated in a portal environment. The research draws also on a historical approach to understand the context within which the portal concept has emerged and how it is pursued today.

What is a portal?

A portal is often seen as a gateway or single log-in point to the internet 'by providing services most often used by Web users'.[3] Davydov argues that portals originated from websites with search engines, which 'have quickly evolved into central information location points for navigating the internet, for gathering relevant information, and, most recently, for collaborative community activities'.[4]

Unification is another key characteristic of the portal. The portal is understood as a coming together of different applications, used in different departments for different purposes, into one large single structure. If the corporation or academic institution has different software applications for different tasks, according to Katz, this framework allows it to overcome the differences between various applications and to integrate them seamlessly to form one large network running through all departments or the corporational or institutional platform. It is a 'fundamental departure from the old entity-centric Web experience [. . .] a basic change in the way we present Web information to users and in which users use the Web'.[5] Strauss even refers to it as the reinvention of the web itself. '[I]t will change the way that university and corporate Web pages are built . . . . a dynamic user-centric collection of everything useful to a particular person'.[6]

These claims reflect the hype surrounding the portal. They portray it as the ideal solution for bringing diverse software installations together to communicate within a single framework. Various verification and password procedures are reversed into a single authentication point when accessing software applications through the portal. The portal is therefore a highly valued tool, achieving seamless integration to form one, big network. This is the claim made by the software vendors.

Different types and models of portals

There are different types of portals. These range from what are generally termed enterprise information portals (EIPs) to specific types of EIP, such as horizontal enterprise portals (HEPs) and vertical enterprise portals (VEPs).[7] Another categorization differentiates between public portals, corporate (or enterprise) portals and personal portals.[8] There is no standardization in the definition. Most commonly, portals, including the institution-wide ones, are referred to as EIPs or enterprise portals (EPs), which were first defined by Shilakes and Tylman in a Merrill Lynch research report in 1998: 'Enterprise Information Portals are applications that enable companies to unlock internally and externally stored information, and provide users a single gateway to personalized information needed to make informed business decisions.'[9] The authors go on to stress that 'EIPs are an amalgamation of software applications that consolidate, manage, analyze and distribute information across and outside of an enterprise'.[10] See Figure 13.1.

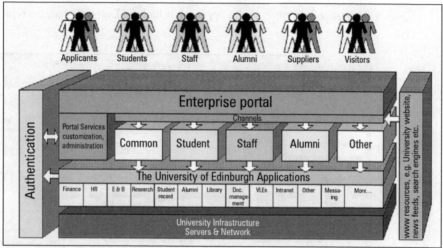

Figure 13.1 The University of Edinburgh's portal model[11]

The role of senior management in setting up the basic parameters of the project is vital:

> The options for Edinburgh being an institutional portal focusing on corporate MIS system integration for varied user groups, or a truly broad implementation that incorporated the wider university institutions such as the Library, Media And Learning Technology Services and the University of Edinburgh Computing Service. In order to ensure that the product select was most suited to the scope of the project, the project team sought guidance from the Vice Principal and Corporate Services Director. The team was given a clear steer that the project aim would be one that maximized inclusiveness.[12]

There are also models focusing on the pedagogic environment – the managed learning environment (MLE): 'The JISC MLE Steering Group has said that the term Managed Learning Environment (MLE) is to be used to include the whole range of information systems and processes of a college (including its VLE if it has one) that contribute directly, or indirectly, to learning and the management of that learning.'[13] One example is 'duo – Durham University Online', implementing the Blackboard community portal. The authors explain the people-centric rather than system-centric approach they took:

> [A]nother aim of the portal is to make it the primary point of entry. This requires it to interface with a range of other established systems and resources. A key part of the Learning Technology Team's input into the development of a student portal has been in its planning. Traditionally VLEs have been planned using a 'system's approach' – connecting data sources and services together.

An oft-cited example of this approach is Richard Everett's diagram reproduced below in Figure 13.2.[14]

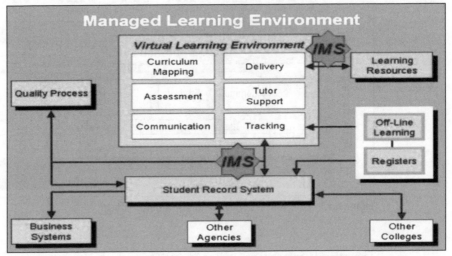

Figure 13.2   JISC's approved MLE structure model, showing the VLE within an institutional portal[15]

They go on to clarify:

> Durham's choice of VLE took a different focus – the product had to meet our pedagogic needs, yet still be simple to use. For it to succeed, duo had to be a tool suitable for all staff and students, promoting learning and teaching. The Community Portal builds on this success.[16]

Institutional key systems and the portal environment

The student record systems (SRSs), virtual learning environments (VLEs), library systems and/or library portals have all been identified as being very important in their own way to understanding institutional portals.

SRSs are usually used to store and manage large quantities of student data. If the SRS is online students have access to their student records, providing them with information about their enrolment, status, personal data, course results and transcripts, as well as financial status. Major SRS software products and suppliers include SITS (Strategic Information Technology Services Ltd), which claims to be the 'UK Market Leader in Academic Management Solutions'.[17] It supplies to HEIs, among other products, SITS:VISION, a student course and administration system, and a self-service web portal called SITS e-Vision.[18] SunGuard SCT Inc. supplies SCT Banner, SCT Luminis (the Luminis Platform III incorporates JA-SIG's open-source portal uPortal) and SCT Campus Pipeline.[19] Another supplier is MicroCompass Systems Ltd, which is an 'established software house and provider of software solutions for more than twenty years'.[20]

VLEs, according to the JISC's *Requirements for a VLE*,[21] supply online learning, including access to learning resources, assessment and guidance; online communications, including e-mail, group discussion and web access; and online tutor support, as well as peer group support. Their principal components include 'mapping of the curriculum into elements (or "chunks") that can be assessed and recorded tracking of student activity and achievement against these elements'.[22] VLEs also 'record certain basic information about students, irrespective of the learning context, such as registration details, course details'.[23]

Clearly, VLEs are essential to student online learning but they also contain basic information about students that could be held in different places and systems, such as the VLE and SRS, creating the potential for data duplication. Consequently, the data occupies not only vast memory space, but also needs regular checking and updating. Some universities have tried to tackle this problem by automating the interface between VLE and SRS. This means that students are automatically added to the correct courses within WebCT by using the module information held against them in SITS. The upload into WebCT takes place every night. Major VLE products and suppliers are WebCT[24] and Blackboard.[25] There are also in-house and open-source products, such as CoSE,[26] Bodington[27] and Merlin.[28]

Library systems and portals are also regarded as essential for students, because they are needed to search for books, journal articles and other resources and to renew and reserve course materials. They also allow students to access their library account online. For library staff they are management tools. Major suppliers are Ex Libris with products such as ALEPH500 and MetaLib,[29] and Talis Information Ltd with the Talis Information Environment and TalisPrism.[30] There are others, such as epixtech, whose products include Horizon, iPac and Dynix.[31] Sirsi Corporation's products include iBistro, iLink, Unicorn Library Management System and Web2.[32] And there is Innovative Interfaces Corp.[33]

Some universities want to go further to start incorporating other applications, such as financial systems, online payment and booking channels, and administrative systems. These are not only beneficial to students, but there is value in extending the integrated online environment to benefit everyone associated with the institution.

Thus the institution-wide portal comes into play with its much vaunted capability of converging separate systems into one single network to promote online access to these systems with single sign-on and 24/7 service. Major portal products and suppliers include Oracle with the Oracle Application Server Portal (Oracle AS Portal),[34] SITS:Vision/SITS e-Vision, SunGuard SCT, Blackboard Portal, Novell's exteNd portal software,[35] and JA-SIG's uPortal.

Analysis of development and integration
Student record systems (SRS)

The SRS landscape is shaped by one major feature, namely the use of commercial products. From the 47 institutions examined, 21 had implemented a SITS product, six had Oracle-based software, and a number of other suppliers had smaller chunks of the market. Hence SRS supplied by commercial vendors had a 70% market share. There were also eight in-house developed SRS systems in the sample. Some of the institutions said that their SRS was Oracle-based, but they had developed it in-house. Others reported that they had a part of their SRS database developed in-house, but other parts were supplied by a commercial vendor. This state of development is reflected in Figure 13.3.

Figure 13.3 underlines one major finding of the investigation reported in this chapter. Many HEIs have started using the portal facility that comes with the product to extend their existing SRS, enhancing their student database into a web-enabled portal environment. This is shown by the following examples. Most HEIs that have

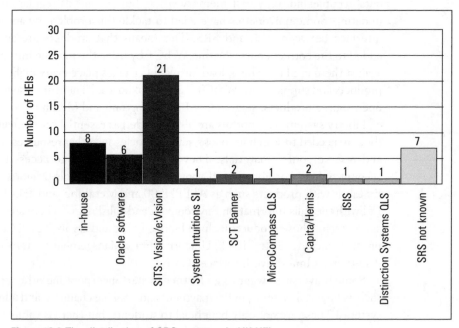

Figure 13.3 The distribution of SRS systems in UK HEIs

been using SITS as their SRS for years, have started to implement SITS e:Vision, the web-enabled SRS access portal. For example, University 1 in the south-east of England has been using SITS as its SRS since 1995. It was looking for online enrolment and had investigated different solutions, but discovered that SITS e:Vision gave it the flexibility it required for its web-enabled enrolment. Now it is rolling out SITS e:Vision to students. It has been very successful and the university says it has only 'touched the tip of the iceberg' in possible applications. The university did not have to move to a brand new SRS to achieve a web-enabled environment, but instead used the product offered by its existing SRS supplier, meaning there was less cost/resource required than would have been the case implementing a totally new system.

Another example is University 2 in Scotland. The head of the Information Strategy Unit was asked about 'how they had developed their portal and if they had evaluated different products before implementing their institution-wide portal'. He replied: 'Our initial reason for introducing a portal was to move staff users from an old student record system to a new one. We saw this as a temporary measure and used Oracle Portal because it was already bundled into our Oracle Campus Licence.' However, the Scottish institution is one of the few British institutions that has introduced the institution-wide set-up of Oracle portal. It has expanded its SRS into an institution-wide portal which has been running successfully for the past three years. In contrast, most universities have only just introduced the SITS e:Vision product with its SRS online capability. Interestingly the university concerned call it a student portal, although it gives students just online access to their records and not to other systems.

This evidence shows that portal projects often start with the idea to integrate new functionality into existing systems. University 1 in the south-east of England had not thought further ahead about providing an institution-wide portal *at that point*; it just considered the extension of its existing SRS. This suggests strongly that a portal is developed out of necessity to give existing systems new functionality. It also shows that, often, a portal is created out of necessity and is not seen as a new and stand-alone product, but is deeply entangled with existing systems. Another interesting aspect of the question of how technical decisions are made became clear when reflecting on the data. From the 21 institutions using SITS as their SRS, 17 are using or are in the process of implementing SITS e:Vision as a point for users to access the student record system online. Apart from that only two institutions have acknowledged so far being committed to use the full SITS:Vision product as an institution-wide portal.

Although only two were committed to implement the full portal, as already pointed out, most other institutions also refer to their new SRS online environment as a portal, although in reality it is actually only a part of a portal in its original sense. For, whereas the idea of the portal is that many different applications are made accessible in one place, here people were actually referring to the extension of their SRS with new functionality as a *student portal*. Even when they mentioned that their portal contained, apart from the SRS login, a list of web links linking to the facilities most important to students, making it navigationally easier to find them instead of 'digging them up' on the external facing website, still it does not mean they have achieved a single sign-on environment to all the listed items. As the Web Editor of University 1 in the south-east of England admits: 'We wish for students to be able to view their individual timetables via e:Vision. It is next on the list to investigate. If we are successful we would probably wish to link WebCT as well. In theory you can link packages via a web link. It could get cumbersome for students/staff if they have to go through various password controls.'

This reflects how far and to what extent at many universities the SRS is intertwined with the notion of the term 'portal'. Nevertheless from this it also becomes clear that even if the only achievement to date is to have the SRS accessible online, it is a beginning and can later lead, with planning, to a successful rollout of a proper institution-wide portal.

Virtual learning environment (VLE)

VLEs have mainly been supplied to UK HEIs by commercial vendors. At the time of the study there were two major suppliers, WebCT and Blackboard, which shared a third of the market each; the suppliers subsequently merged during 2005. The other third consists of various brands and suppliers, some in-house and some open-source developments such as the open-source Bodington Common VLE. See Figure 13.4. Bodington has been developed by Leeds University and has been used by two other universities.

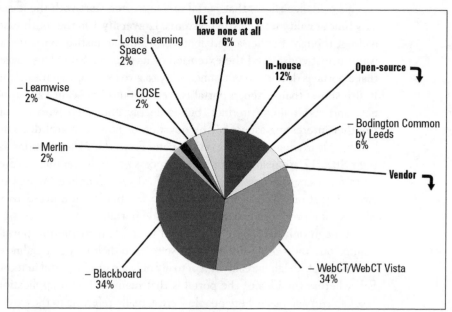

Figure 13.4   VLE systems in use in UK HEIs

WebCT and Blackboard also have portal products on offer and some universities have either already expanded or are interested in expanding their existing VLE towards an institutionalized portal. Four of the investigated institutions fall into this category. Institution-wide portals again develop out of existing systems. The reasons for this, according to the head of Learning Technology at University 3 in central England, are cost- and resource-related factors.

Library catalogues and library portals or gateways

Many different library systems are in use. As a result, the overall portal landscape in HEI libraries is not as easy to spot or categorize as in case of the VLEs or SRSs. There are also the questions of what a library portal is and how far it is compatible with institution-wide portals or, indeed, whether could it also be expanded itself to be an institutional portal.

Library portals are often referred to as library oriented portals (LOPs).[36] They are systems that allow libraries to manage access to electronic resources. They are enhancements, add-ons or stand-alone products developed by suppliers of library management systems (LMSs) and others. They integrate the diverse licensed and owned electronic holdings of libraries and offer tools for the librarian to manage the collection as a whole.

Why is there need for LOPs? Aren't institution-wide portals sufficient? It's because:

- Multiplication of electronic resources is a problem for end-users.
- Users face difficulties in finding the most appropriate database or resource to search for information relevant to their needs.
- It is confusing that there are different search interfaces and different passwords to different databases lead to unsatisfying search experiences.
- LOPs provide better integration with other database-driven information resources.
- They give more effective navigation of complex, multiple, disparate collections.
- They provide reliable, objective, well ordered access to scholarly and educational internet resources.
- Users can customize their research tools and gain more efficient access to e-resources.

Institution-wide portal versus specialized portals

What are the potential conflicts arising from developing both an institution-wide portal and specialized portals?

- Multiple and diverse portal solutions in different departments jeopardize an institutional portal's core characteristics, i.e. single sign-on, simplified search processes, integration of data, standardization of interfaces.

- Wider institutional initiatives could come after the library develops its own.
- If university policy shifts to access everything via an institution-wide portal it could be very costly if the LOP has to be abandoned.

By not clarifying an institution-wide strategy, universities are in danger of creating dilemmas for libraries, which have a requirement to expand their services. Such expansion can only be safely planned where the institution-wide development path is relatively clear. Even if the arguments above seem to militate against it many HE libraries have invested in their own LOP. Reasons for this are often related to the lack of institution-wide strategies and/or lack of working portals. Often there are no plans or strategies by the institution to develop a portal in the near future and thus the library's needs cannot be sufficiently dealt with. On the other side, there are the vendors supplying library system upgrades and licences, which have portal capability ready to be rolled-out with the upgrade.

Consequently, a trend towards wider implementation of library-oriented portals can be identified. However, there is no visible evidence or obvious tendency for LOPs to be expanded or evolved into institution-wide portals, as seems to be the case with VLE and SRS developments. To a certain extent it has been rather a notable trend to let the LOP co-exist with the institutionalized portal, in some cases even accessible within it.

Just to name a few examples, University 4 in the east of England wanted to expand towards a full institution-wide SITS portal, but has also acquired the MetaLib/SFX portal. University 5 in Scotland had rolled-out MetaLib and also implemented an institution-wide Oracle portal. University 6 in the north of England runs MetaLib, SITS e:Vision as its SRS portal, *and* was about to think about a third software as its overall institution-wide portal solution. It was at the evaluation stage of different products, including the Oracle portal. In the examination of portal development, no institution within this study had mentioned a possible abandonment of its LOP because of institution-wide developments. If institutions saw it as likely that multiplication of portals in one organization would lead to some of the services being abandoned, then probably fewer LOPs would have been implemented, simply for financial reasons. The worst-case scenario, in this case, might be that the LOP would not be interfaced with the institutionalized portal, but would appear as a mere web link within a container or channel in the portal environment, requiring separate sign-on.

Evidence from this study shows that HEI libraries are in a very lively process of acquiring and rolling-out LOPs. A substantial number of HE libraries have implemented ALEPH from Ex Libris as their library catalogue. Ex Libris has also MetaLib in its product range. At the time of the survey, from 13 HE libraries acquiring ALEPH, nearly all of them had also either implemented or were planning to implement MetaLib in the next couple of months. Eleven were working already, one was to be rolled-out very soon and one university was interested in acquiring it. Apart from this it has also been found that although most ALEPH users have also installed MetaLib, four institutions acquired MetaLib, but not the ALEPH library system. They used other catalogue systems such as iPac/Horizon Information Portal by Dynix or iBistro WebCat by Sirsi Corporation. MetaLib has a surprisingly large market share of 18%.

In fact to complement the above argument about the progression of 'multiple portal systems', the study gives clear evidence of the misunderstanding of the portal concept. In acquiring MetaLib surely there should not be any need for another portal for the same service department; actually it should be only one for the whole of the institution. However, for the sake of the argument and to exemplify the mishandling of the term 'portal' in reality, evidence can be found that multiple portals can exist even in the same service department. For example, University 6 in the north-England library has acquired MetaLib and also the iPac/Horizon Information Portal by Dynix as its cataloguing system. Both products are labelled as being a portal. If the concept of the portal is supposed to represent all services in a form of a one-stop shop with single sign-on, this is clearly a misuse of the term 'portal'. In consequence, there should be only one offering one-stop access to all services, but here two products co-exist literally next to each other.

Talis Ltd is another important supplier of HE library systems. Its Talis Information Environment includes TalisPrism, which is, according to the vendor's information, a portal. This again underlines not only a trend towards the multiplication of portals, but also that portal capability is implemented as a means of extending and upgrading existing systems. All nine institutions that had systems based on a Talis product were also in the process of implementing or had already rolled-out TalisPrism. This indicates a clear trend towards offering a broader range of services and also a new format towards the presentation and personalization of services. Although LOPs might not contribute towards an institution-wide expansion, their very existence signals a change in the key characteristic of the portal, namely that 'one-portal-is-not-enough-for-everything', and that within an institution-wide portal framework multiple portals continue to exist.

The stages of portal development and integration

The above shows that there is a clear trend at HEIs to implement portal software out of necessity to add more functionality to existing systems. In most cases institutions were entering the process without a clearly defined portal strategy or project. In some cases out of this 'extension process' the institution-wide portal has been developed. In other cases multiple and individualized portal developments have taken place without expanding into an institution-wide framework and by working next to each other.

However, in the investigation, another pattern of activity can also be clearly identified, that is where institutions were demonstrating a clear tendency towards the establishment of portal strategies, pilot projects and also working portals, devoted entirely to the successful implementation of the portal at an institution.

This does obviously involve large budgets and specialized teams assigned solely to work on the portal implementation in their institution; in-house or third-party related. Although these projects are often cost and resource-intensive, the evidence shows that some institutions have been running an institution-wide portal successfully for the past three years, as University 2 in Scotland has demonstrated.

In the examination of portal integration stages, different levels of development have been identified and outlined in Table 13.1. At the time of the survey 28 institutions had a running portal. More than 50% of them had a working student portal. This includes 'SRS online access points', such as SITS e:Vision, which are called portals, but have merely been used to integrate other applications and to move towards single sign-on. They have been classified in this way, even if they had not yet been able to automate the interface, for example between SRS and VLE, as long as there was an indication of a planned expansion in the near future.

At the same time 22 institutions were at the project stage. They had released either pilot portals or test versions to a number of users and/or were just in the evaluation stage. Some institutions might have had one form of a working portal, for example aimed at students, but could also be considered to be at the project stage because they were currently working on a staff or institution-wide portal.

Only one institution was at the portal strategy stage, but had not yet moved onto the project stage. The explanation seemed to be that most institutions that had moved to the portal or live portal stage had defined their strategy while starting the portal project. Thus, in most cases, the definition of a portal is intertwined with the portal project itself and cannot be separated as a process on its own; that is without a project in place. One institution had no portal or strategy at all; there were others that had not outlined one at the time, but did not rule out the possibility of one in the near future. This accounted for 4% of the overall portal activity.

An intranet category was defined, because intranets can cause confusion and be mixed up with portals. There were institutions that had an intranet in place for staff and students, but there was no indication that this was to lead to a portal. An intranet is a network connecting an affiliated set of clients using standard internet protocols, notably TCP/IP and HTTP. A portal is a user interface configuration presenting a unified view into multiple corporate information systems.[37] However, it has to be pointed out that some experts now also refer to the concept of 'intranet portals', that is 'these portals can tame the unruly chaos on internal company networks. Intranet portals overcome many internet portal limitations, and might be the best hope for productivity and a unified user experience.'[38] This is found, in this study, to be one reason that many institutions are keen on putting up a so-called portal environment. They call them portals, but they are based on their existing intranet and they are hardly portals in the original sense. The purpose is to get rid of the navigational jungle and to give users a much better presentation point to access the information important to the user, but with the same old problems. Often these institutions make users log into the 'portal' that gives them seamless access to one or two services, but within this environment other services are presented as a mere list of links; they do still require multiple authentication. University 7 in the south-east of England for example had nine different authentication systems in common use. This is a real problem for users. This does not mean that it is wrong to set them up, if over time these problems are tackled and a real portal environment is created. But investigations in the study showed that often, especially in cases of student portals with SRS accessibility, there was no further strategy to continue the development. Thus again either the development is stagnating or multiple portal developments take place to compensate for the lack of the institution-wide portal.

There were 'other' cases of portal development, but the extent of development could not be identified. This accounted for seven institutions of the universities examined.

Table 13.1 HEIs and the stages in portal development

Portal development	Number of HEIs
Have a *working portal*	
– student portal	15
– staff portal	6
– institution-wide working portal	8
Have a *portal project/pilot portal*	
– for a student portal	5
– for a staff portal	6
– for institution-wide portal	6
– in the evaluation stage	5
Have a *portal strategy*	
– for a student portal	0
– for a staff portal	0
– for institution-wide portal	1
Have *no* portal or strategy	
– at all	1
– for institution-wide portal	0
– outlined at the moment, but likely to develop one in the future	3
Have an intranet	2
– for students	1
– for staff	2
Portal development stage, *extent unknown*	7

Portal software products

The portal software product distribution in UK HEIs has developed into three major strands, accounting for 59% of the overall market. The investigation shows that the main products implemented or under consideration were SITS e:Vision, JA-SIG open-source solution uPortal, and Oracle software. Seventeen HEIs were using or in the process of implementing the web-enabled SITS e:Vision for accessing student record systems online. However, only two universities were identified as planning to implement the full version of SITS:Vision as an institution-wide portal facility. JA-SIG uPortal and Oracle-based software had each been considered by ten HEIs, as well as Blackboard software by four. However, 19 institutions considered the possibility or had already implemented multiple portal systems. This is 38% of the total of institutions examined. See Figure 13.5.

As outlined above, the term 'multiple' or 'combined portals' means that some of the institutions implemented one form of a portal, for example SITS e:Vision to access SRS, but were also thinking about an institution-wide portal supported by another software product, for example by Oracle Portal. Within this institution-wide portal framework the other portal (SITS) would be accessible, too. A similar phenomenon was mentioned earlier in relation to the LOP integration in HEI libraries. According to the web developer of University 8 in Wales, the University's 'main approach is to pull information from separate portals into one central portal and then provide single sign-on to allow the user to jump between the other full blown portals for each product when they need more functionality'. It had SITS e:Vision and Blackboard running, but at the same time was in the investigation stage of Novell software as a student and staff portal.

Another example is University 9 in the north of England, which had an open-source Zope/Plone portal and within this institutionalized portal framework SITS e:Vision and WebCT were accessible. Additionally it had implemented TalisPrism. Here neither the SRS nor library portal had been expanded, but a separate one acted as the institution-wide portal. University 6 of the north of England had a similar approach. According to the Support and Development Manager, it had not yet made

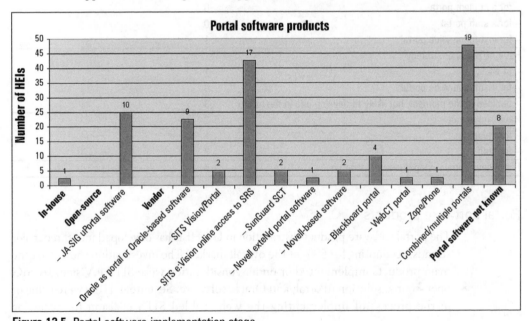

Figure 13.5 Portal software implementation stage

any decision about an institution-wide portal, but the line of investigation was in a similar direction, suggesting that it might use Oracle technology as the institution-wide portal and hold SITS e:Vision within it. It had also rolled-out the MetaLib portal.

Conclusion

This chapter has examined the stage of portal integration at 45 universities and two university sector colleges in the UK. It has established a set of criteria and applied it to the different institutions. Different stages of software integration within the institution have been outlined followed by the investigation of their level of integration into the portal environment. Software applications analysed included the SRS, VLE, library catalogue, library portal and the institution-wide portal.

Summarizing the analysis, it is clear that the development of portal integration at UK HEIs has been gradual. Although it has been established that institution-wide portals have been running successfully for quite some time, the majority of portal developments in HEIs have been rather an extension of existing services. In many cases the SRS has been the main driver for implementing the technology. It has also been shown that many institutions have been quick to speak of having a working portal, when actually they have just implemented a web-enabling feature giving users online access to their SRS database. In some cases online accessibility was the equivalent of a portal, revealing how much those terms are intertwined with each other. Furthermore it reflects how far the term 'portal' has spread, but at the same time how little the portal concept has been understood, thus leading to the misconception that one service available online constitutes a portal. Apart from the misinterpretation that sees mere web enablement of an existing system as a portal, a portal has often been understood as just a presentation layer of services important to users. A typical example was to make one or two services available via one authentication process, such as the SRS and webmail, but other services were added as a list of links and they still required separate sign-on. It is stretching a point to refer to this as a portal. The portal is supposed to overcome the multiple authentication process reversed into one single sign-on. It is also supposed to give users a one-stop-shop facility, where they have access to services 24/7.

However, even in the case of misunderstanding and false labelling it appears that if an institution has done no more than put the SRS online, it is a beginning and can lead later to a successful roll-out of an institution-wide portal. This trend has been clearly identified by some institutions trying to roll out one service such as the 'SRS portal' to interface it with other applications, such as the VLE, and gradually shaping it into a portal. Such a pattern of development can also be seen in the case of the VLE. VLE-based portal projects are an example of how portals can be developed out of necessity to give existing systems new functionality. It also reveals that often, in reality, portals are created out of a logical need and without being considered as a new and stand-alone product, but deeply entangled with existing systems. As far as the need for expansion of existing systems is concerned, portals are developed not for the sake of having a portal, but out of necessity. This is also reflected in the profile of the portal landscape, where the majority of institutions have either a working student and/or staff portal or are in the process of implementation.

Another clear trend attacks the roots of the key characteristic of the portal concept. It has been identified that libraries try to offer a broader range of services integrating new formats towards the presentation and personalization of services by setting up a LOP. The LOP might not contribute towards an institution-wide expansion as the SRS and VLE can do. However, they are a major sign of how portals are perceived at a majority of UK HEIs. The very notion of a 'one-portal-is-enough-for-all-ideal' is about to change. Although the portal ideal, outlined by JA-SIG Consortium, speaks of the portal as being unifying and acting as pulling together different applications into one, big and single structure with single sign-on, here it is revealed that the portal development is maturing, showing a new direction towards which the portal community is about to turn. The case of the libraries that set up a LOP, regardless of the fact that they do not contribute to major institution-wide portal developments and might be at risk of being abandoned later, show how immune separate portal developments have become and that they are starting to have co-existence with the institution-wide portal. It is perhaps a significant change in the concept of the portal showing that different types of portals can co-exist and that it is possible to have more than one portal running at the same institution. This can also be said in the SRS case, because often they are implemented and treated as a separate portal, not contributing to the institution-wide portal, but accessible within the overall framework.

In some institutions the development path might lead to the integration of three different portal types, one for the SRS, one for the library and one institution-wide portal, accessible either via the overall institution-wide portal or separately via the institutional website. In some cases it is a deliberate process; in others it has happened without much notice being given to it. In general it appears that the services can co-exist with the knowledge that single sign-on has not been achieved between them yet or might even not be possible at all. And still they are called portals. Such portals seem more to act as an information point displaying lists of services important to students and staff. These services are first displayed as the user signs onto the portal home page. In many cases they seem to link many more resources in a much clearer navigational structure than the existing website might have ever produced. Consequently, the change in the concept could be a strength, in that even if there is no single sign-on with many applications included, it has the capability to produce a far better organization of resources than it has been possible with the common institutional website.

Certainly, from the appearance of different portal types, no portal product seems to be superior to the other. What is preferred depends on how the product complements the existing structure, most notably in the case of the SRS, one of the university's most valuable assets.

Notes

1   *UK Universities and Colleges: an alphabetical list of universities and colleges in the United Kingdom*, www.scit.wlv.ac.uk/ukinfo/alpha.html.
2   Ibid.
3   Davydov (2001), 125.
4   Ibid., 128.
5   Katz (2002), 7.
6   Strauss (2002), 33.
7   Strauss (2002), 35.
8   Davydov (2001), 137.
9   Shilakes and Tylman in Firestone (1999), 2; and. Shilakes and Tylman (1998).
10 Ibid
11 JISC Institution-wide and Library Portal Case Studies (2003–4), *Case Studies of Portal Implementation in FE and HE Institution Wide Portal – The University of Edinburgh: 'A broad vision for the individual's needs'*, www.jisc.ac.uk/project_portal_casestudies.html.
12 Ibid.
13 JISC Briefing Paper 1, *MLEs and VLEs Explained*, www.jisc.ac.uk/index.cfm?name=mle_briefings_1.
14 JISC Institution-wide and Library Portal Case Studies (2003–4), *duo – Durham University Online: implementing the Blackboard™ Community Portal*, www.jisc.ac.uk/project_portal_casestudies.html.
15 JISC Briefing Paper 1, MLEs and VLEs Explained (1999) www.jisc.ac.uk/index.cfm?name-mle_briefings_1.Becta.
16 JISC *duo*.
17 SITS, www.sits.co.uk/.
18 Ibid., www.sits.co.uk/html/SITS-Product.htm.
19 SunGuard SCT, www.sct.com/index.html.
20 MicroCompass, www.microcompass.com/NR/exeres/2E6CDB0D-B1EF-45C9-9A70-90F0B8323B58.htm and www.distinction-systems.co.uk/NR/exeres/2577720C-0FBA-475B-8CF7-D8AD699D4662.htm.
21 JISC, *Requirements for a VLE*, www.jisc.ac.uk/index.cfm?name=mle_related_vle.
22 Ibid.
23 Ibid.
24 WebCT, www.webct.com.
25 Blackboard Learning System (LS), Blackboard, www.blackboard.com.

26   Information about CoSE, www.ltsn-01.ac.uk/resources/vle/CoSE.
27   Information at LSE website,
     http://teaching.lse.ac.uk/tech/technologies.htm#vle and
     http://www.bodington.org.
28   Information at LSE website,
     http://teaching.lse.ac.uk/tech/technologies.htm#vle.
29   Ex Libris, www.exlibris.co.il.
30   Talis Information Ltd, www.talis.com.
31   epixtech, www.epixtech.com/global.asp.
32   Sirsi Corporation, www.sirsi.com.
33   Innovative Interfaces Corp., www.iii.com/.
34   Oracle,
     http://portalstudio.oracle.com/pls/ops/docs/FOLDER/COMMUNITY/
     OTN_CONTENT/MAINPAGE/KEYFEATURES_BENEFITS/
     ORACLEAS_PORTAL_10G_FAQ.HTM.
35   Novell's exteNd portal,
     www.novell.com/solutions/extend/what_is_extend.html.
36   Cox and Yeates (2002).
37   Corporate Portals vs Corporate Intranet,
     www.intranetjournal.com/ix/msg/36073.html.
38   Nielsen (2003).

Bibliography

Britain, S. and Liber, O. (1999) *A Framework for Pedagogical Evaluation of Virtual Learning Environments*, JTAP Report, October 09, www.jtap.ac.uk/reports/htm/jtap-041.html.

Cox, A. and Yeates, R. (2002) *Library Orientated Portals Solutions*, TSW 2–3, August, www.jisc.ac.uk/uploaded_documents/tsw_02-03.doc.

Davydov, M. (2001) *Corporate Portals and e-Business Integration*, New York, McGraw-Hill.

Firestone, J. M. (1999) *Defining the Enterprise Information Portal*, White Paper 13, 31 July, www.dkms.com/papers/eipdef.pdf.

JISC (2001) *MLEs and VLEs Explained*: Briefing Paper 1, 24 April 2001, www.jisc.ac.uk/index.cfm?name=mle_briefings_1.

JISC (2002) *MLEs and VLEs Explained*, Briefing Paper 1, www.jisc.ac.uk/index.cfm?name=mle_briefings_1.

JISC (2002) *Requirements for a VLE*, www.jisc.ac.uk/index.cfm?name=mle_related_vle.

JISC Institution-wide and Library Portal Case Studies (2003–4), *Case Studies of Portal Implementation in FE and HE Institution Wide Portal – The University of Edinburgh: 'A broad vision for the individual's needs'*, www.jisc.ac.uk/project_portal_casestudies.html.

Katz, R. (2002) 'It's a Bird! It's a Plane! It's a . . . Portal?'. In Katz, R. and Associates (eds), *Web Portals in Higher Education*, San Francisco, Jossey-Bass.

Murray, M. (2003) *duo – Durham University Online: implementing the Blackboard™ Community Portal*, www.jisc.ac.uk/uploaded_documents/Durham_case_study2.doc.

Nielsen, J. (2003) *Intranet Portals*, www.useit.com/alertbox/20030331.html.

Shilakes, C. and Tylman, J. (1998) *Enterprise Information Portals*, New York, Merrill Lynch, Inc.

Strauss, H. (2002) All About Web Portals – a home page doth not a portal make. In Katz, R. and Associates (eds), *Web Portals in Higher Education*, San Francisco, Jossey-Bass.

UK Universities and Colleges: an alphabetical list of universities and colleges in the United Kingdom, www.scit.wlv.ac.uk/ukinfo/alpha.html.

Online sources about vendors and product ranges

Since the research was carried out a number of significant changes have taken place in the industry. These are reflected in the references below, which were checked in March 2006.

Blackboard Learning System (LS), Blackboard, www.blackboard.com.

Bodington Common, at LSE website, http://teaching.lse.ac.uk/tech/technologies. htm#vle, as well as www.bodington.org.

Corporate Portals vs Corporate Intranet, www.intranetjournal.com/ix/msg/36073.html.

Cose, www.staffs.ac.uk/COSE/.

Dynix/epixtech is now SirsiDynix, www.sirsidynix.com.

Ex Libris, www.exlibris.co.il.

Information source for all library suppliers: Biblio Tech Review, www.biblio-tech.com.

JA-SIG uPortal, www.uportal.org/ and www.ja-sig.org.uk/.

Merlin, http://teaching.lse.ac.uk/tech/technologies.htm#vle.

MicroCompass Systems Ltd, www.microcompass.com/NR/exeres/2E6CDB0D-B1EF-45C9-9A70-90F0B8323B58.htm and www.distinction-systems.co.uk.

Novell's exteNd portal software, www.novell.com/products/extend/index.html.

Oracle Application Server Portal, http://portalstudio.oracle.com/pls/ops/docs/FOLDER/COMMUNITY/OTN_CONTENT/MAINPAGE/KEYFEATURES_BENEFITS/ORACLEAS_PORTAL_10G_FAQ.HTM.

Sirsi Corporation is now SirsiDynix, www.sirsidynix.com.

SITS is now offered by Tribal,
www.tribaltechnology.co.uk/html/products/education_systems/sits_vision.
htm.
SunGuard SCT, www.sct.com/index.html.
Talis Information Ltd, www.talis.com.
WebCT, www.webct.com.

Academic institutions in the UK consulted in the study

University of Aberdeen, www.abdn.ac.uk
University of St Andrews, www.st-andrews.ac.uk
Anglia Polytechnic University, www.apu.ac.uk
University of Birmingham, www.bham.ac.uk
University of Bradford, www.brad.ac.uk
University of Brighton, www.bton.ac.uk
University of Bristol, www.bristol.ac.uk
Brunel University, www.brunel.ac.uk
Cardiff University, www.cf.ac.uk
University of Coventry, www.coventry.ac.uk
University of Cranfield, www.cranfield.ac.uk
DeMontfort University, www.dmu.ac.uk
University of Derby, www.derby.ac.uk
University of Dundee, www.dundee.ac.uk
University of Durham, www.dur.ac.uk
University of East Anglia, www.uea.ac.uk
University of East London, www.uel.ac.uk
University of Edinburgh, www.ed.ac.uk
University of Exeter, www.ex.ac.uk
Glasgow Caledonian University, www.gcal.ac.uk
University of Huddersfield, www.hud.ac.uk
University of Hull, www.hull.ac.uk
King's College London, www.kcl.ac.uk
Kingston University London, www.kingston.ac.uk
University of Leeds, www.leeds.ac.uk
University of Leicester, www.le.ac.uk
Liverpool University, www.liverpool.ac.uk
London Metropolitan University, www.londonmet.ac.uk
University of Loughborough, www.loughborough.ac.uk
University of Manchester, www.man.ac.uk
Napier University, www.napier.ac.uk
Norwich School of Art and Design, www.nsad.ac.uk/index.php
University of Nottingham, www.nottingham.ac.uk
University of Oxford, www.ox.ac.uk

Queen Mary University College, Edinburgh, www.qmuc.ac.uk
Royal Holloway College, www.rhul.ac.uk
University of Sheffield, www.sheffield.ac.uk
School of Oriental and African Studies, www.soas.ac.uk
University College London, www.ucl.ac.uk
University of Sunderland, http://welcome.sunderland.ac.uk
University of Surrey, www.surrey.ac.uk
University of Wales Institute, Cardiff, www.uwic.ac.uk
University of Warwick, www.warwick.ac.uk
University of Wolverhampton, www.wlv.ac.uk
University of York, www.york.ac.uk
NIIMLE, www.niimle.ac.uk

14

MyUU: a case study of the Utrecht University portal

Peter Schelleman

Utrecht University and the beginning of MyUU

Utrecht University was established in 1636. Utrecht is the largest research university in the Netherlands and ranks fourth in Europe in research. There are more than 8000 staff and the University enrolls the largest number of students in the country, about 28,000 in all. Annual turnover amounts to €630 million.

University administration has been decentralized for more than 20 years, with considerable powers for faculty boards and support organizations while central administration is organized along the lines of a holding company. The University Board has been recentralizing for some years now because of budgetary pressures and the need for a more business-like approach to university policies.

Utrecht University is unique in Europe in having outsourced its central IT organization to a commercial IT provider, Capgemini. The reasons for this move in 1999 were complex. The central IT department had been competing poorly with faculty computing centres and a move towards offering IT services to outside organizations failed. The central IT organization was also seen as demand driven, rather than customer oriented. The outsourcing process was guided by the establishment of a new but small strategic IT department at central office with a chief information officer (CIO) reporting directly to the University Board. The CIO drew up the first five-year strategic IT plan of the University, which was adopted by the University decision makers, Board, Deans and Council, in 2000. In the plan customer web services were given strategic priority and a university-wide intranet with the name MyUU was announced. This intranet would come into being by portal technology. At the time portal software was still in its infancy, but the University Board and the CIO had seen a rudimentary portal developed by Capgemini, called MyGalaxy, and it was thought that this could provide the link between the individual applications of the departments and be of strategic value in the battle for students in Holland. Moreover, portal technology promised to offer a contribution to a closer interaction of faculties and central office through a common intranet. Although the strategic plan met with wide approval, it was not declared binding for faculty and central departments, but considered a roadmap for the strategic central IT department. This lack of strong governance was not specific to IT, but generic to Utrecht University in most administrative matters.

The new CIO soon discovered three electronic learning environments in use at the university, three ERP systems, numerous HRM systems and many other examples of fragmentation. Focus in the first two years of the IT strategic plan was therefore given to improvement of student services by rolling out central administration of study grades to all faculties, making services web-enabled and by introducing a uniform authentication and authorization system for all students. Such a system was seen as a clear prerequisite for introducing a university-wide portal.

MyUU – studies, plans and progress

In the 2001 budget the University Board allocated €250,000 to cover outside project costs for the MyUU portal to go live in 2003. The allocation was not based on any real estimate of costs, but more on an educated guess of how much could be needed. Internal costs should be covered by switching priorities in central office departments.

The MyUU project was assigned to the Central Communication Department, which was also in charge of the University website. The IT department was asked to support the project from a technical point of view and to advise on the selection of software, hardware and technical development. Capgemini, the IT outsourcer, offered full support for the development and implementation stage and also support to the internal project manager. As is usual in such projects at Dutch universities a steering committee of the strategic directors was set up. Communication chairing the committee with, as members, the CIO, representatives of Central Administration and faculty representatives. A student consultant group was also organized. The University Board, however, did not participate directly in the steering committee, because at the time the Board saw itself as the arbiter between central office departments and faculty organizations. Later on this absence was seen as not showing enough interest in the MyUU project at the top level.

The academic year 2001–2 was occupied by talking to stakeholders in the venture, i.e. faculties and departments, by consulting student groups and by looking at developments in other universities in the Netherlands and abroad. The situation proved to differ widely from faculty to faculty. Some faculties had already set up information services for students on their faculty website, while others did not even have an information function at faculty level and left it to their individual departments to inform students and staff. Information services could sometimes be reached on the internet, but many departments still relied on trusted notice boards in the corridors. Self-service for employees was virtually nonexistent.

Although the idea of a portal was widely embraced, huge differences arose as to how the portal should look, what services to offer and when to offer what. The list of requirements grew by the day and it began to dawn on the steering committee that expectations ran so high that any portal, however well designed, would fall short of the need-to-haves, let alone the far longer list of nice-to-have items. Moreover, at the time – near the end of 2001 – the Communication Department ran into difficulties with the University website, especially with its content management system and a debate started about priorities in allocation of manpower and funds. The Communication Department strongly argued that the university website and its content management system should be improved first before the portal could be developed. The debate about whether to put portal or web content first – developing it together with a common content management system or developing it jointly but with different content management systems – raged on in 2002. And still there was no portal. Such a situation is not uncommon though. Prof. Hugo Strauss from Princeton University, one of the portal gurus, reported the same about Princeton in the Educause pre-conference of 2002: lots of discussion, changing goals and choices and, after a number of years, still no portal.

The CIO advised the steering committee that the choice of portal software depended partially on the directory that would be used to generate user profiles and roles and partly on single sign-on requirements. Costs would be high and considerably higher than the budget allocated. As to directories the University faced a bewildering choice. The personnel records of most, but not all, university staff members were kept in SAP. Student records made use of a home-grown system with Oracle as its database. Authentication and authorization to the internet were done through a SUN directory while quite a number of departments made use of Exchange-Outlook by means of Microsoft Active Directory. All these software firms offered their own portal versions, none of them compatible.

At the time the central IT department had undertaken an innovative project linking the different source databases together through means of a meta-directory, a rule box to synchronize the SAP personnel data and the student Oracle records with different electronic learning environments such as Blackboard and WebCT, with the SUN authentication directory and with the Active Directory from Microsoft. Redesigning the services in a consistent way was deemed too costly, so the meta-directory approach proved both cost and time effective. However, the synchronization project had clearly demonstrated the complexity of the different systems and the problem of tying it all together and keeping it synchronized. Therefore, creating yet another directory, as some portal software would entail, was too unpleasant a prospect to contemplate. The choice therefore narrowed down to the SUN ONE portal because of its integration with the authentication and authorization software and Microsoft Sharepoint portal, because of the possibilities of linking it to the MS Active Directory and the use of other Microsoft software such as calendaring, mail and word processing. Many faculty IT departments, however, were wary of Microsoft products due to security issues and the MS big brother approach, and argued strongly for either open-source systems or Unix-based software.

The CIO finally recommended the choice of SUN portal technology. An important factor in his advice was that other Dutch universities had gone through the same selection process and were making the same choice. Erasmus University in Rotterdam was deploying a portal with SUN technology and the University of Amsterdam was prototyping its portal with the same software. The three chief information officers met and decided to share information and co-operate in portal development.

By the time all the reports were in, the year 2002 was passing away and the steering committee was divided on how to proceed. The committee finally reported to the Board that portal technology was still in its infancy and that it would be better to build a technical intranet and then choose an integrated content management system for both web and portal before building a portal. From the perspective of the steering committee this seemed wise advice. No large university-wide portals had been shown to work well; no standard had been set as to how applications should be hooked into the portal; and knowledge of portal software was rudimentary in the Netherlands. The committee had also looked abroad and found no instances of fully fledged university-wide portals.

The University Board, however, rejected the advice of the steering committee out of hand. The Board stressed that the University had been promised a portal; that the name MyUU had been circulating for some time and that serious money had been spent in the preliminary stages. It disbanded the steering committee and asked the CIO to come up with an alternative plan for a live portal at the end of the current year, 2003. The CIO and the outsourcing firm Capgemini talked things over and decided to build a demo version of a portal, to go live after the summer vacation. The idea was to build the framework for a portal, demonstrate the strength of the portal vision and then sell the portal concept to the University community. It was realized that this went counter to the strategic policy of a customer-oriented approach to IT services, but no other alternative looked viable within the constraints of time and money.

To keep costs down the first portal version should be oriented towards students and not staff, the main reasons being that self-service possibilities were virtually absent and that for students there was a proper authentication system, while for staff there were still a number of different systems. Second, the design of the portal should not try to duplicate services that were already offered in existing applications, but should provide links to these applications, if possible with single sign-on (SSO). For the design of the portal use should be made of the web University designs and no extra design costs should be incurred. A simple and cheap content management system should be introduced for the portal in such a way that a later decision for a combined content management system for portal and web should not be hindered by the choice made. As to hardware sizing the CIO decided that the installed hardware should be double the advice of the hardware consultants; the main worry here being that the system should be robust enough to cater for more than 30,000 users. Previous experience had shown that scaling up later on was difficult and expensive. Reports had also come in from Erasmus University in Rotterdam that it was running into scaling problems. The University of Amsterdam reported that it had run out of money in the prototyping phase and decided to shelve its portal project for at least a year. So suddenly Utrecht found itself at the head of portal development in the Netherlands.

The development of the demo portal went well, especially in designing the layout, and providing a number of basic services. The demo version was first demonstrated in October 2003 at the national higher education convention and attracted considerable interest. In December 2003 it was felt that the first version was sufficiently developed to go live in a pilot to be used by students and staff to try out and comment on. The pilot version did not contain any single sign-on elements but provided web links to the IT services and was personalized through integration with the University electronic directory. It also contained rudimentary elements of what was called MyLibrary, offering access to electronic library documents through the portal. This was a service long wished for by most scholars, scientists and advanced students, but up to that time not possible because publishing firms demanded strong authentication for getting access to the scholarly and scientific journals. The portal provided such a means of authentication. Finally the portal contained a simple content management system to publish news items. Many departmental offices of the University were happy with this because after a brief training they could publish news items on the portal which they could not do on the University web. Everything looked set for a grand announcement of the pilot portal version on New Year's Day 2004.

Selling the portal

When faculty administrations were notified of the progress and plans for the pilot portal, reactions were, mildly put, mixed. In particular, directors of larger faculties with their own websites felt that going public in the way the CIO was suggesting would be premature and confusing to staff and students. They argued strongly that proper single sign-on should be realized before the portal could be used by large numbers of students and they listed three prerequisites for SSO that should be fulfilled before the portal should be rolled out. The benefit that individual departments could publish news items on the fly was not seen as an advantage, but as a service which could disrupt faculty information services. The CIO argued that the portal software would make it possible to shows such notices only to the students of the individual department, but not to faculty members as a whole. It soon became clear that understanding of portal strengths and weaknesses was rudimentary at faculty level, and portal demonstrations were scheduled. Faculty managers remained adamant, however, that SSO should be improved before faculties would use the portal.

The first SSO demand was a link to the electronic learning environments Blackboard and WebCT, implemented in such a way that students following

WebCT courses would gain automatic entrance to the WebCT environment and the same for Blackboard courses.

The second request was for an SSO to the student and course registration software OSIRIS. OSIRIS is the home-grown software student and course administration of Utrecht University and rather successful in Dutch higher education. It also has its own authentication and authorization built in. The third requirement was that Exchange-Outlook services such as calendaring and mail should be fully integrated into the portal and not just shown in a window as in the demo portal.

The University Board decided that the portal could go live in a pilot version for a small group of students, but should not be rolled out to the University community until further work had been done on single sign-on. This proved more costly and time-consuming than expected.

SSO services for Blackboard and WebCT went live in the first quarter of 2004, but new software versions of these applications meant rebuilding the SSO links and it took some time and effort to convince the various faculties that new software versions of the applications had to be tested on SSO compliance before being installed.

Single sign-on to OSIRIS, the student and course registration software, proved more difficult. Although SSO could be implemented, it could not be maintained during a portal session. The Osiris software had a built in safety system which terminated the application if users did not enter any transaction within five minutes after signing in. Even more worrying was the load that portal SSO put on the application. OSIRIS was a strategic tool of the university curriculum, but unfortunately at the time not known for its stability, and linking it to the portal resulted in delays for users that were unacceptable. Although work was carried on into 2005, no proper solution to the problems was found. An alternative approach, of showing an alert in the portal as soon as a datum (e.g. a mark for a subject) had been entered into Osiris, is still being explored. Students showed understanding of the problems and accepted that they had to authenticate themselves again when consulting OSIRIS. Faculty directors, however, saw the problems as evidence that the portal project was not ready for deployment.

The third requirement, full implementation of Microsoft Exchange-Outlook functions in the portal, proved impossible to realize. A world-wide search for software listed only one firm that could provide a solution, but at huge costs and with serious doubts as to whether it would work under load. Here one of the main problems of proprietary software was demonstrated. SUN pointed towards its own mail system for a solution; Microsoft pointed towards Sharepoint portal while interchangeability through standardization was a vivid topic at international gatherings, but by the middle of 2005 not yet accomplished in any of the commercial portal offerings.

Faculty boards showed dissatisfaction with the lack of progress and pointed out that the electronic learning environments had their own portal versions which could satisfy their needs quite nicely. By 2004 many faculty boards had another reason for delaying portal acceptance: the University Board announced a sweeping reorganization of the University structure, reducing the number of faculties from 14 to seven and forcing the faculty offices into merging, the reorganization to be completed in 2006. Projects came to a virtual standstill during the reorganization.

A few large faculties which were not touched by organizational changes embraced the MyUU portal, mainly because they wanted to strengthen their ties to their community members and make use of portal goodies such as intranet portal versions with forums for specific interest groups. This function had been built into the MyUU portal from the beginning, because elements of the portal had been designed as an erector set. Special interest groups could sign up for specific components of the set to tailor the portal to the different user groups. Authority for setting up such an interest group had been delegated to the faculties and departments and by 2005 been highly automated, so that all kinds of portal communities came into being.

Oddly enough, the portal project was almost brought to its knees and yet saved by still another SSO challenge. One of the portal services offered was strong authentication to the library electronic publications. This proved hugely successful, although it took time, more effort and even more money to put the different publications online. Some set cookies, which others again rejected and SSO had to be designed in a different way for almost all individual publishers but, within six months, 90% of the electronic publications were made accessible. Word spread quickly that this opened up the marvellous possibility of working at home while still having access to library sources, and the use of the MyUU portal rapidly rose per day and per hour. By the summer of 2004 more than 2000 staff members and more than 10,000 students used the portal once or more per week for prolonged periods of time, while in 2005 portal usage increased by 10% every month. This caused delays and instability in the portal software in 2004. The brute force approach of installing more hardware seemed to work at the beginning, but did not solve the root of the problem which was caused by the software not being able to handle a large number of concurrent users. Upgrading the software to new versions was advised, but meant redesigning many SSO links and also installing new versions of the content management software; new versions which proved not compatible with previous ones. The University had built an excellent and very costly single point of failure, as someone pointed out. Costs rose in 2004 to double the budget allocated, although by 2005 costs kept level while unit cost per user dropped dramatically, due to increased usage. It was also clear that there was no way back: too many users were happy with the library services and gradually more faculty departments were making use of the community functions in the portal for their own needs.

By 2005 the Utrecht MyUU portal was finally stabilized with the help of SUN. Many months had gone by, however, in tackling the instability, and impetus had been lost in developing new functions within the portal. In the summer of 2005 the student portal was widely used within the University, while the staff portal project was under reevaluation.

In 2004 the Dutch national IT higher education foundation, SURF, published its BIBA report on portals and content management systems. The report is available in pdf form, although only in Dutch (www.surf.nl/download/BIBAmanrapportagejan2005.pdf), while the evaluation categories can be found under (www.surf.nl/download/BIBArapp061004.pdf).

The report illustrated that portals still had a long way to go to become fully functional. One of the main findings was that portal software was oriented towards commercial enterprises and that much work needed to be done on deployment in the educational sector. There were few integrated application suites in the educational sphere which made proper SSO difficult and standards were still emerging, rather than providing guidance for portal choices. More emphasis should be put on IT architecture and on standardizing authentication processes.

This is true for the whole IT sector in higher education. Most development takes place at the cutting edge of technology and follows new trends, but relatively little effort is put into maintaining and upgrading existing educational software. Portal deployment at university level therefore suffers.

These findings are not restricted to the Netherlands. SURF and its sister UK organization, JISC, agreed to exchange information about their portal developments, but also concluded at a joint conference in 2005 that developments did not yet meet expectations. JISC focuses in a number of projects on use of Shibboleth authentication in portals, especially UPortal, for authentication across university borders. For the JISC project, see www.jisc.ac.uk/index.cfm?name=project_perseus, while information on Shibboleth can be found at http://shibboleth.internet2.edu. However, in the USA Internet 2 conference in May 2005 it became clear that Shibboleth compliance in new portal software versions would not be guaranteed by commercial vendors; the system remains firmly, though unfortunately, in the academic domain.

Portal evaluation

MyUU portal evaluation took place at different times and on different levels. The portal design was twice tested by student panels who were asked to perform tasks in the portal and were monitored on their usage. This led to redesign of some portal elements, because they were not as intuitive as intended. On the whole acceptance by students of the MyUU portal was high and student panels often urged a more forward approach in promoting and implementing the portal at faculty level. On the staff side things looked less sunny. Only relatively small central departments had embraced the portal and no self-service elements have come online. This absence of relevant services for staff proved not to be a portal problem, but a failure of the administrative departments at central and faculty level, which shied away from introducing self-service. The University Board recognized the problem and decided to reorganize the administrative organization, bringing all administrative IT services under direct control of the CIO.

Findings

The MyUU portal project demonstrated the shortcomings of fragmented administrative systems, the problems with incompatible software and the need for strong governance in deploying software and especially portal software. It also demonstrated the problems in portal software at the moment.

Users do not accept poorly working software and do not care whether it is the underlying application that is at fault or the portal software itself. Nor should they have to know what the root of the problem is; it is up to the IT organization to provide a faultless service.

Single sign-on is frequently vaunted as one of the main advantages of portal usage. It proved far more difficult to do well and to maintain the SSO links than expected, due to the large number of different software packages in use. This calls for an architectural approach to software portfolio development, before full use can be made of portal enterprise possibilities. SSO also places demands on organizational integration, because underlying application versions contain changes that often influence the portal SSO. It also raises the question about portal hype and substance. The Gartner curve on new IT products is well known and in 2003 portals were still in the high expectation, but also hype segment. In 2005 the situation is not that different in the Netherlands, although gradually more institutes of higher education are beginning to deploy portals, most of them with the aid of Microsoft Sharepoint.

An important lesson is that portal deployment is not a panacea for organizational problems. It clearly shows shortfalls in the administrative systems, but cannot remedy them. The hope of the University Board that the MyUU portal would link the individual departments into a common enterprise proved wishful thinking. It is Board power and strong governance, not portal technology, that can bring about such a change.

Portal costs are high and will remain high. This is not a specific Utrecht experience, but is reported by many other public institutions and companies undertaking portal projects. The high costs are not caused by the portal software itself, but by the difficult process of interlocking with other software and by serving the needs and wishes of many different customer groups. At university level these problems are exacerbated, because users do not pay for better services; university fees are fixed by governmental decree, in the Netherlands and the UK. This led to an interesting discussion with one of the commercial portal providers which still bases its licensing cost on the number of users and argued to put the accrued costs on the student bills! Such licensing fees are prohibitive to proper portal deployment across educational organizations, since we want to increase student numbers and lower costs, not raise them.

There are also considerable portal benefits. The access through stronger authentication of library services resulted in a huge demand for portal access by visiting staff from abroad, by temporary staff and by the hospital research staff, who previously wanted little to do with the University as a whole. This helped introducing a University-wide staff authorization and authentication system, which previously had been opposed by faculty boards with their own systems of granting access to their services through the web. The lesson here is that flexibility in portal design can attract new groups of users who can be offered their own portal version at relatively little extra cost. On the benefit side this counts twice: portal unit costs will drop because of increased number of users, while the business impact can be considerable if users like the portal and spread the word. Many parents of students mentioned the MyUU portal as one of the distinctive services of Utrecht University; they had seen the portal and liked it.

Self-service systems also stand to benefit from portal deployment. Frequently asked questions can be tailored to the portal user groups so that FAQs are already pre-sorted as to the category of users. This helps in producing a high number of correct answers at the first go and raises customer satisfaction. Forum services can be provided easily and special interest groups can be served according to their needs.

Are enterprise portals worth doing?

The Utrecht case demonstrates that one needs to offer clear user benefits to make a portal worthwhile. As is often the case in IT, return on investment (ROI) is difficult to calculate, if possible at all. A number of organizational points make a portal project easier or more difficult to undertake. Strong governance helps; weak governance leads to the question whether it is not better to introduce portals geared to specific services, rather than introducing an enterprise-wide portal. A clear IT architecture is required to keep costs within bounds and help portal development along. No portal can be implemented without a good directory of users, which also lists their specific roles and functions in order to tailor access to those services that the user is entitled to and to personalize the portal. Proper design of identification, authentication and authorization is needed and this should be accompanied by standardized attributes to register specific roles and give access to specific applications, depending on role and degree of authorization. Portal technology should be robust and adhere to international standards; application software that links into the portal through single sign-on should also be standardized to make access not only possible but easy to build and maintain.

Finally, a portal project is never finished: every new IT service means changing the portal; every new group of users has ideas about how a portal should look and how they will use it. This makes portals difficult to do well, but also gratifying to be involved with. In the end it boils down to the orientation towards customer services: a portal – if well designed – makes the use of IT services easier for many customers. At Utrecht University one of the things that the MyUU portal demonstrated was that many students were not aware of all the IT services offered to them and that making them available through the portal increased usage considerably.

This may well be the true benefit of an enterprise portal: presenting the services in a clear and concise way, tailored to customer role and usage so that the user feels at home both as an individual and a member of the communities he belongs to. An enterprise portal is successful if the portal address is used as the starting page for the web services of the organization. In this respect MyUU portal still has some way to go.

Section 5

The future

The assiduous reader of the previous chapters will already have gathered many notes about the future(s) of the portal. To pick out a few points: Franklin specified some next steps within the possibilities of the emerging technology. Winship reviewed the vast array of functions and services appearing in web portals, all candidates to be the killer application that sells a new organizational portal to users. Hepworth, Probets, Qutaishat and Walton pondered the possibilities wrapped up in the concept of personalization, concluding with a positive view of the forces gathering behind it. Sugianto and Tojib argued that a major trend will be towards facilitating access to the portal from anywhere with any device. Several of the public sector chapters seem to suggest that a portal is nearly always something that is going to happen, as much as something available now.

The chapters in this last section of the volume pick up these issues and look exclusively at future trends. The first is from the perspective of a dynamic force in the tertiary education sector, JISC. Notay takes a look at cross-sectoral developments which will probably create the infrastructure on which diverse web portals and local portals will be built. Bryson examines the potential role of portals for the arts and humanities, in the context of the Grid and e-Research. In the concluding chapter, Awre explores the possibilities held in the buzzworld of Web 2.0.

In the rest of this section introduction we consider another direction of development. Firestone and others have argued that the Enterprise Information Portal will evolve into a 'knowledge portal' (e.g. Firestone, 2003). What precisely that means is unclear, though Firestone makes his own suggestions. One thing that knowledge management has contributed to our view of the world is to reinforce our understanding of the diversity of information/knowledge that people need in the workplace – beyond books and data, even internal reports. It may be important and possible to in some sense manage knowledge in people's heads and knowledge that is bound up in communities. We have already seen in Musgrave's chapter how the development of portals needs to take into account pre-existing communities and cultures. This concept focuses more on the portal as a host and creator of communities. So knowledge portals are likely to include directories of experts/interests to recognize that knowledge is owned by individuals. Databases and resources generated by communities themselves will be an important part of a portal, recognizing that people can be encouraged to share specialist information and create new information sources as communities. Collaboration tools will allow swift connections between individuals. Presumably all this will be more than just a few forums and shared calendars. The knowledge portal will enable communities to form and develop.

The community-of-practice concept captures some of these possibilities. The most intelligent exponent of this idea is its co-originator Etienne Wenger. And it is useful to consider his early (2001) study of the requirements for a technology to support communities of practice as a way of thinking about what a community perspective on portals would tell us.

In his paper Wenger identifies a number of different processes that communities require to exist and thrive, and some suggestions of the types of tool available to achieve this. The stress is on the function to be supported, less a simple list of tools:

- presence and visibility (place): e.g. Yellow Pages, member directory, presence awareness
- rhythm (both daily and rituals): calendar, reminders, invitations, e-mail newsletters
- knowledge-generating interactions: document sharing, meeting/conference facilities
- efficiency of involvement: integration with desktop, archiving conversations, tracking of pieces of information
- short-term value: FAQs, expert ranking, brainstorming
- long-term value: repositories, taxonomies
- connection to the world: news feeds
- personal identity: profiling, personalization, personal space
- communal identity: 'about' section, news
- belonging and relationships: levels of interaction
- complex boundaries: security
- evolution – maturation and integration: expandable systems
- active community building: statistics, polls and votes.

Thinking through these processes is a challenging way of looking at how technologies can be made habitable. Wenger's notion of rhythm points to the need to generate patterns of activity over time within portals to keep people returning and interested. His notion of personal identity stresses giving people tools to declare what they are interested in and to describe themselves as part of participating in the community. His notion of belonging and relationships points to the need to create different sorts of social spaces, some of which are open stages, others of which are private backstages where it is worked out how to perform. His notion of evolution points to the need for a portal to evolve over time in response to the internal development of the community. Seen through Wenger's work, developing a knowledge portal as a host of communities is likely to involve a lot of work. Looking at the academic context the concept of the virtual research environment (VRE) (Fraser, 2005) may build out of such concepts.

Of course the concept of community is as malleable as the word 'portal'. There are therefore many ways of understanding the implications of seeing a portal as representing communities. Thus, in contrast to the notion of community as network, a community feeling may be simply a sense of the presence of others. For example, it may be that the reason why the public library is so liked is not just for its role in sustaining communities as networks, but simply that it is a pleasant public space in which it feels safe to be with people. This is a more indirect sense of community. The beauty of sitting in a library is that one is surrounded by a pleasantly stimulating level of noise and activity, without necessarily any connection to others. If this is to be re-created in the library portal this could be simply through reflecting the traces of the presence and activity of others – such as who else is logged on or recent searches.

These arguments suggest that though technological possibilities and limits are still important, people issues are going to seem increasingly central to the development of services like portals. This goes beyond the idea of user needs and usability testing, though these are important concepts. Portals may increasingly be seen as creating and servicing communities.

References

Firestone, J. M. (2003) *Enterprise Information Portals and Knowledge Management*, London, Butterworth-Heinemann.

Fraser, M. (2005) Virtual Research Environments: overview and activity, *Ariadne*, 44 [online], www.ariadne.ac.uk/issue44/fraser/ [accessed 21 December 2005].

Wenger, E. (2001) *Supporting Communities of Practice: a survey of community-oriented technologies*, www.ewenger.com/tech/index.htm [accessed 1 July 2004].

15
The future of portals?

Balviar Notay

Introduction

There are many types of portal: from library portals, institutional portals, subject portals and community portals to virtual research environments with portal functionality. This chapter focuses on the national portal developments at the UK's Joint information Systems Committee (JISC)[1] and looks at the new standards that have come into recent prominence that allow embedding of portal services at a local level.

We must first acknowledge that the word 'portal' is not a straightforward term; it is used to cover a rather broad spectrum of products and information use scenarios. And in an environment that has grown richer in networked services a clear definition of what a portal is and does is not easy to articulate. It is difficult to predict where we might end up, but from current developments we can try to make some educated guesses and also look to what might be needed for this future.

JISC developments

The JISC has concentrated on the development of portals on a national level and focused on how to discover national resources. We could say this has so far been more of a top-down approach as opposed to the bottom-up approach of supporting portal developments within a local institutional environment. The JISC Portals Programme[2] has so far developed portal projects in media, subject and community formats. The associated Presentation Programme[3] aims to investigate and discover how different types of resources can be presented within a variety of web environments in ways that best benefit users. A number of studies have also been conducted in this area. Both of these programme areas aim to address the presentation and fusion layers of the Information Environment Architecture[4] developed by UKOLN.[5]

Figure 15.1 shows that the presentation and fusion layers comprise a series of user-facing systems that include different types of portals (presentation services). National portals are, then, just one type of presentation service. The architecture actually allows for more diversity, e.g. virtual learning environments and library systems.

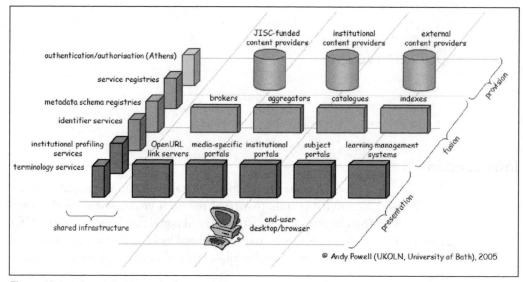

Figure 15.1 Information Environment Architecture

The portals developed within the JISC programme have a number of key features, encapsulated in a Baseline Portal Functional Specification.[6] Thus, portals within the Information Environment are primarily discovery tools; they hold no content locally but provide access to dispersed content; they provide a common means of access to varied content sources; and they have a focus on the presentation of information to the user. All additional functionality should, in principle, be delivered by systems other than the portal itself. A range of JISC portals, each with its own emphasis (for example, subject based), has been developed to support access to information. Three strands exist within the programme, each addressing a particular emphasis.

Subject-based portals

The Subject Portals Project (SPP)[7] has been based around the subject-based hubs of the Resource Discovery Network (RDN)[8] and has investigated how extended services might be added to internet resource catalogues (IRCs) that are already provided. The emphasis in the project has been on how a portal can provide a subject-based view of content. The solution proposed has been to use a Java-based portal framework, Jetspeed/uPortal, through which individual services, or portlets, can be surfaced. Portlet functionality includes aggregated cross-search, access management, user profiling, alerting services, e-journal access, newsfeeds, etc. This structure provides flexibility and extensibility for the future. Searching is carried out mainly using Z39.50, although the newsfeed portlet used RSS. An additional e-journal portlet was developed but not fully implemented.

Media-based portals

Three projects have focused more on how portals can facilitate access to different types of content, irrespective of subject. The Pixus Image Portal Project[9] has worked on the issues surrounding access to images. An important aspect here in supporting searching was the level of metadata attached to each image. Nevertheless, users found that the simple Dublin Core records used were sufficient for access to images. The portal combined the use of Z39.50 searching and OAI-PMH harvesting, although users were presented with a seamless interface that hid this underlying complexity.

In addition to the above project the JISC has recently (September 2005) funded the Visual and Sound Material (VSM) Portal Scoping Study and Demonstrator Project[10] based at EDINA.[11] Initially it will conduct a scoping study to explore the functional, software, collection and user needs requirements of a portal to cross-search/harvest both still images and time-based media from a single interface. The project will also explore new technology and trends, for example content-based image retrieval (CBIR). The second phase of the project will be to build the portal demonstrator based on the scoping study recommendations; the project will conclude in February 2007. The primary purpose of this work is to stimulate and advance thinking in this area, to develop a firm understanding of user requirements and to use this as a basis for specifying a range of useful portal functions.

The Go-Geo! Geospatial Portal project[12] has focused on providing access to any content that has a geographical reference in it. The portal allows the user to ask 'where?' as well as 'what?'. The portal is underpinned by the Geo-X-walk[13] service, which takes a search query and translates this into different geographical terms to widen the search. For example, enter a town and Geo-X-walk will map this to postcodes, parish boundaries, local councils, etc. and then search dispersed content sources and present the results in Go-Geo! As geographical terms in different forms may occur in all types of content, interrogation by geo-reference can be used in this way to retrieve a wider range of material than would normally be located through simple untranslated keyword searching.

The Xgrain project[14] (now branded as GetRef) developed a portal and broker that cross-searches abstracting and indexing databases of bibliographic journal information. This is achieved predominantly using Z39.50, although the system is designed so that it can make use of a range of search technologies such as SRU and

SRW. It has also been designed with both machine-to-machine and user interfaces, allowing it be used flexibly in different environments.

Community-based portals

The Connect Learning and Teaching Portal project[15] is a joint initiative with the HE Academy, and is focused on providing a portal to support a distinct user community, in this case those working in support of learning and teaching across higher education. In this light, discovery services are relevant, but not central to the aim and role of the portal, which has also developed discussion forums and services on relevant organizations and funding opportunities. The portal has been developed not as a single entity, but as a collection of portal services that can be flexibly combined and used in different environments as required.

Standards such as JSR-168 for local embedding within institutions and web services for remote portals (WSRP) for the use of portal services remotely have recently come into prominence. These enable the delivery of a more seamless experience to users and allow services to be tailored to organizational priorities and goals. For example, tools have been developed to allow stand-alone portal services to be embedded within an institutional portal or other web environments. The Contextual Resource Evaluation Environment project (CREE)[16] based at Hull is examining the use of internet search tools within portal and non-portal environments and investigating the use of the JSR-168 and WSRP standards for presenting search tools within a portal framework. The Connect Learning and Teaching Portal has structured its development around the concept of a portal made up from an aggregation of portal or portlet services that can be used in other environments. These range from a simple URL link to a Javascript-embedded search box, to using WSRP. The SPP mentioned above also utilized JSR-168 in the latter stages of the project and the VSM Portal Scoping Study and Demonstrator Project, also mentioned above, will be exploring the feasibility of both these standards within the project. This is an area the JISC is looking to investigate further since, although the discrete website approach is a valid model and continues to serve many audiences successfully, contextualizing the portal in the user environment – for example institutional websites, virtual learning environments and library portals – will facilitate integrated access to information and discovery services. Both approaches are seen as valid and necessary.

The need for portals in many contexts

Various portal activities are taking place across the e-research, e-learning and digital library communities and there is a need to look and see if it is possible for discrete portal functionality (portal toolkits) to cut across these communities. For example, some projects in the JISC Virtual Research Environments (VRE) Programme are looking at adapting existing portal functionality using uPortal and

GridSphere while others are creating new portal technology. There is also interest to see if Information Environment portals could serve the e-science community.[17] The JISC e-Learning Framework Programme[18] supports the integration of various services in a flexible fashion. WSRP is one of the means of presentation of these services, for example scheduling, cross-search and messaging. The intention is to facilitate the integration of commercial, home-grown and open-source components and applications within institutions and regional federations, by agreeing common service definitions, data models and protocols. A few projects from this programme have created open-source portal toolkits to facilitate embedding of these services, for example the Portal Service Embedder Project (PSE),[19] which developed the Connect Learning and Teaching WSRP portlet referred to above.

User needs

Among the many complexities of technical development we must also remember the user's needs. The user is faced with a plethora of choices including central institutional database applications, library systems, library portals, institutional portals, learning management systems, communication applications, web pages, websites and external content. More evidence is needed to assist with the assessment and implementation of portals and portal functionality from the user's perspective, and must co-exist with the technical developments. Indeed the JISC Portals Programme has a strand of work to run alongside portal and resource discovery developments that will focus on user needs and requirements analysis. Within this complex resource discovery landscape it has also become increasingly evident that we need to take into account the dominant use of search engines within the academic context and how this is affecting user behaviour. While the use of search engine functionality and services such as Google is being further investigated, we should also look at innovations like text mining, semantic web and automated metadata extraction, and how these might influence the direction of future developments.

Conclusion

Many of the above developments this chapter has discussed involve an element of personalization, and the notion of a personal learning environment (PLE) is another area of growing interest. They could be seen as the next-generation learning management system and have the potential to serve the needs of the lifelong learner more effectively. How portal services interact with such environments is yet to be fully explored. Furthermore, going beyond user environments, applications could also potentially have the capability to access portal services. For example, if one were writing a course assignment and wanted to insert a reference, it might be feasible to access a portal service such as a cross-search of bibliographic databases within the application and insert the reference, rather than going outside the document.[20]

The portal future is not easy to predict, but the major challenge ahead will be how to offer and integrate meaningful portal services in a complex user landscape. With the use of open standards to provide interoperability and flexibility the JISC wishes to facilitate not just a top-down approach but portal services that support the bottom-up approach at a local portal implementation level.

Notes

1   Joint Information Systems Committee (www.jisc.ac.uk).

2   Portal Programme (www.jisc.ac.uk/index.cfm?name=programme_portals).

3   Presentation Programme
(www.jisc.ac.uk/index.cfm?name=programme_presentation).

4   JISC Information Environment Architecture
(www.ukoln.ac.uk/distributed-systems/jisc-ie/arch/).

5   UKOLN (www.ukoln.ac.uk/).

6   JISC Baseline Portal Specification (www.ukoln.ac.uk/distributed-systems/
jisc-ie/arch/portal/spec/).

7   Subject Portals Project (www.portal.ac.uk/spp/).

8   Resource Discovery Network (www.rdn.ac.uk/).

9   PIXUS Image Portal Project (www.pixus.scran.ac.uk).

10   Visual and Sound Material Portal Scoping Study and Demonstrator
Project (www.jisc.ac.uk/index.cfm?name=project_vsmporta).

11   EDINA (http://edina.ac.uk/).

12   Go Geo! Data Portal (http://hds.essex.ac.uk/Go-Geo/Background.htm).

13   Geo-X-walk (http://hds.essex.ac.uk/geo-X-walk/).

14   Xgrian/GetRef (http://edina.ed.ac.uk/projects/joinup/xgrain/).

15   Connect Learning and Teaching Portal (www.heacademy.ac.uk/48.htm).

16   Contextual Resource Evaluation Environment
(www.hull.ac.uk/esig/cree/).

17   *Portals and Portlets*, 2003
(www.nesc.ac.uk/action/esi/contribution.cfm?Title=261).

18   JISC e-Learning Frameworks Programme
(www.jisc.ac.uk/elearning_framework.html).

19   Portal Service Embedder Project (www.jisc.ac.uk/index.cfm?name=pse).

20   Lorcan Dempsey (2004) *Pick Up a Portal*, CILIP,
www.cilip.org.uk/publications/updatemagazine/archive/archive2004/
october/lorcan.htm.

16

Managing web-based information in an arts and humanities research environment

Jared Bryson

Digital research tools in higher education

Institutions of higher education traditionally occupy themselves with teaching an established corpus of wisdom to the next generation, and in the process of doing so produce and manage vast quantities of information. They have benefited immeasurably from information and communication technology (ICT), which allows them to manage their enormous resources better, while their administration and teaching have been transformed by new digital tools. However, some faculties have taken advantage of the revolution more than others. For universities research is big business. Those who can stay ahead of the innovation curve stand to benefit immensely. The fields of science and engineering stand out, both competing with and collaborating with commercial and governmental research and development projects for the latest applications of information and computer technology. Their research culture is attuned to collaborative working and large sets of raw data. The internet and the world wide web are themselves the product of disciplinary needs within these sectors, and many of the rapidly developing e-science or grid computing programmes have been under way in the science and engineering field for over a decade.[1]

Portal technology quickly became a useful strategy for managing the vast array of information becoming available through the internet on the world wide web.[2] As a tool something akin to the Swiss army knife, portals offered to do many things for the user, but with none of them dedicated to a single task. The work of portals has evolved from what might be termed 'thin' portals (also called gateways or hubs), which contain pages of links or web-searching tools, to 'thick' portals, which rely on grid technologies to aggregate many forms of data into a single, personalized interface, facilitating communication and collaboration by using high speed data transfers and alerting services. Portal technologies sit atop the complex network architecture supplied by grid computing and web services, and provide a simple entry-point into a range of networked computational tools. This convergence of portals and grid computing is beginning to shape various new initiatives throughout the higher education sector known as 'e-research'.

Web research tools resources for the arts and humanities

If e-research technologies could be thought of as being in their adolescence for science and engineering, they are in their infancy within the arts and humanities.[3] In the UK the Arts and Humanities Research Council (AHRC) exists to provide funding to researchers and postgraduate students for a range of subjects considered to be part of the arts and humanities. As a consequence of having power over funds, it also takes on a critical role in steering policy. The Council's areas of concern are covered by eight broad subject panels:

Panel 1: Classics, Ancient History and Archaeology
Panel 2: Visual Arts and Media: practice, history and theory
Panel 3: English Language and Literature
Panel 4: Medieval and Modern History
Panel 5: Modern Languages and Linguistics
Panel 6: Librarianship, Information and Museum Studies
Panel 7: Music and Performing Arts
Panel 8: Philosophy, Law and Religious Studies.　　　　(AHRC, 2006)

A report on virtual research environments in the arts and humanities (Anderson, Dunn and Hughes, 2005) noted that, since 1998, about £50m has been spent on projects that produced digital outputs. This pales in comparison with the US National Science Foundation's more than £350m dedicated to computer science and engineering projects in just one year (2006).

The Arts and Humanities Research Council

Momentum is slowly beginning to build behind the power of portal and grid technologies to shape the research agenda within the arts and humanities. However, that momentum must overcome a number of barriers, from funding structures within higher education, to the degree of conservatism and ignorance over the affordances of such new tools. Currently, some researchers who hold seniority in the field are of a generation for whom the web is still 'new' technology. These researchers may find it uncomfortable to have to master new skills, and may be hindered by the adoption of innovative ICTs within their specialist field. To the extent that the arts and humanities have fewer 'early adapters', immature portal applications are considered more of a distraction than an enabler of core research goals. Table 16.1 captures some of the distinctive elements of many of the disciplines across higher education, with humanities highlighted.

Table 16.1 Taxonomy of knowledge structures (from Sparks, 2005, after Becher, 1989)

Group	Knowledge	Culture
Physical Sciences e.g. Physics	Cumulative; atomistic (crystalline/tree-like); concerned with particulars, qualities, simplification; resulting in discovery/explanation	Competitive, gregarious; politically well organised; high publication rate; task-oriented
Humanities (e.g. history) and Pure Social Sciences (e.g. anthropology)	Reiterative; holistic (organic/river-like); concerned with particulars, qualities, complication; resulting in understanding/interpretation	Individualistic, pluralistic; loosely structured; low publication rate; person-oriented
Applied Sciences (e.g. mechanical engineering) 'hard-applied'	Purposive, pragmatic (know-how via hard knowledge); concerned with mastery of physical environment; resulting in products and techniques	Entrepreneurial, cosmopolitan; dominated by professional values; patents substitutable for publications; role oriented
Applied Social Sciences (e.g. education) 'soft-applied'	Functional, utilitarian (know-how via soft knowledge) concerned with enhancement of (semi-) professional practice; resulting in protocols and procedures	Outward-looking; uncertain in status; dominated by intellectual fashions; publication rates reduced by consultancies; power oriented

In examining how academic cultures shape the use of ICTs, Jenny Fry (2004) has noted that,

> Failure to develop ICT policy that is informed by systematic comparative research could seriously disadvantage fields that do not map onto the physical science model of communication and knowledge production.

She also discusses Becher's taxonomy (see Table 16.1 above) when applied to interdisciplinary subject fields. This has important implications for funding access, since many of the research councils favour cross-cutting projects because they appear to offer value for money.

In an e-research seminar convened to probe the application of e-research technologies to the arts and humanities, rapporteur Sheila Anderson noted that there was a fundamental difference in methodology for the sciences, which test hypotheses against a set of data. For the arts and humanities, the research is about

> criticism and meaning, about interpretation, reinterpretation, and extracting meaning. In order to undertake this kind of analysis 'deep' access into the content of resources is required, often at the level of individual words or phrases, or images or sounds. Moreover, this level of access may well be required at the 'locate' stage of the process in order to assess the relevance and usability of a particular resource.   (Anderson, 2004, 2)

She goes on to point out a further difference in the raw materials of research in the arts and humanities. Unlike those in the sciences, they are complex and partial, being 'created for a different purpose of audience, and over which they have little or no control in their creation' (Anderson, 2004, 2–3). That same report goes on to point out that there is a relatively low awareness and understanding of the potential for web-based tools for research. This situation had changed little a year later when Dunn and Dunning (2005) visited 19 research centres dedicated to work in the arts and humanities. Typically, these centres applied ICT in one of two ways: for communication and collaboration, or for digitization and analysis. For these tasks, portal and grid technologies could be applied with great effect, as long as the necessary infrastructure was in place, including funding and training.

Strategic initiatives of the AHRC

In recognition of this situation, the AHRC has been attempting to transform these fields through a series of web initiatives, often in collaboration with the Joint Information Systems Committee (JISC), in order to explore and support needs across all eight of their subject fields. Since ICT and web-based technologies are moving at a blistering pace, there is a balancing act to be performed between 'jumping on the latest technology bandwagon' and being left behind. The Research Council stands between national government, which controls its grant package, and the individual university institutions. This mediating role means that it has to gauge long-term needs and impacts without falling behind to such an extent that it would be nearly impossible to catch up. The following initiatives are attempting to build a solid infrastructure to both innovate and sustain ICT in the arts and humanities:

- **ARIA** is the arts and humanities' ICT awareness and training programme, which provides a broad overview of ICT tools and resources, and offers help in learning how to use them.
- **The Methods Network** offers advanced expertise on how to exploit and analyse digital resources, focusing on research processes, questions and methods, as well as on uses of data.
- **E-Science** is a shared initiative of the AHRC and JISC that aims to develop VREs and grid computing technologies. These involve internet-enabled collaboration systems for researchers from different institutions, offering secure access to distributed data, computing power and software.
- **AHDS** (Arts and Humanities Data Service) archives significant collections of electronic texts, databases, images and mixed media resources.
- **HUMBUL** and **ARTIFACT** are 'thin' portals (or hubs/links pages) which offer expertly mediated web links specific to academic subjects. This entails collection-level descriptions of extensive online resources, and various value-added services including online tutorials, alerting services, and customizable resource finders.

Both HUMBUL and ARTIFACT are members of a series of eight mediated access nodes co-ordinated by the Research Discovery Network (RDN, 2006). In mid-2006 the RDN will be re-branded INTUTE, and the eight gateways will be merged into four. The RDN is

> a collaboration of over seventy educational and research organisations, including the Natural History Museum and the British Library, and builds upon the foundations of the subject gateway activity carried out under JISC's (Joint Information Systems Committee) eLib programme. (RDN, 2006)

The eLib programme began life in 1994, just as the world wide web was gaining in popularity. Its efforts were an attempt to access high quality internet resources and manage the nearly overwhelming tide of information. This, however, was before the emergence of the mighty search databases held by companies such as Google and Yahoo! The RDN hubs are intended to offer added value by carefully selecting sites targeted at researchers within specific academic disciplines. The mediation role of these gateways is one of their crucial functions. They are intended to act as a quality control on the myriad of available resources that have come to populate the world wide web. Their role is to sort out the validated information from the non-validated; the high school history project from the scholarly peer-reviewed journal.

The expectation is that as these various initiatives begin to mature and develop the digital technologies, a new level of innovative research can be undertaken. Previously unimagined – or at least unworkable – questions can be tackled, and the disciplinary isolation that often marks the arts and humanities will begin to collapse. When the tools become available and comfortable to use the question can then be asked: What could be created by the advent of large-scale computational manipulations conducted through the collaborative efforts of multi-institutional research teams within the various subject fields of the arts and humanities?

Some subjects will benefit more than others. Subjects that are fuzzy at the disciplinary boundaries, such as archaeology or computational linguistics, share a number of research methodologies with the pure sciences. The Silchester VRE project (Fulford and Rains, 2006) seeks not only to provide a public face to archaeological field techniques and day-to-day discoveries, but also real-time data logging by technicians excavating the finds. The project's communication facilities allow the officers in the field to discuss finds and check progress with experts all over the UK.

Research Portals in the Arts and Humanities (RePAH)

The AHRC is reviewing its long term ICT strategy with the aim of understanding the needs of the arts and humanities research community and of finding ways to be alongside, if not ahead, of the innovation curve that is following web technology.

One of the projects arising from this review is a collaborative project involving the University of Sheffield's Humanities Research Institute and De Montfort University's Knowledge Media Unit. The Research Portals in the Arts and Humanities (RePAH)[5] project is evaluating the web resource requirements of various research communities, focusing specifically on ways in which portal technology might be adapted to provide a useful virtual research environment.

Following the well-trodden path of other user requirement reviews, the project will approach the data collection and analysis process using methodological triangulation. This produces a layering of several techniques developed to locate weaknesses and to improve the overall quality of the project. It plans to conduct an extensive literature review, including a range of other user requirements reports, across a variety of academic disciplines. The review will focus on both institutional and subject portal projects. It will carry out log analysis of the AHRC's subject gateways, HUMBUL and ARTIFACT, as well as the AHDS. This will be followed by a web-based questionnaire, interviews, focus groups and a Delphi-style iterative discovery process. This process will help to develop a series of demonstration portals that will incorporate key features such as database searching and aggregation, as well as tools that provide news-alerts and assist collaboration. These will then be evaluated and fed back into an analytical report to the AHRC.

From the outset of the project it became apparent that some fundamental issues were being raised. Apart from usability factors with regard to the portal system's user interface, the rather intangible political concerns over the ability to create, sustain and 'police' the content seemed to be the most intractable. Allied to this concern were the economic and pedagogical factors of sustainable funding and long-term training for those who would use such systems. In *Building Collaborative e-Research Environments* (Cox, 2004, 2) it was noted that disciplines will 'have to identify the possibilities for them in the technology, to overcome cultural obstacles to collaboration and be retrained in relevant skills'. The benefits of access and communication also brought with them worries over security for intellectual property, as well as quality control and validation of data.

Academic careers are built upon publishing in the correct journals and the ability to produce a scholarly monograph. Allowing open access to publications complicates the freedom to share ideas that is so vital to innovative research. Nevertheless, publishing houses invest a great deal of resources in producing high quality documents, and access, for the time being, has a cost. Given this problem, how can the website be filled with accurate and useful content, and then maintained in near-perpetuity?

The aggregating capability of portal software holds out the promise of being able to access and manipulate disparate datasets such as images, maps and texts; and the ability to work on the same data in real time with fellow researchers at a distance has also generated a great deal of interest. Not only do the arts and humanities have their own research cultures, but increasingly funding for research is encouraging cross-disciplinary projects. This adds a further layer to any ICT development, but also creates new opportunities for innovation.

Since the RePAH project was aimed at understanding the requirements for researchers, as opposed to teachers or administrators, there was a focus on the nature and commonality of the research process shared across all eight subject areas. As Oxford University began to explore its users' requirements, its findings produced a list of needs, including project management, resource access, collaboration, and communication tools such as wikis,[6] shared calendars, chat facilities and alerting services (Kirkham and Pybus, 2005).

Portal features and applications

There follow below a few features and scenarios of how portal features and applications might be put to use by scholars within the arts and humanities fields. Each subject specialist may find different ways of applying the same features, but this short list provides some idea of the possibilities if portals were put to full use in a virtual research environment:

Scenario 1: A team of three palaeographers working at three universities are examining medieval texts and want to compare simultaneously digital images of illuminated manuscripts from eight different libraries from around the world. Discussions over key words across several texts are held by videoconference from each researcher's desktop.

Features: Cross database search

               Online collaboration tools

               Desktop video conferencing

Scenario 2: An archaeologist wants to see geographical information system (GIS) data for ten Iron Age sites across Britain – containing maps, images of artefacts, measured drawings of site structures, and even field logs of excavations – in order to develop a synthetic picture of past material culture.

Features: Aggregation of data

               Cross database search

               Grid connection/services

Scenario 3: A professor of English Renaissance literature wants to know how many editions of Edmund Spenser's Shepherd's Calendar were in existence during Queen Elizabeth I's time. The search yields websites and journal articles with grades of reliability based on a universal standard of validation, setting the search against a list of all potential hits with reasons for not including them in the validated list.

Features: Peer review facility

               Quality control and ranking system

Scenario 4: A small team of researchers from drama, archaeology and Japanese studies at an interdisciplinary AHRC-funded centre need to access an array of secondary literature, some of which is not taken by the centre's host university library. The portal provides access to journals, including those discovered serendipitously and held by commercial subscription services. It also advises on copyright access and use of specific images, and audio and video downloads.

Features: Access to all journals

               ·Copyright management

Scenario 5: A senior lecturer in modern history, hoping to sustain his efforts for continued research into Afghanistan in the post-Cold War era, picks up funding alerts from various sources, including research councils, government agencies, private foundations and international organizations. The same alerting service provides regular notification of conferences, calls for papers and new publications in the historian's field of interest. His portal interface allows fast-finding of his personal web bookmarks.

Features: Pushed alerts for funding/conferences/papers

               Personalization and bookmarking

Most of these features already exist in isolation, and with some degree of maturity; however, at the moment it is the political and cultural will that is needed to move them into a coherent reality. For instance, creating databases that offer the range of archaeological information requested in Scenario 2 (above) would require a common standard of archaeological information to be collected and inputted from both previous and future excavations across the UK. It would also require the ability to transfer the information from a network of storage 'servers' to the researcher's desktop portal. Furthermore, the system would need to sustain high quantity file transfers at equally high rates in order to render the images and maps used to produce the synthesis. The population of databases with content essential for operating aggregating portal grids can be executed using community-based systems such as wikis, but this again depends on the existence of a cultural requirement that will drive the research need. The economics of the process certainly cannot be overlooked. If projects are funded for a limited duration, sustaining systems that require regular updating and continuous monitoring will fail shortly after the funding stream dries up.

The e-research seminar mentioned on page 211 establishes a further set of criteria:

> The development and implementation of tools and software that enabled interrogation and exploration of resources, and that formed a key part of the research process, rather than as tools to search, sort and retrieve, would be key to the further integration of ICT into arts and humanities research. It was argued that an arts and humanities e-research agenda could play an important part in driving this issue forward because it could concentrate on methods and processes and the technologies required to support these, rather than focusing on research outputs in the more traditional sense.   (Anderson, 2004)

The short list of features given in the scenarios above are meant to function for each specific subject field's special research area, rather than as the present the thin portals which cover the entire breadth of the arts and humanities fields. The arts and humanities gateway was meant as a single system to serve the needs of all of the various subjects within the arts and humanities, but this broad-brush approach can also mean that some critical pieces of information may not be captured in specific subject areas. However, 'thin' portals are meant to post links that are reviewed by subject specialists, thus intending to add a level of trust for the resources on offer. This mediating feature is the thin portal's crucial 'selling point', but researchers who use them must be willing to access resources which by their very nature are limited by forces not under their control.

At the present time the powerful search features of Google renders these thin portals far less attractive. If subject-specific, thick portals sitting atop a networking grid were to mature and be taken up by the various fields, it would be at that point that new questions could be asked and research could be driven forward.

Conclusion

The development of ICT in higher education has come in fits and starts. Some fields have raced ahead, establishing benchmarks for applying the latest, fastest and most 'friendly' systems. Others have lagged behind, but through the experience of awaiting progress have been able to learn lessons and perhaps glean wisdom. The research culture of the arts and humanities, given as it is to complex and 'fuzzy' research questions, will shortly be able to add thick portals and grid computing to its quiver of ICT arrows.

The work of the AHRC may be critical to encouraging those fields that lag behind and steering those out in front so that all might benefit. As these new digital tools are built and become a reality, perhaps conversations about 'humanity' may take on entirely new dimensions.

Notes

1   Work in the UK linking radar arrays during World War II, and the development of the American ARPANET in the mid-1960s, were driven by the need for military communication. The first nodes of ARPANET were based at Stanford, UCLA, University of California Santa Barbara and the University of Utah.

Tim Berners-Lee at CERN, the Centre for European Nuclear Research's (2006) National Center for Supercomputing Applications (NCSA) at the University of Illinois in Urbana-Champaign began with the concept of 'metacomputing', coined by its director Larry Smarr in the late 1980s. NCSA also produced MOSAIC, one of the first web browsers for use on the NSA Usenet (WIKIpedia, 2006a, 2006b).

A quick check of the internet can turn up many definitions for 'grid computing'. The collaborative web encyclopaedia, WIKIpedia, has this to say:

Grid computing is an emerging computing model that provides the ability to perform higher throughput computing by taking advantage of many networked computers to model a virtual computer architecture that is able to distribute process execution across a parallel infrastructure. Grids use the resources of many separate computers connected by a network (usually the internet) to solve large-scale computation problems. Grids provide the ability to perform computations on large data sets, by breaking them down into many smaller ones, or provide the ability to perform many more computations at once than would be possible on a single computer, by modeling a parallel division of labour between processes . . .

Grid computing has the design goal of *solving problems* too big for any single *supercomputer*, whilst retaining the flexibility to work on multiple smaller problems. Thus grid computing provides a multi-user environment. Its secondary aims are: better exploitation of the available computing power, and catering for the intermittent demands of large computational exercises.

The agenda for e-research based on grid and portal technologies can be seen in the AHRC's report in May of 2004:

- Using technology to do what couldn't be done otherwise
- Enabling global collaboration
- Grid technologies to provide access to distributed resources of data, computing power, storage space, and applications
- Utility computing to provide integration of remote heterogeneous data, automated capture of metadata, real time data capture
- Dealing with complexity – access and finding tools, semantic web and shared vocabularies, ontologies
- The Access Grid to provide video communications, virtual networks and collaborations   (Anderson, 2004, p1)

2   Before the widespread use of search engines, the best way to move about within the world wide web was to use commercial web services such as Yahoo!, AOL or Compuserv. Today Google's search engine seems to be the tool of choice for locating web resources. Its vast database of sites trumps most others (www.google.co.uk/corporate/facts.html).

3   The number of sites dedicated to arts and humanities computing within UK universities is small by comparison with other disciplines. A list of institutions for humanities computing is given at www.allc.org/imhc/.

4   National Science Foundation (2006) *Budget for Computer and Information Science and Engineering*.

5 RePAH project online, http://rpah.dmu.ac.uk/.
6 From WIKIpedia:
'A wiki is a type of *website* that allows users to easily add and edit content and is especially suited for *collaborative writing*. The name is based on the *Hawaiian* term wiki, meaning 'quick', 'fast', or 'to hasten' (*Hawaiian dictionary*). Sometimes the *reduplication* **wikiwiki** (or **Wikiwiki**) is used instead of *wiki* (*Hawaiian dictionary*)' (Wikipedia, 2006c).

References

Anderson, S. (2004) *E-Science (E-Research) Expert Seminar: report on proceedings*, http://ahds.ac.uk/e-science-seminar-2004.pdf [accessed March 2006].

Anderson, S., Dunn, S. and Hughes, L. M. (2005) VREs in the Arts and Humanities, *Proceedings of the All Hands Meeting*, www.ahrcict.rdg.ac.uk/info/vre/AHM05_paper.pdf [accessed February 2006].

Arts and Humanities Research Council (2006), www.ahrc.ac.uk [accessed February 2006].

Becher, T. (1989) *Academic Tribes and Territories: intellectual enquiry and the cultures of disciplines*, Buckingham, Study for Research into Higher Education (SRHE) and the Open University Press.

CERN (2006) *What are CERN's Greatest Achievements?*, http://public.web.cern.ch/Public/Content/Chapters/AboutCERN/ Achievements/WorldWideWeb/WWW-en.html [accessed March 2006].

Cox, A. (2004) *Building Collaborative eResearch Environments*, www.jisc.ac.uk/index.cfm?name=event_report_eresearch [accessed February 2006].

Dunn, S. and Dunning, A. (2005) *AHRC Research Centres and the Use of ICT*, Arts and Humanities Research Council and Arts and Humanities Data Service, www.ahrcict.rdg.ac.uk/info/centres_projects/phase1.pdf [accessed February 2006].

Fry, J. (2004) The Cultural Shaping of ICTs within Academic Fields: corpus-based linguistics as a case study, *Literary and Linguistic Computing*, **19** (3).

Fulford, M. and Rains, M. (2006) *A Virtual Research Environment for Archaeology*, Silchester Insula IX, Reading, Department of Archaeology, Reading University, www.silchester.rdg.ac.uk/ and www.silchester.reading.ac.uk/vre/ [accessed March 2006].

Kirkham, R. and Pybus, J. (2005) *Building a Virtual Research Environment for the Humanities: interim results of the user survey*, Building a Virtual Research Environment for the Humanities, University of Oxford,

http://bvreh.humanities.ox.ac.uk/BVREH_Interim_Results_of_User_
Survey_Report_web.pdf [accessed February 2006].

National Science Foundation (2006) *Budget for Computer and Information Science
and Engineering*, www.nsf.gov/about/budget/fy2006/pdf/
4-ResearchandRelatedActivities/2-
ComputerandInformationScienceandEngineering/17-FY2006.pdf [accessed
March 2006].

Pearce, L. (2003) *Institutional Portals: a review of outputs*, Hull, University of
Hull, www.fair-portal.hull.ac.uk/downloads/iportaloutputs.pdf [accessed
February 2006].

Resource Discovery Network (2006) About RDN, www.rdn.ac.uk/about
[accessed February 2006].

Sparks, S. (2005) *JISC Disciplinary Differences Report*, Rightscom Ltd for JISC
Client Scholary Services Group,
www.jisc.ac.uk/uploaded_documents/Disciplinary%20Differences%20and
%20Needs.doc [accessed February 2006].

WIKIpedia (2006a) History of the Internet,
http://en.wikipedia.org/wiki/History_of_the_Internet [accessed March
2006].

WIKIpedia (2006b) Grid Computing,
http://en.wikipedia.org/wiki/Grid_computing [accessed March 2006].

WIKIpedia (2006c) WIKI, http://en.wikipedia.org/wiki/Wiki [accessed March
2006].

17

Portals and Web 2.0

Chris Awre

Introduction

The discussion of portals throughout this book has revolved around the delivery of portal functionality through the world wide web. Portals have rarely been discussed in the context of client software that needs to be installed and run from the desktop. Certainly individual areas of functionality that are associated with portals – searching, news, information gathering – do have many desktop tools associated with them, but when it comes to drawing them together the web has been the platform of choice.

Bearing this in mind it is sometimes hard to believe that the web has been around for little over a decade in the form that we know and love. In that time there has been enormous change and the pace of this change shows no signs of stopping. From an innovation viewpoint this promises to deliver ever more powerful and flexible services: from a user's viewpoint this advance may be tempered by a concern that what is available today will simply be superseded tomorrow, requiring constant adjustment to the web landscape.

In a presentation entitled 'The Open Source Paradigm Shift', and later in a paper with the same title published on his website,[1] Tim O'Reilly picked out a number of changes and developments in the field of open-source software development that had taken place in recent years, and identified some key trends. These were:

- software as commodity
- network-enabled collaboration
- customizability or software-as-service.

To sum these up software can no longer be regarded as the end in itself in building a solution. Software is the commodity that enables services to be developed, often by customizing and/or combining different pieces of software to build something new. This flexible and organic development path is facilitated through collaboration and it is the network that provides the means for that collaboration among developers across the world.

Although these trends were focused on open-source software they also have relevance to the development of the web, and indeed it is quite possibly the web, being the network it is, that has led open-source software in the direction he describes. In a subsequent paper published in 2005, 'What is Web 2.0: design patterns and business models for the next generation of software',[2] O'Reilly makes this connection and gives the trend the label in the title of the paper: Web 2.0. This chapter examines the Web 2.0 trend and assesses how it might influence web portal development in the years to come.

What is Web 2.0?

The first thing that can be said about Web 2.0 is that it is not a specific technology but more a concept. It is also a term that can simply be used as a label to describe the trends taking place in web development. It was first coined by Dale Dougherty, a vice-president at the publishers O'Reilly, when they were developing a conference on web trends in 2004, and the name eventually stuck to the extent that the second Web 2.0 conference took place in October 2005, attended by over 800 delegates.[3] Many have decried the term as simply marketing hype, a way of rebranding web technologies to make them sound more attractive. Nevertheless, the term is here to stay for at least some time. To fully understand what it represents, though, you do need to strip it away and look more closely at the trends taking place.

In trying to capture the essence of Web 2.0 Tim O'Reilly produced a 'meme map' of what can be covered by this umbrella term (see Figure 17.1). Many of the trends identified for open-source software are present here. Services are core rather than software, the network is the platform for collaborating and building these services, and there is ability to remix or customize existing services to suit needs and to help build better services.

Key to all of these trends is the involvement of people. In an article for *Information Today* in November 2005[4] Robin Peek emphasizes that the web has enabled many to do what was previously the preserve of the few. In the field of publishing, only those with the know-how and appropriate technology were once able to prepare and disseminate content. The web effectively provided this capability for anyone with an internet connection. People were given power to inform, comment and debate in new, flexible and powerful ways. E-mail and web pages have matured into blogs and Wikis as routes through which discussion takes place and information disseminated. And people have taken advantage of this by the millions. As of December 2005 the Technorati blog search site provided access to over 23 million blogs from around the world.

People make the web what it is, and services that allow them to do so are proving to be the most popular. One of Amazon's most loved and used features is the user

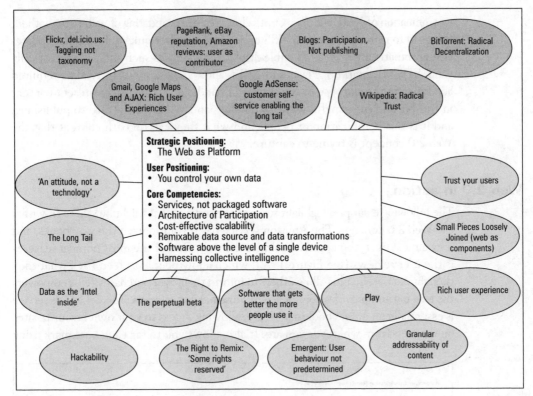

Figure 17.1   Tim O'Reilly's Web 2.0 'meme map'

reviews. Flickr and del.icio.us allow users to construct and organize their own collections online. The online encyclopedia Wikipedia has been built entirely by people simply wishing to contribute. It appears that if you make a service easily usable and trust people to use it as they see fit (within appropriate rules) people will do just that and produce services and information of value. This trend has been labelled as 'opening up the long tail', the collective power of individuals who provide the majority of sites on the web.

For most people, web publishing is as far as they will go. But for many the ability to build new services is equally attractive. The web, the network, has provided a platform through which this can be achieved. Where services on the web have made available their APIs for others to build on new services have been developed, adding value to the original. The two most famous companies to do this are Amazon[5] and Google.[6] Both do this through the use of Web Services, an increasingly common technology underpinning the web and applications that are delivered via this platform. As with publishing, give people the opportunity to take part and they will.

The use of Web Services is one clear way in which technology developments are supporting the Web 2.0 trend. They allow a user to interact with an existing service and use the output for their own means, creating a richer user experience when using the web. However, other technologies are also facilitating this. AJAX, a combination of XML and Javascript, allows real-time updating of web pages without the need to refresh the screen. RSS or Atom feeds offer quick information updates that automatically refresh. Flexible display technologies such as CSS, semantically valid XHTML markup, Flash and XSLT allow data to be displayed as required according to the purpose of the service at hand. All of these help present content in flexible and meaningful ways, as do blogs and Wikis with regard to publishing, and it is this combination of people and what they can do with content that the Web 2.0 concept is trying to capture.

Web 2.0 in action

The following examples highlight some of the services that might be said to fit within the Web 2.0 concept. The Amazon service has revolutionized the way books, and now almost everything, can be sold via the web. One of the most popular features is the user reviews (see Figure 17.2), which allow people to feed back what they thought of an item, plus allow others to inform their own purchases. This empowers the long tail and provides confidence to subsequent customers. The del.icio.us service is essentially an online bookmark store, allowing access to your own favourite sites on the web from wherever you are. It also allows you to tag each bookmark using

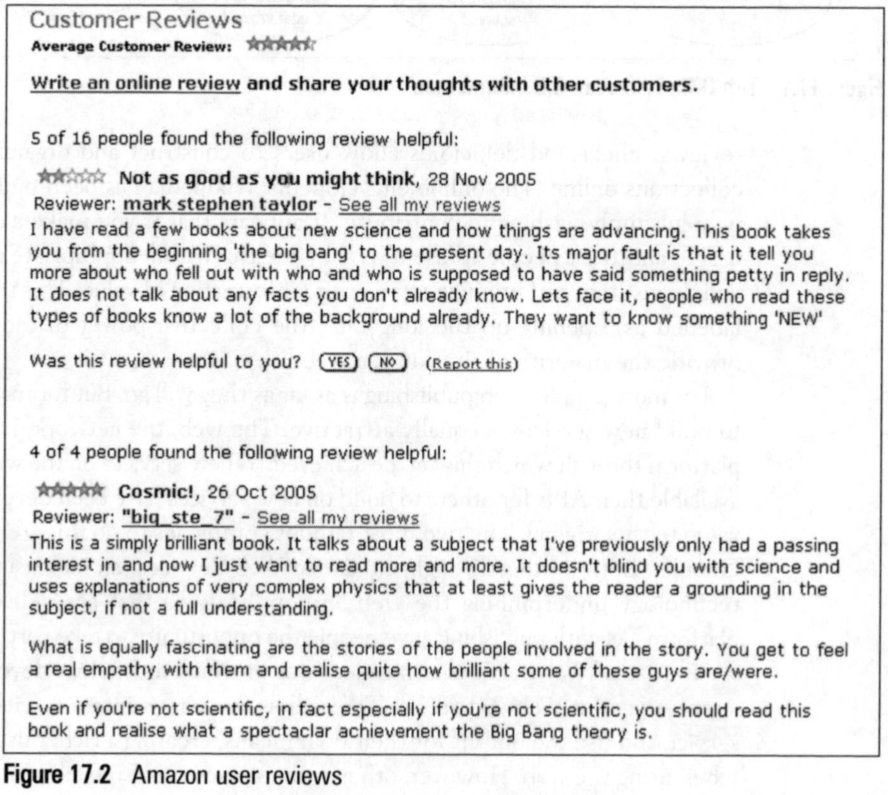

Customer Reviews

Average Customer Review: ★★★★☆

<u>Write an online review</u> **and share your thoughts with other customers.**

5 of 16 people found the following review helpful:

★☆☆☆☆ **Not as good as you might think**, 28 Nov 2005
Reviewer: <u>mark stephen taylor</u> - <u>See all my reviews</u>
I have read a few books about new science and how things are advancing. This book takes you from the beginning 'the big bang' to the present day. Its major fault is that it tell you more about who fell out with who and who is supposed to have said something petty in reply. It does not talk about any facts you don't already know. Lets face it, people who read these types of books know a lot of the background already. They want to know something 'NEW'

Was this review helpful to you? (YES) (NO) (<u>Report this</u>)

4 of 4 people found the following review helpful:

★★★★★ **Cosmic!**, 26 Oct 2005
Reviewer: <u>"big_ste_7"</u> - <u>See all my reviews</u>
This is a simply brilliant book. It talks about a subject that I've previously only had a passing interest in and now I just want to read more and more. It doesn't blind you with science and uses explanations of very complex physics that at least gives the reader a grounding in the subject, if not a full understanding.

What is equally fascinating are the stories of the people involved in the story. You get to feel a real empathy with them and realise quite how brilliant some of these guys are/were.

Even if you're not scientific, in fact especially if you're not scientific, you should read this book and realise what a spectaclar achievement the Big Bang theory is.

Figure 17.2   Amazon user reviews

your own terms, and organize them using these tags. This is useful as an individual service. But del.icio.us also lets other people see your bookmarks and search for useful sites using the tags you apply. It allows you to create content and then let that content be reused to possibly greater effect (see Figure 17.3).

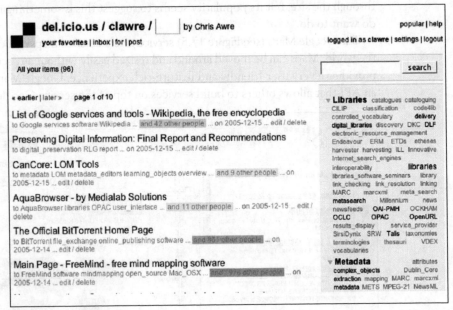

Figure 17.3   del.icio.us
Reproduced with permission of Yahoo! Inc. © 2006 by Yahoo! Inc. YAHOO! and the YAHOO! logo are trademarks of Yahoo! Inc.

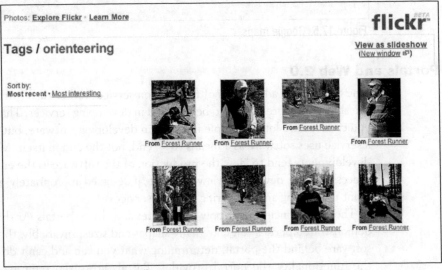

Figure 17.4   Flickr image gallery
Reproduced with permission of Yahoo! Inc. © 2006 by Yahoo! Inc. FLICKR and the FLICKR logo are trademarks of Yahoo! Inc.

It is not only textual content that can be shared in the way del.icio.us facilitates the sharing of bookmarks. Flickr (see Figure 17.4) offers a way for people to present their photographs and tag them in the same way for others to then view and use. There is an assumption that individuals wish to share their content through the site, but its popularity seems to suggest this is something many people do want to do.

The Google Maps (see Figure 17.5) service offers detailed maps of locations across the world. Maps can be moved around and resized easily without any screen refresh, providing a very user-friendly and feature-rich experience. Google Maps also offers an API that allows others to build services on top of the service Google provides.

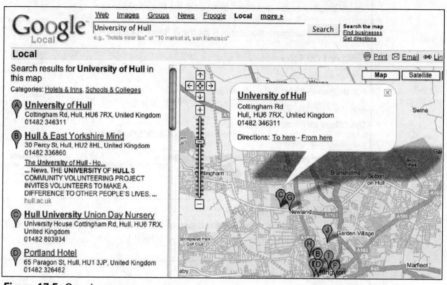

Figure 17.5 Google maps

Portals and Web 2.0

One of the main advantages of focusing on services rather than software per se is the ability for more people to be involved in developing services. That is not to say you cannot have lots of people involved in developing software, but that building a service uses software as a means to an end, not the end in itself. Many software developments tend to view the production of the software as the endpoint in the process. Service developers view software, if designed appropriately, as the starting point to building and delivering flexible services.

The same principle can apply to websites and also to portals. As this volume has demonstrated portals can take many shapes and sizes. Invariably, though, there is software behind the portal, determining what you can and can't do according to the functionality the portal provides. Portals are often seen as endpoints in themselves, providing a pre-set service to the end-user and no more. But what if portals could be designed as services, acting not as the endpoint but as the starting point for allowing end-users to build new services? This is already occurring in some cases. Amazon is sometimes regarded as a portal, but has sparked off much more than the www.amazon.com itself offers through making its Web Services APIs available.

Could Web 2.0 replace portals as a concept? This remains to be seen. Yet, whereas portals have often worked according to the one-stop-shop model, the Web 2.0 environment promises a more fluid model, where there are no 'stops' but simply a continuum of services that people move between as required. Portal functionality as currently delivered, however, will almost certainly benefit the Web 2.0 concept and its associated technologies. Indeed, some examples of 'Web 2.0 portals' exist already in services offered by Netvibes and at www.google.com/ig.

Many of the characteristics of Web 2.0 epitomize what portals are intended to be: the provision of a rich user experience through interaction with a range of services, applications and information; the personalization of services allowing users to control their own content and structure; the contribution or publication of content for the individual and others to benefit from in the future; and the ability to take existing functionality and remix it to serve a specific need. Technologies to support these services now exist and portals can take advantage of them. Opening up one's system used to be fraught with fears about loss of identity. While this risk will still be present, making a portal available to the long tail could also bring dividends.

Library 2.0

In his overview of Web 2.0 principles[7] Paul Miller moves on to discuss the applicability of Web 2.0 to libraries. The term Library 2.0 was coined by Michael Casey in, suitably, his blog LibraryCrunch in September 2005.[8] In one posting he argues that from his library OPAC he wants to:

> have it remember me, either through a login or other, simple, method. I want my bookmarks, my saved titles, my search history. I want to be able to write reviews and make suggestions, I want to add friends to my social network and let them see my reviews and what I've liked and disliked. I want a built-in, fully customizable aggregator, a to-do list, a place to take notes and save files, and I want access to this from any computer in the world, not just the one at my library. All this exists, of course, in bits and pieces – all of it through Web 2.0.

This request is a key example of what opening up a system to the long tail means. It gives ownership to people to allow them to use services on the web as they want to use them, not just as the service lets them. There are implications for how this is managed to ensure data propriety and accuracy, but it is certainly putting the user at the centre of library services.

What does Web 2.0 mean for libraries themselves? Libraries manage large collections of content, and much of this is either available or described digitally.

Access to this content is made available through a myriad of routes, including portals. Applying the Web 2.0 concept to this would allow the end-user to do much as Michael Casey suggests. It might also mean being able to search and collate information in a flexible manner, or even to allow new services to be built on top of the library's content to serve specific needs. In essence it means taking the content available and making the best use of it, making it work harder. Many of the tools available to make this content work harder are available and it will be interesting to see how they are picked up and used in the years to come.

As for portals, Web 2.0 for libraries requires them to open up. There is still risk associated with doing this, but also dividends in terms of what libraries can potentially offer their end-users and people in general. Applying the Web 2.0 concept can also establish the library as part of the wider web that their end-users use. Lorcan Dempsey has argued[9] that librarians should not treat their own services on the web as the sole focus of a user's attention, but as part of a broader web. Web 2.0 offers a route towards this, making the library a connected part of this wider view.

Future development

As its recent history demonstrates, Web 2.0 is very much in its infancy and it remains to be seen how much it becomes an established concept. The technologies behind the concept have been developing for some time, and there is no reason to think they will not continue to do so. It is how they are utilized that remains unclear, though this is down to the imagination of the long tail. It is a tantalizing prospect.

The more the technology permits complex services to be served via the web, the more there appears to be blurring between the web and the desktop, with the former becoming able to replicate the usability of the latter. There are also examples of integration between the two: the inclusion of RSS readers in browser software such as Internet Explorer 7 and Firefox, and the integration of del.icio.us with the Firefox browser clone Flock. It is also likely that this ability to combine the benefits of the desktop and the web will continue.

For many services delivered via the web there is no doubt that Google acts as a yardstick for many innovations, particularly in the way it is collecting content so that it can deliver this in flexible ways (e.g. Google Print and Google Base) and it is notable that they, and now also the Open Content Alliance, are working with libraries to enable this. One thing is certain: development will not be slow. For Web 2.0 future development, therefore, it is probably best to leave it at: Watch this space!

Conclusions

Web 1.0, a term retrofitted to the last decade of web development, produced a lot in a short space of time. Web 2.0 proposes how we can take the development of the web further and offers a path for the future development of portals toward making them a full realization of what they can be. Web 2.0 is marketing hype to some degree: the O'Reilly papers are looking at industry trends as much as trends overall, and an article in *Wired* in August 2005 described exactly the same trends without needing to mention Web 2.0 at all.[10] But it is also a valuable picture of how we can make the best use of the web in the future. One of the keys to this is 'we', as O'Reilly encourages an 'architecture of participation' where everyone who wishes to get involved can do so. The challenge is laid down.

References

1   O'Reilly, T. (2004) *The Open Source Paradigm Shift*, www.oreillynet.com/pub/a/oreilly/tim/opensource/paradigmshift_0504.html.

2   O'Reilly, T. (2005) *What is Web 2.0: design patterns and business models for the next generation of software*, www.oreillynet.com/pub/a/oreilly/tim/news/2005/09/30/what-is-web20.html.

3   Web 2.0 conference 2005, www.web2con.com/.

4   Peek, R. (2005) Web Publishing 2.0, *Information Today*, **22** (10), 17–18.

5   Salkever, A. (2003) How Amazon Opens Up and Cleans Up, *Business Week Online*, 24 June, www.businessweek.com/technology/content/jun2003/tc20030624_9735_tc113.htm.

6   Hof, R. D. (2005) Mix, Match, and Mutate, *Business Week Online*, 25 July, www.businessweek.com/magazine/content/05_30/b3944108_mz063.htm.

7   Miller, P. (2005) Web 2.0: building the new library, *Ariadne*, **45**, October, www.ariadne.ac.uk/issue45/miller/intro.html.

8   LibraryCrunch (2005) *Library 2.0*, blog by Michael Casey, www.librarycrunch.com/, quote from entry for 23 September.

9   Dempsey, L. (2005) *The Sole Focus of a User's Attention*, 3 January, http://orweblog.oclc.org/archives/000529.html.

10 Kelly, K. (2005) We Are the Web, *Wired*, **13**, 8 August, www.wired.com/wired/archive/13.08/tech_pr.html.

The contributors

Chris Awre is Integration Architect with the e-Services Integration Group, University of Hull, where he has a remit to examine, advise on and facilitate the integration of existing and future university systems and processes, particularly those being delivered through the University portal. He was Project Manager of the UK Joint Information Systems Committee's CREE (Contextual Resource Evaluation Environment) project, investigating how users wish to have library-based resources and services presented to them in portal and non-portal environments. Before joining the University of Hull in 2004, he was JISC's Programme Manager for a variety of development programmes. These included the Portals and Presentation Programme, involving exploration of how portals can be used to serve information needs and their role as a presentation medium, and the Focus on Access to Institutional Resources (FAIR) Programme, involving the exploration of methodologies for depositing and disclosing institutional assets.

Andrew Cox is a lecturer in Information Management at the Department of Information Studies, Sheffield University. He lectures in the areas of knowledge management and the organizational and social impact of new communication technologies. His doctorate, from the Department of Information Science, Loughborough Unviersity, applied community of practice theory to online and professional communities, examining their role in information and knowledge sharing and professional identity. Previous jobs include working for the digital library research centre, LITC, at London South Bank University, and he was for many years editor of the practitioner journal *Vine*, which tracked new techologies in the library sector. In 2002 he was author of a JISC techwatch report on portals, and he has maintained an interest in the portal field since then, through involvement in projects and conference papers.

Jared Bryson is a user requirements analyst currently undertaking work for the Research Portals in the Arts and Humanities (RePAH) project, collecting data for the AHRC's strategic review of ICT. He is also pursuing graduate research at Brunel University's Centre for Intelligence and Security Studies. This is part of a major career transition since most of his work over the past decade has been in the heritage sector as an archaeologist and museum educator. After taking a bachelor's degree in archaeology he worked as a professional archaeologist, excavating sites along the eastern seaboard of the United States for clients such as the National Park Service and the National Trust for Historic Preservation. He has excavated in Turkey on the upper Euphrates River exploring the emergence of urbanism in the region, as well as in Jordan investigating the transition from Christian to Islamic society. He received an MA in Museum Education from the College of William and Mary and subsequently worked as a community archaeologist and curator of education for the city of Alexandria, Virginia. This experience allowed him to join a research team at the Centre for the Public Library and Information in Society (CPLIS) in the University of Sheffield's Department of Information Studies. While there he produced several reports of national significance, which evaluated the social impact of museums, archives and libraries throughout the UK.

Ron Davies is an independent consultant based in Brussels. He has more than 20 years' experience in the design, development, selection, implementation and support of information systems, including library systems, thesaurus management applications, subject gateways and portals. A Canadian as well as a British citizen, he has worked for private, governmental and international organizations in more than a dozen countries. He regularly teaches courses in library portals, digital repositories and new information technologies and has consulted or developed portals for government departments and international organizations in areas as diverse as trade, agriculture, labour and social policy.

Aspasia Dellaporta is User Experience Specialist at Cimex Media Ltd. She has a background in psychology, and extensive experience in usability and accessibility methods and practices for web and software interactive systems. She leads the user experience research and development at Cimex, applying usability and accessibility to the design and development of corporate and e-learning projects, with a focus on web applications. Her interests include web accessibility, evaluation methods for innovative e-learning applications for children, audio-based e-learning for visually impaired users and information architecture design. Key projects include: BBC Jam PE learning resource, Need2Know website for the DfES, CC4G for Eskills UK, LGiU website, Gambling Commission website and HMRC (accessibility testing). Before joining Cimex she was a senior research assistant at City University, researching web accessibility and e-learning. She is a member of the Usability Professionals Association (UPA) and holds an MSc in Human–Computer Interaction with Ergonomics from UCL.

Stephen Emmott is Head of Web Services at the London School of Economics and Political Science (LSE). He has developed extensive experience of web management in higher education (HE) since serving as the first Editor of Web Services at King's College London (1997–2000). He regularly advises other UK universities and is currently a member of the organizing committee for the annual Institutional Web Management Workshop (IWMW). Before this he was the producer/project manager for a variety of websites including *Which?* Online, Lloyds Bank and Lufthansa UK. After completing his MSc in Cognitive Science, Stephen served as a visiting lecturer before entering the new media industry in 1994.

Tom Franklin of Franklin Consulting has worked in learning technology for over ten years and has been particularly concerned with user needs in the design and implementation of systems. He was one of the earliest people to be involved in the development of virtual learning environments (VLEs) and managed learning environments (MLEs). He has overseen the development of three VLEs and supported work in MLEs in over a dozen universities and colleges. He has been instrumental in the design of a national educational portal and has provided consultancy to several universities on portal design, selection and implementation. He has also worked in accessibility, usability and standards, including supporting the development of IMS specifications. He is now an independent consultant with Franklin Consulting, providing strategic advice on the use of portals, integration of systems as well as VLEs and MLEs.

Mark Hepworth is a lecturer in Information Retrieval and the Development of User-oriented Information Services at the Department of Information Science, Loughborough University. A first degree in Social Anthropology and African History sparked Mark's people-centred approach to understanding communities and information behaviour. These skills were channelled into an interest in how people learn and interact with information at Sheffield University. This led to work for the first European full-text online database company, Datasolve Ltd, and later R&D for the *Financial Times* electronic information services. He then took a senior lectureship in Information Studies in Singapore. After six years he returned to the UK to join the Department of Information Science at Loughborough. During the last five years he has led research projects on the information needs of informal carers, hospital social workers and people with multiple sclerosis. He currently supervises PhD projects concerning the teaching of information literacy in schools and tertiary institutions, personalized web-based information delivery, information systems implementation in Kenya and the information needs of children with parents with cancer in Malaysia. Other recent work has focused on the communication needs of people with severe learning disabilities, and the accessibility of library portals for people without sight.

Yvonne Klein is Portal Consultant with the University of East London (UEL). She is currently involved in portal strategy implementation and has been working with the UEL on a number of developmental and research projects for the past five years. Between 2001 and 2002 she worked and delivered an internally funded research project about student web portals in higher education institutions for the JISC joint

UEL, APU and UNL managed learning environment (MLE) project called 'A partnership approach to developing an environment for managed learning' (www.jisc.ac.uk/index.cfm?name=project_partnership_ml). The findings informed information policy, particularly the Web Portal Strategy, which led to the implementation of the current UEL student portal. It has been rolled-out successfully to undergraduate students since September 2004. In January 2005 Yvonne joined the Rix Centre, a cutting-edge multimedia research and development centre for people with learning disabilities. She is working on the development of a specialist portal for people with learning disabilities using innovative intellectual approaches and state-of-the-art multimedia applications.

John A. MacColl is Head of the Digital Library Division at the University of Edinburgh, where he has worked since 1998. His work involves the strategic management of library systems, e-resources and help services. He is also closely involved with the development of an Edinburgh-based consortium of libraries sharing digital services. His career has been spent in the universities of Glasgow, Aberdeen, Abertay Dundee and Edinburgh, and includes experience in libraries, converged information services, a computing service and a UK data centre. He was the founding editor of *Ariadne* magazine in 1996, and his experience in digital and research library issues has led to consultancies in different parts of the world. He served on the CURL Task Force on Scholarly Publishing and the CURL Task Force on Digital Content Creation and Curation, and is a member of the new joint SCONUL/CURL Task Force on e-Research. He has extensive experience of JISC-funded projects in digital libraries, scholarly communications, e-research and e-learning, acting as project manager on some projects, and as director on several.

Andrew Madden began his research career as an ecologist and published several articles in agricultural journals, mostly on aspects of pest control. In 1995 he joined a group at the University of Aberdeen that was developing software to teach about land use and environmental sciences. This led him to develop an interest in the role of computers in education. Since then, Dr Madden has studied the impact of ICT on teaching and learning at Sheffield Hallam University; he was part of a team that advised lecturers at Barnsley College on the use of computers in teaching; and he set up and ran a library/learning resources centre at a school in north London. Since November 2001, he has been based in the Department of Information Studies at Sheffield University, where he has carried out research on the information-seeking habits of school children, and the internet search practices of members of the general public.

Dean Mohamedally is a PhD research student at the Centre for Human–Computer Interaction Design, City University, London. Before starting his PhD he worked as a mobile software R&D consultant, and completed an internship at Philips Research Laboratories, UK. During his BSc in Computer Science at King's College London, he developed multi-platform development tools and software components for mobile systems. His current research focus is on mobile and web software tools to support e-science in human–computer interaction methods. He is a registered community developer for several high-profile organizations and has academic ties with Sun Microsystems, Microsoft (.Net platform, Windows Mobile, TabletPC), Palm, IBM Websphere, Nokia, Sony Ericsson and Symbian.

Stephen Musgrave is the IT Manager at Blackpool and The Fylde College in the north-west of England. He is Deputy Chair of the UK national Joint Information Systems Committee on the Integrated Information Environment (JIIE), and a member of the UK Parliamentary IT Committee (PITCOM). He holds a BSc (Hons) in Computing with Electronics, an MSc in Information Systems, and a PhD in the Computer Science of Telematics from the Open University (OU). His research interest is community portals in the context of community informatics in the UK, investigating people and technology issues of implementing portals in the civic and civil society domains. Formerly an electronics officer in the UK merchant navy, he has also taught Communication Engineering as a principal lecturer in the UK further education sector.

Balviar Notay has been JISC Programme Manager for Resource Discovery, Portals and Presentation since 2004. The Portals Programme has so far developed portal projects in media, subject and community formats (www.jisc.ac.uk/ index.cfm?name =programme_portals). The Presentation Programme (www.jisc.ac.uk/ index.cfm?name=programme_presentation) aims to investigate and discover how different types of resources can be presented within a variety of web environments in ways that best benefit users. Both of these programme areas aim to address the presentation and fusion layers of the JISC Information Environment Technical Architecture (www.ukoln.ac.uk/distributed-systems/jisc-ie/arch/). Before this post Balviar worked on the JISC 5/99 Learning and Teaching Programme (www.jisc.ac.uk/index.cfm?name=programme_learning_teaching), which made content, learning and teaching materials and tools available in the area of images, moving pictures and sound, data, museum collections and e-books.

Steve Probets joined the Department of Information Science at Loughborough University in 2001. He lectures in e-business and electronic publishing. He is currently a member of the Knowledge Management Group at Loughborough and the Electronic Publishing Innovation Centre. Before this he was a member of the Electronic Publishing Research Group at Nottingham University. His research interests lie in metadata, structured documents and the electronic publishing industry. He is currently working on a research project investigating the representation of publisher copyright agreements in a formal manner. He has supervised Masters and PhD students investigating personalized information provision in the health domain and ways of managing metadata diversity within library portals, and he has an interest in using metadata to determine the most appropriate method for content delivery.

Fadi Qutaishat is a PhD research student in the Department of Information Science, Loughborough University. He received a Bachelors degree in Computer Science from Amman University in Jordan in 1997. He then worked for Al-Balqa Applied University as a computer lab supervisor. He joined Loughborough University in 2002 as a Masters student and was awarded his Masters degree in Information and Knowledge Management in 2003. He then went on to commence a doctorate, concerned with investigating the attitudes towards and the impact of information personalization on the multiple sclerosis (MS) community. Fadi's research is expected to deliver practical and theoretical outcomes that could be advantageous for people with MS. After finishing the PhD, he will return to his home country of Jordan to join Al-Balqa Applied University as a Lecturer in the Management Information Systems programme.

Peter Schelleman started his professional career at the English Department of Utrecht University as an associate professor in English Language teaching. After a number of further academic and strategic roles at the University, including responsibility for the establishment of a multimedia centre and new fields of disciplinary studies, he was asked in 1998 to become the first chief information officer of the University in charge of strategic planning and with the task of outsourcing the IT department to Capgemini – the first such move in higher education. He was twice nominated as IT manager of the year, in 2001 by a CIO panel, and in 2004 by the telecom industry. In 2002 he was one of the founding members of the Dutch CIO council for Higher Education. Utrecht University IT services were considered to be one of the eight best practice examples in European higher education in a 2003 European Council survey. The unique outsourcing model, and the way in which research in teaching development with the aid of IT had been implemented at Utrecht, was singled out for praise. He served on a number of national IT boards and chaired the User Board for the Dutch high speed computing grid Gigaport Next Generation. He was appointed to a number of other boards in regional and national organizations such as NIVE, the Dutch quality-management organization for industry. He was elevated to the rank of knight in the order of Oranje Nassau in 2005 by the Queen of the Netherlands for his services to Utrecht University and IT in higher education. He has recently retired from the University at the age of 62, but is still active on national IT committees.

Ly Fie Sugianto is a senior lecturer at the Faculty of Information Technology, Monash University, Australia. She holds a Bachelor of Computer Systems Engineering degree from Curtin University and a Doctorate of Philosophy in Electrical Engineering from Monash University, both in Australia. She has published over 50 research papers in optimization technique, fuzzy mathematics, decision support systems and e-commerce. She has also received several grants to conduct research in electricity markets and information systems. She has been nominated as an expert of international standing by the Australian Research Council College of Experts for her work in the electricity market.

Dewi Rooslani Tojib is a research student at the School of Information Technology, Monash University, Australia. She received her Bachelor of Business Systems degree from Monash University in 2003. She is currently a PhD candidate at the Clayton School of Information Technology, Monash University. Her research interests include business-to-employee portals, instrument development and user satisfaction.

Geoff Walton is Subject and Learning Support Librarian at Loughborough University. He is a Chartered Librarian, a SEDA (Staff & Educational Development Association) accredited teacher, a member of the HEA (Higher Education Academy) and a Learning and Teaching Fellow at Staffordshire University. He has worked as an academic librarian for 12 years, before which he worked as a librarian with Staffordshire County Council. As a subject librarian he supports the Faculty of Health and Sciences (Psychology and Mental Health and Sport and Exercise, in particular). He was the project manager charged with developing a Level 1 information skills module (which has run for ten years) and was instrumental in migrating this to a virtual learning environment, in particular COSE (Creation Of Study Environments). He is currently reading for a PhD at Loughborough University. This research is focused on developing a strategy for delivering information literacy in an online setting.

Martin White is Managing Director of Intranet Focus Ltd (www.intranetfocus.com), which he established in 1999 after 30 years' experience in information management, electronic publishing, market research and management consulting. He consults on the design and management of intranets, enterprise web strategy, and the specification, selection and implementation of content management and search software for clients in the UK, Europe, the USA and the Middle East. Since 2001 Martin has written the 'Behind the Firewall' column on intranet management issues for the US magazine *EContent* (www.econtentmag.org) for which he is a contributing editor, a position he also holds for *Intranets: Enterprise Strategies and Solutions* (www.intranetstoday.com). He is also a member of the Editorial Board of the *International Journal of Information Management*. His book, *The Content Management Handbook*, was published by Facet Publishing in 2005. Martin has been Chairman of the Online Information Conference since 1999. He is a visiting professor at the Department of Information Studies, University of Sheffield (www.shef.ac.uk/is), and a member of the Governing Board of CAB International (www.cabi.org). Martin is an Honorary Fellow of the Chartered Institute of Library and Information Professionals, and was President of the Institute of Information

Scientists in 1993/4. He was the recipient of the Lifetime Achievement Award at the 2005 Information Industry Awards.

Ian Winship retired from Northumbria University in 2005 after over 30 years' working in the University Library. For much of that time he was involved in electronic resources from dial-up online searching in the 1970s to the evaluation of library portals more recently. Initially he also had responsibilities for stock and services in science and technology and later led a specialist team developing electronic library services. Currently he does some work as a consultant and is an associate lecturer at the Open University. He is also a visiting scholar in University Library and Learning Services at Northumbria. He is the joint author of two books published by Facet Publishing: *The Student's Guide to the Internet*, which reached three editions, and *The Public Librarian's Guide to the Internet*. He has also written and presented on topics as diverse as information skills teaching, online searching in academic libraries, web searching, internet radio, information resources and e-learning, plagiarism detection, weblogs and RSS.

Panayiotis Zaphiris is a senior lecturer at the Centre for Human–Computer Interaction Design, School of Informatics, City University, London. Before joining City University he was a researcher at the Institute of Gerontology at Wayne State University, where he obtained a PhD in Human Computer Interaction (HCI). His research interests lie in HCI, with an emphasis on inclusive design and social aspects of computing. He is especially interested in HCI issues related to the elderly and people with disabilities. He is also interested in internet-related research. He was the principal investigator of the JISC Information Visualization Foundation Study and a co-investigator on the Disability Rights Commission (DRC) Formal Investigation into Web Site Accessibility (managing the automatic testing of 1000 websites) and on the JISC Usability Studies for JISC Services and Information Environment projects.

Index